Tell It Slant

Tell ^{It} Slant

Creating, Refining, and Publishing Creative Nonfiction

Second Edition

Brenda Miller and Suzanne Paola

New York   Chicago   San Francisco   Lisbon   London   Madrid   Mexico City
Milan   New Delhi   San Juan   Seoul   Singapore   Sydney   Toronto

12 13 14 15 16   QFR   21 20 19 18 17

ISBN   978-0-07-178177-0
MHID   0-07-178177-3

e-ISBN   978-0-07-178178-7
e-MHID   0-07-178178-1

Library of Congress Cataloging-in-Publication Data

Tell it slant / Brenda Miller and Suzanne Paola. -- 2nd ed.
       p.   cm.
   Includes index.
   ISBN 0-07-178177-3 (alk. paper)
      1. English language—Rhetoric.   2. Reportage literature—Authorship.
   3. Reportage literature, English.   4. Journalism—Authorship.5. Investigative
   reporting.   6. Creative writing.   7. Report writing.   8. Creative
   nonfiction.   I. Paola, Suzanne.   II. Title.

   PE1408.M548   2012
   808'.042—dc23   2011051744

See the authors' Facebook page for information about the revised *Tell It Slant* website.

Emily Dickinson poem (p. v) reprinted by permission of the publishers and the trustees of Amherst College from *The Poems of Emily Dickinson*, Thomas H. Johnson, ed., Cambridge: Mass.: The Belknap Press of Harvard University Press, copyright © 1951, 1955, 1979, 1983 by the president and fellows of Harvard College.

Tell all the Truth but tell it Slant—
Success in Circuit lies
Too bright for our infirm Delight
The Truth's superb surprise
As Lightening to the Children eased
With explanation kind
The Truth must dazzle gradually
Or every man be blind—

—EMILY DICKINSON

Contents

Preface

Since the initial publication of the textbook version of *Tell It Slant* in 2003, the landscape of creative nonfiction has evolved. Creative nonfiction courses are now being taught at virtually all universities and colleges, and the esteemed magazine *Poets and Writers* has finally recognized creative nonfiction as a category—along with fiction and poetry—in its Directory of Writers. No longer must creative nonfiction justify itself as a solid literary genre; rather, "creative nonfictionists" are generating some of the most exciting new works in literature—as well as some of the most intriguing controversies.

Creative nonfiction writers have embraced new ways of forming their texts—including online technologies—because the genre lends itself to grand experimentation. Dozens of new journals have sprung up—both in print and online—that feature creative nonfiction prominently in their offerings. The biennial NonfictioNow conference, sponsored by the creative nonfiction program at the University of Iowa, brings together leading luminaries in the field, along with hundreds of creative nonfiction practitioners eager to connect with one another and deepen their study of this endlessly fascinating genre.

Once a lone instructional text in a field of personal essay anthologies, the original edition of *Tell It Slant* foresaw the way creative nonfiction teachers and new writers would need some guidance in the basics of creative nonfiction in order to create a strong foundation for this evolution. The book became the go-to text for universities, garnering a following of thousands of students and writers who found the personal voices of the authors an engaging way to enter this field, using the text in creative nonfiction and composition studies. Now, several more fine textbooks have emerged to share the shelf with *Tell It Slant,* but this book remains a favorite for those who rely on its thorough examination of the many forms creative nonfiction can take.

Unfortunately, in 2010, the textbook edition of *Tell It Slant,* which included an anthology section, went out of print, but the trade edition remains a preferred book for those seeking accessible guidance on the many subjects and stances that creative nonfiction can explore. So this seemed the perfect time to update the book you have in your hands, not only to help academics use this combined text and trade edition for their classes, but also to keep pace with the growth in creative nonfiction forms, ethical controversies, and publication outlets for exciting new work.

We have updated references throughout the book to include more recent work in the field, as well as highlighted innovative creative nonfiction that plays with the boundaries of experimentation and form. We've added new "Try It" exercises that have been field tested with great success in the classroom, and we've updated the chapter titled "The Particular Challenges of Creative Nonfiction" to include references to James Frey and other controversies regarding nonfiction ethics, with material for generating rich discussion on the topic.

We've expanded the chapter previously titled "The Basics of Personal Reportage," now called "Using Research to Expand Your Perspective," in order to show the way "topical" nonfiction, or nonfiction on a particular subject—scent, meals, particular plants, etc.—has recently come to the forefront of the nonfiction field. We show how research methods—using the Internet, interview, and immersion—have evolved along with developments in technology, and we've enhanced our discussion on *how* to use research to generate powerful writing.

The chapters on the "personal essay" and "lyric essay" now include emerging forms such as the "found" essay, the mixed-media essay, and the graphic memoir. We've also included a new chapter—"Writing Online: Hypertext and Social Media"—that explores the many ways creative nonfiction genres are evolving along with technology, including hypermedia, literary blogs, and Twitter. Finally, we've added a comprehensive chapter on publication that highlights the many new venues that now exist for creative nonfiction writers.

As an appendix to the book, we've also included two essays of our own— "The Hazing of Swans" by Suzanne and "A Braided Heart: Shaping the Lyric Essay" by Brenda—as personal examples of how we approached some of the concepts we describe. We reference many, many other readings in *Tell It Slant*, and we have compiled a comprehensive list—of both individual essays and useful anthologies—that is available on the *Tell It Slant* website.

For teachers—or for writers who would like to structure their own individual writing course—we have provided several sample syllabi on the *Tell It*

Slant website. In these syllabi, you will see how one can use this book flexibly for different purposes: for an introductory nonfiction class, for a more advanced topical class, for a composition class, for a short-term workshop, or for a long-term writing group. We give you ideas for using one of the many fine anthologies that exist as a supplement to the instructional material in *Tell It Slant*, as well as point you in the direction of many excellent online readings and resources. We are also available on our Facebook page to answer your questions about using this book in a way that works best for you. Our Facebook page is also a good way to access updates and pedagogical resources.

We see all the chapters in this book as presenting a series of introductions, lessons, sometimes provocations in the art of writing creative nonfiction. We aim to present the most comprehensive information about creative nonfiction possible, in an accessible form, with a sense of how these techniques have played out in the lives of working writers. We also want all of the concepts we present to be translatable immediately into actual writing ideas, so each chapter begins with a short personal narrative to give you a sense of how we, the authors, have negotiated the territory. Because we recognize the limits of what we know, we have provided tips from many of the best nonfiction writers working today—Bernard Cooper, Robin Hemley, Lawrence Sutin, to name a few—to expand our expertise in particular areas of creative nonfiction. At the end of each chapter, we provide a series of prompts to help you put into action the principles we've explained. Use them as starting points to create your own brand of creative nonfiction.

Also on the *Tell It Slant* website you'll find an updated bibliography. In this resource, we've included work that you can find in books and online; we hope you will add your own favorites to this list and continue to be a lifelong learner in this genre. If you are a teacher or workshop leader, this bibliography can be the resource you use to create a comprehensive course, using *Tell It Slant* in tandem with either one of the excellent anthologies we recommend, relying on the substantial readings available at or via our website, or putting together your own print or online reader.

We believe that deep within you is a work of art only you can breathe into being. We can coach you and help you develop the muscles you need, but we trust that you will find, between the lines here, the prompts that spur only you, the book that begins where ours ends. Breathe deeply! Now let's begin.

Introduction

Where to Begin

Here's how it happens: I'm at a party, or sitting quietly in my seat on an airplane, or milling around at a family reunion, and someone finally asks me the question: "So, you're a writer. What do you write?" It's a deceptively simple question. And seems to demand a simple response.

But in the split second before I can answer, I go through all the possible replies in my head. "Well," I could say, "I write essays." But essays sound too much like academic papers and articles. I could say, simply, "Nonfiction," but then they might think I write celebrity biographies, cookbooks, or historical treatises on World War II. I could try to take the easy way out and say I write autobiography or memoir, but people would raise their eyebrows and say, "Memoir? Aren't you too young to write your memoirs?" Besides, not all of what I write is memoir; in fact, many of my pieces are not based in private memory at all.

All this is too much for casual party chat. I need a term that, once deployed, will answer all their questions for good. But I know that if I answer with the correct phrase—creative nonfiction—I'm in for a long night. My interrogator will warm up to the debate, throwing out the opening volley: "Creative nonfiction? Isn't that an oxymoron?" His forehead crinkles, and his eyes search my own, trying to understand what, exactly, I'm talking about.

I want to tell him that I love writing creative nonfiction precisely because of this ambiguity. I love the way writing creative nonfiction allows me to straddle a kind of "borderland" where I can discover new aspects of myself and the world, forge surprising metaphors, and create artistic order out of life's chaos. I'm never bored when I write in this genre, always jazzed by the new ways I can stretch my writing muscles. But I rarely trust my listener will understand. So, more often than not, I smile and say, "Maybe I'll show you sometime." Then I execute a pirouette and turn his attention toward the view out the window or to the lovely fruit punch in its cut-glass bowl. I direct his attention to the myriad things of this world, and maybe that is the correct answer after all.

—BRENDA

When Emily Dickinson wrote, "Tell all the Truth but tell it Slant / Success in Circuit lies . . ." what did she mean by these lines? We think she meant that truth takes on many guises; the truth of art can be very different from the truth of day-to-day life. Her poems and letters, after all, reveal her deft observation of the outer world, but it is "slanted" through the poet's distinctive vision. We chose her poem as both title and epigraph for this book because it so aptly describes the task of the creative nonfiction writer: to tell the truth, yes, but to become more than a mere transcriber of life's factual experiences.

Every few years, National Public Radio checks in on a man who feels compelled to record every minute of his day in a diary. As you can imagine, the task is gargantuan and ultimately imprisons him. He becomes a slave to this recording act and can no longer function in the world. The transcription he leaves may be a comprehensive and "truthful" one, but it remains completely unreadable; after all, who cares to read reams and reams of such notes? What value do they hold apart from the author? In nonfiction, if we place a premium on fact, then this man's diary would be the ultimate masterpiece. But in literature and art, we applaud style, meaning, and effect over the bare facts. We go to literature—and perhaps especially creative nonfiction literature—to learn not about the author, but about ourselves; we want to be *moved* in some way. That emotional resonance happens only through skillful use of artistic techniques. As Salman Rushdie put it, "Literature is where I go to explore the highest and lowest places in human society and in the human spirit, where I hope to find not absolute truth but the truth of the tale, of the imagination and of the heart."

Simply by choosing to write in this genre, and to present your work as nonfiction, you make an artistic statement. You're saying that the work is rooted in the "real" world. Though the essay might contain some elements of fabrication, it is directly connected to you as the author behind the text. There is a truth to it that you want to claim as your own, a bond of trust between reader and writer. If you present a piece as fiction, you are saying that the work is rooted in the world of the imagination. Though the story may contain autobiographical elements, the reader cannot assume that it has a direct bearing on the truth of the writer's life or experience. At some point, every writer needs to decide how she wants to place herself in relationship to the reader; the choice of genre establishes that relationship and the rules of engagement.

The more you read and study, the more you will discover that creative nonfiction assumes a particular, creating *self* behind the nonfiction prose. When you set about to write creative nonfiction about any subject, you bring to this endeavor a strong voice and a singular vision. This voice must be loud and interesting enough to be heard among the noise coming at us in everyday life. If you succeed, you and the reader will find yourself in a close, if not intimate, relationship that demands honesty and a willingness to risk a kind of exposure you may never venture in face-to-face encounters.

This is not to say that creative nonfiction must be "self-centered." On the contrary, creative nonfiction often focuses on material outside the life of the author, and it certainly need not use a personal "I" speaker. It's the "creative" part of the term *creative nonfiction* that means a single, active imagination is behind the piece of reality this author will unfold. Essayist Scott Russell Sanders wrote, "Feeling overwhelmed by data, random information, the flotsam and jetsam of mass culture, we relish the spectacle of a single consciousness making sense of a portion of the chaos. . . . The essay is a haven for the private, idiosyncratic voice in an era of anonymous babble."

This "idiosyncratic voice" uses all the literary devices available to fiction writers and poets—vivid images, scenes, metaphors, dialogue, satisfying rhythms of language, and so forth—while still remaining true to experience and the world. Or, as novelist and essayist Cynthia Ozick put it, "Like a poem, a genuine essay is made out of language and character and mood and temperament and pluck and chance."

Creative nonfiction can focus on either private experience or public domain, but in either case, the inner self provides the vision and the shaping influence to infuse the work with this sense of "pluck and chance." In many cases, the essayist may find himself "thinking aloud" on the page. Then the essay becomes a continual process of unexpected discovery. The creative nonfiction writer continually chooses to question and expand his or her own limited perceptions.

Lee Gutkind, who edits the journal *Creative Nonfiction*, says creative non-fiction "heightens the whole concept and idea of essay writing." He has come up with the "the five Rs" of creative nonfiction: Real Life, Reflection, Research, Reading, and 'Riting. That second "R," Reflection, means that in contrast to traditional objective journalism, creative nonfiction allows for and encourages "a writer's feelings and responses . . . as long as what [writers] think is written to embrace the reader in a variety of ways." Imagination coupled with facts form this hybrid genre that is both so exciting and so challenging to write.

As in any creative enterprise, the most difficult challenge to writing creative nonfiction lies in knowing where to begin. One might think that creative nonfiction would provide an easy out for this question. After all, someone might chide, all the material is at your fingertips. It's nonfiction after all; the world is yours for the taking. But the minute creative nonfiction writers put pen to paper, they realize a truth both invigorating and disheartening: we are not the rote recorder of life experience. We are artists creating artifice. And as such, we have difficult choices to make every step of the way.

Memoir may seem more straightforward, but as William Zinsser articulates in his introduction to *Inventing the Truth: The Art and Craft of Memoir*, "Good memoirs are a careful act of construction. We like to think that an interesting life will simply fall into place on the page. It won't. . . . Memoir writers must manufacture a text, imposing narrative order on a jumble of half-remembered events."

We've designed this book to help you gain access to your particular stories and memories—your particular voice—while also providing suggestions for turning your gaze onto the world in a way that will allow you to find material outside of the self. We begin with memory and move steadily outward to family, environment, spirituality, history, the arts, and the world. In this way, we hope you will begin to consider both your individual life and our collective lives as material for creative nonfiction. Readers will want to read your work not because they wish to lend a sympathetic ear to a stranger, but because of the way your truth-filled stories may illuminate their own lives and perceptions of the world.

Tell It Slant

PART 1

UNEARTHING YOUR MATERIAL

If there's a book you really want to read, but it hasn't been written yet, then you must write it.

—TONI MORRISON

1

The Body of Memory

Memory begins to qualify the imagination, to give it another
formation, one that is peculiar to the self. . . . If I were to remember
other things, I should be someone else.

—N. Scott Momaday

In my earliest memory, I'm a four-year-old girl waking slowly from anesthe-
sia. I lift my head off the damp pillow and gaze blearily out the bars of my
hospital crib. I can see a dim hallway with a golden light burning; somehow
I know in that hallway my mother will appear any minute now, bearing ice
cream and 7-Up. She told me as much before the operation: "All good girls
get ice cream and 7-Up when their tonsils come out," she said, stroking my
hair. "It's your reward for being brave." I'm vaguely aware of another little
girl screaming for her mother in the crib next to mine, but otherwise the
room remains dark and hushed, buffered by the footfalls of nurses who stop
a moment at the doorway and move on.

I do not turn to face my neighbor, afraid her terror will infect me; I can
feel the tickling urge to cry burbling up in my wounded throat, and that
might be the end of me, of all my purported bravery and the promised ice
cream. I keep my gaze fixed on that hallway, but something glints in my
peripheral vision and I turn to face the bedside table. There, in a mason jar,
my tonsils float. They rotate in the liquid: misshapen ovals, pink and nubbly,
grotesque.

And now my mother has simply appeared, with no warning or
announcement. Her head leans close to the crib, and she gently plies the
spoon between the bars, places it between my lips, and holds it there while

3

I swallow. I keep my gaze fixed on her face, and she keeps her gaze on mine, though I know we're both aware of those tonsils floating out of reach. The nurses pad about, and one of them enters the room bearing my "Badge of Courage." It's a certificate with a lion in the middle surrounded by laurels, my name scripted in black ink below. My mother holds it out to me, through the bars, and I run a finger across my name, across the lion's mane, across the dry yellowed parchment.

—Brenda

The Earliest Memory

What is your earliest memory? What is the memory that always emerges from the dim reaches of your consciousness as the *first one*, the beginning to this life you call your own? Most of us can pinpoint them, these images that assume a privileged station in our life's story. Some of these early memories have the vague aspect of a dream, some the vivid clarity of a photograph. In whatever form they take, they tend to exert on us a mysterious fascination.

Memory itself could be called its own bit of creative nonfiction. We continually—often unconsciously—renovate our memories, shaping them into stories that bring coherence to chaos. Memory has been called the ultimate "mythmaker," continually seeking meaning in the random and often unfathomable events in our lives. "A myth," writes John Kotre, author of *White Gloves: How We Create Ourselves Through Memory*, "is not a falsehood but a comprehensive view of reality. It's a story that speaks to the heart as well as the mind, seeking to generate conviction about what it thinks is true."

The first memory then becomes the starting point in our own narratives of the self. "Our first memories are like the creation stories that humans have always told about the origins of the earth," Kotre writes. "In a similar way, the individual self—knowing how the story is coming out—selects its earliest memories to say, 'This is who I am because this is how I began.'" As writers, we naturally return again and again to these beginnings and scrutinize them. By paying attention to the illogical, unexpected details, we just might light upon the odd yet precise images that help our lives make sense, at least long enough for our purposes as writers.

The prominent fiction writer and essayist David James Duncan calls such autobiographical images "river teeth." Using the image of knots of dense wood that remain in a river years after a fallen tree disintegrates, Duncan creates a metaphor of how memory, too, retains vivid moments that stay in mind long after the events that spurred them have been forgotten. He writes:

> There are hard, cross-grained whorls of memory that remain inexplicably lodged in us long after the straight-grained narrative material that housed them has washed away. Most of these whorls are not stories, exactly: more often they're self-contained moments of shock or of inordinate empathy. . . . These are our "river teeth"—the time-defying knots of experience that remain in us after most of our autobiographies are gone.

Virginia Woolf had her own term for such "shocks" of memory. She calls them "moments of being," and they become essential to our very sense of self. They are the times when we get jolted out of our everyday complacency to really *see* the world and all that it contains. This shock-receiving capacity is essential for the writer's disposition. "I hazard the explanation," she writes, "that a shock is at once in my case followed by the desire to explain it. . . . I make it real by putting it into words." Woolf's early moments of being, the vivid first memories from childhood, are of the smallest, most ordinary things: the pattern of her mother's dress, for example, or the pull cord of the window blind skittering across the floor of their beach house.

The memories that can have the most emotional impact for the writer are those we don't really understand, the images that rise up before us quite without our volition. For example, the flash of our mother's face as she sips from a cooled cup of coffee, her eyes betraying some private grief you've never seen before; or the smell of grapefruit ripening on a tree outside your bedroom window. Perhaps the touch of a stranger's hand reminds you of the way your grandmother casually grasped your hand in her own, the palm so soft but the knuckles so rough, as you sat together watching television, not speaking a word.

These are the "river teeth," or the moments of being, the ones that suck your breath away. What repository of memory do you hold in your heart rather than your head? What are the pictures that rise up to the surface without your bidding? Take these as your cue. Pick up your pen, your net, your magnet, whatever it takes. Be on alert. This is where you begin.

Metaphorical Memory

A metaphor is a way at getting at a truth that exists beyond the literal. By pinpointing certain images as *symbolic*, writers can go deeper than surface truths and create essays that work on many levels at once. This is what writers are up to all the time, not only with memory but with the material of experience and the world. We resurrect the details to describe not only the surface appearance, but also to make intuitive connections, to articulate some truth that cannot be spoken of directly.

Many writers allow early memories to "impress themselves" on the mind. They do not dismiss them as passing details but rather probe them for any insights they may contain. They ask not only "what?" but "why?" "Why do I remember the things I do? Why these memories and not others?"

Let's go back to that first memory of the tonsils, that early river tooth in the personal essay at the beginning of this chapter. For me, Brenda, as a writer it is not important *what* I remember—or even the factual accuracy of the scene—but *why* I recall it the way I do. And, I keep coming back to that incongruous jar of tonsils. I doubt the doctors did such a thing (my mother has no recollection of it), but it remains the most stubborn and intractable part of the scene. What I like about this part of my memory is its very illegibility. The best material cannot be deciphered in an instant, with a fixed meaning that, once pinned down, remains immutable. No. As essayists, we want the rich stuff, the inscrutable images whose meaning is never clear at first, second, or third glance.

I could interpret that jar of tonsils in any number of ways, but this is the one I light on most frequently. When I woke from having my tonsils removed, I knew for the first time that my body was not necessarily a whole unit, always intact. At that moment, I understood the courage that it will take to bear this body into a world that will most certainly cause it harm. Of course, as a child I realized no such thing. But, as an adult—*as a writer preserving this memory in language*—I begin to create a metaphor that will infiltrate both my writing and my sense of self from here on out.

Think back on that early memory of yours, the one that came to mind instantly. Illuminate the details, shine a spotlight on them until they begin to yield a sense of truth revealed. Where is your body in this memory? What kind of language does it speak? What metaphor does it offer for you to puzzle out in writing?

Muscle Memory

The body, memory, and mind exist in sublime interdependence, each part wholly twined with the others. There is a phrase used in dancing, athletics, parachuting, and other fields that require sharp training of the body: *muscle memory*. Once the body learns the repetitive gestures of a certain movement or skill, the memory of how to execute these movements will be encoded in the muscles. That is why, for instance, we never forget how to ride a bike. Or why, years after tap dance lessons, one can still execute a convincing shuffle-hop-step across a kitchen floor.

One cannot speak of memory—and of bodily memory in particular—without trotting out Marcel Proust and his famous madeleine. Proust dips his cookie in the lime-blossom tea, and *Remembrance of Things Past* springs forth, all six volumes of it. Because memory is so firmly fixed in the body, it takes an object that appeals to the senses to dislodge memory and allow it to float freely into the mind or onto the page. *These* memories will have resonance precisely because they have not been forced into being by a mind insistent on fixed meanings. It is the body's story and so one that resonates with a sense of an inadvertent truth revealed. As writer Terry Tempest Williams has said, the most potent images and stories are those that "bypass rhetoric and pierce the heart."

So, as far as memory devices go, you could do worse than turn to the body for guidance. The body can offer an inexhaustible store of triggers to begin any number of essays, each of which will have greater significance than what appears on the surface. Sometimes, what matters to us most is what has mattered to the body. Memory may pretend to live in the cerebral cortex, but it requires muscle—real muscle—to animate it again for the page.

The Five Senses of Memory

By paying attention to the sensory gateways of the body, you also begin to write in a way that naturally *embodies* experience, making it tactile for the reader. Readers tend to care deeply only about those things they *feel* in the body at a visceral level. And so as a writer consider your vocation as that of a translator: one who renders the abstract into the concrete. We experience the world through our senses. We must translate that experience into the language of the senses as well.

Smell

"Smell is a potent wizard that transports us across thousands of miles and all the years we have lived," wrote Helen Keller in her autobiography. "The odors of fruits waft me to my southern home, to my childhood frolics in the peach orchard. Other odors, instantaneous and fleeting, cause my heart to dilate joyously or contract with remembered grief."

Though Helen Keller's words are made more poignant by the fact that she was blind and deaf, we all have this innate connection to smell. Smell seems to travel to our brains directly, without logical or intellectual interference. Physiologically, we *do* apprehend smells more quickly than the other sensations, and the images aroused by smell act as beacons leading to our richest memories, our most private selves. Smell is so intimately tied up with *breath*, after all, a function of our bodies that works continually, day and night, keeping us alive. And so smell keys us into the memories that evoke the continual ebb and flow of experience. The richest smells can be the most innocent: the smell of a Barbie doll; Play-Doh; the house right after your mother has cleaned (the hot dust inside the vacuum, the tart scent of Lemon Pledge); or the shoes in your father's closet, redolent of old polish. Or, the smells can be more complex: the aftershave your father wore the day he lost his job or the scent of your baby's head when you first held her in your arms.

What are the smells you remember that even in memory make you stop a moment and breathe deeply, or that make your heart beat more vigorously, your palms ache for what's been lost? Write these down. Write as quickly as you can, seeing how one smell leads to another. What kinds of images, memories, or stories might arise from this sensory trigger?

Taste

Food is one of the most social gifts we have. The bond between mother and child forms over the feeding of that child, either at the breast or at the bottle, the infant body held close, the eyes intent on the parent's face. When you sit down to unburden yourself to a friend, you often do so over a meal prepared together in the kitchen, the two of you chopping vegetables or sipping wine as you articulate whatever troubles have come to haunt you. When these predicaments grow overwhelming, we turn to comfort food, meals that spark in us a memory of an idealized, secure childhood. When we are falling in love, we offer food as our first timid gesture toward intimacy.

In his famous essay "Afternoon of an American Boy," E. B. White vividly remembers the taste of cinnamon toast in conjunction with the first stumbling overtures of a boyhood crush. In "A Thing Shared," food aficionado M. F. K. Fisher uses something as simple and commonplace as the taste of a peach pie—"the warm round peach pie and cool yellow cream"—to describe a memory of her father and sister the first time they found themselves alone without the mediating influence of their mother. The food acts as more than mere sustenance; it becomes a moment of communion. "That night I not only saw my father for the first time as a person. I saw the golden hills and the live oaks as clearly as I have ever seen them since; and I saw the dimples in my little sister's fat hands in a way that still moves me because of that first time; and I saw food as something beautiful to be shared with people instead of as a thrice-daily necessity." This scene becomes an illustration of how we awaken to one another. It's less about her own family than about the fleeting moments of connection that can transpire in *all* families, in one way or another.

What are the tastes that carry the most emotion for you? The tastes that, even in memory, make you stop a moment and run your tongue over your lips and swallow hard? Write these down, as quickly as you can. Which scenes, memories, associations come to the surface?

Hearing

Sounds often go unnoticed. Because we cannot consciously cut off our hearing unless we plug our ears, we've learned to filter sounds, picking and choosing the ones that are important, becoming inured to the rest. But these sounds often make up a subliminal backdrop to our lives, and even the faintest echo can tug back moments from the past in their entirety.

For example, in his short gem of an essay, "The Fine Art of Sighing," memoirist Bernard Cooper uses a sound as subtle as a sigh to elucidate his relationship to his family, himself, and the world. He describes how his father sighs, how his mother sighs, and how he, himself, sighs. And, paradoxically, by focusing in on this small, simple act, Cooper is able to reveal much larger things: his mother's dissatisfaction with domestic life, his father's gruff sensual nature, and Cooper's ambivalence about his own body and sexuality. "A friend of mine once mentioned that I was given to long and ponderous sighs. Once I became aware of this habit, I heard my father's sighs in my own and knew for a moment his small satisfactions. At other times, I felt my mother's restlessness and wished I could leave my body with my breath, or be happy in the body my breath left behind."

Music is not so subtle but rather acts as a blaring soundtrack to our emotional lives. Think about the bonds you formed with friends over common musical passions, the days spent listening to the same song over and over as you learned the mundane yet painful lessons of love. Sometimes you turned up that song as loud as you could so that it might communicate to the world—and to your deepest, deafest self—*exactly* the measure of your emotion.

We often orchestrate our memories around the music that accompanied those pivotal eras of our lives. In his essay "A Voice for the Lonely," Stephen Corey writes movingly about how a certain Roy Orbison song can always call him back to his sophomore year of high school, to his friendship with a boy as outcast as himself. He characterizes those moments as "The right singer, the right sadness, the right silence." When you have the soundtrack down, the rest of life seems to fall into place.

Touch

Hospitals rely on volunteers to hold babies on the infant wards. Their only job is to hold and rock any baby that is crying or in distress. The nurses, of course, do not have time for such constant care, but they know this type of touch is essential as medicine for their patients' healing. As we grow, this need for touch does not diminish, and thus our raging desires for contact, our subtle and not-so-subtle maneuvers that lead us into skin-to-skin encounters with other living beings.

We are constantly aware of our bodies, of how they feel as they move through the world. Without this sense we become lost, disoriented in space and time. And the people who have affected us the most are the ones who have *touched* us in some way, who have reached beyond this barrier of skin and made contact with our small, isolated selves.

Sometimes an essayist can focus on the tactile feel of objects as a way to explore deeper emotions or memories. For instance, in his short essay "Buckeye," Scott Russell Sanders focuses on the feel of the buckeye seeds that his father carried with him to ward off arthritis. They are "hollow," he says, "hard as pebbles, yet they still gleam from the polish of his hands." Sanders then allows the sensation of touch to be the way we get to know his father:

> My father never paid much heed to pain. Near the end, when his worn knee often slipped out of joint, he would pound it back in place with a rubber mallet. If a splinter worked into his flesh beyond the reach of tweezers, he would heat the blade of his knife over a cigarette lighter and slice through the skin.

Such sensory details bring the reader almost into the father's body, feeling the pound of that mallet, the slice of the skin. He never needs to tell us his father was a tough man; the images do all the work for him. These details also allow us to see the narrator, Sanders, watching his father closely, and so this scene also conveys at least a part of their relationship and its emotional tenor.

Think about the people in your life who have touched you deeply. What was the quality of their physical touch on your body? How did they touch the objects around them? Why do you think this touch lingers in memory?

Sight

How do you see the world? How do you see yourself? Even linguistically, our sense of sight seems so tied up in our perceptions, stance, opinions, personalities, and knowledge of the world. To see something often means to finally understand, to be enlightened, to have our vision cleared. What we choose to see—and *not* to see—often says more about us than anything else.

When we "look back" in memory, we *see* those memories. Our minds have catalogued an inexhaustible storehouse of visual images. Now the trick is for you to render those images in writing. Pay attention to the smallest details: the way a tree limb cuts its jagged edge against a winter sky or the dull canary yellow of the bulldozer that leveled your favorite house on the street. Close your eyes to see these images more clearly. Trace the shape of your favorite toy or the outline of a beloved's face. Turn up the lights in the living room. Go out walking under a full moon. Keep looking.

For Annie Dillard, in her jubilant essay "Seeing" (from *Pilgrim at Tinker Creek*), being able to see truly is akin to spiritual awakening:

> One day I was walking along Tinker Creek thinking of nothing at all and I saw the tree with the lights in it. I saw the backyard cedar where the mourning doves roost charged and transfigured, each cell buzzing with flame. . . . It was less like seeing than like being for the first time seen, knocked breathless by a powerful glance. . . . I had been my whole life a bell, and never knew it until at that moment I was lifted and struck.

What are the moments in your life that have "struck" you? How have they been engraved in memory?

Fortunately, we live in an age where visual memories are routinely preserved in photographs and on video. Sometimes these photos and films can act not only as triggers for your memory—reminding you of the visual details of the experience—but they can also prompt you to delve more deeply below the surface.

TRY IT

1. Write a scene of a very early, vivid memory. What calls out for further examination? Are you realistic? What are the odd details, the ones that don't seem to fit with other people's versions of the story? What in this scene seems to matter to you? Should it? What are you leaving out? If you get stuck, keep repeating the phrase "I remember" to start off your sentences; allow this rhythm to take you further than you thought you could go.

> VARIATION 1: Do you have an ideal "earliest memory"? Write this out, and see how your imagination and your memory intersect or diverge. Is there an essay in the process of memory itself?

> VARIATION 2: Talk with family members about *their* memories of the time you pinpoint as your first memory. How do they corroborate or deny your own memory? How can you create a "collaborative" memory that includes their versions of the events? How does this memory enact a family "myth"? Is there an essay about the way these divergent accounts work together?

2. In the preface to his anthology *The Business of Memory*, Charles Baxter writes, "What we talk about when we talk about memory is—often—what we have forgotten and what has been lost. The passion and torment and significance seem to lie in that direction." What have you forgotten in your life? What are the moments that keep sliding out of reach? Write for twenty minutes, using the phrase "I can't remember" to start off each sentence. Where does such an examination lead you?

You may find that by using this exercise you can back into the scenes and images you *do* remember but never knew how to approach. You can write some very powerful essays based on this prompt, exploring material that seemed too dangerous to examine head-on.

> **VARIATION:** After you've lighted on some events or times you can't fully articulate, do a little research. Ask others about their memories of that time. Find documents or photographs that may shed some light on the issue. Be a detective, looking for clues. After you've gathered enough evidence, write an essay that focuses on the way your memory and the "reality" either differ or coincide. Why have you forgotten the things you did?

3. How many different "firsts" can you remember in your life? The first meal you remember enjoying, the first smell you remember wanting to smell again, the first day of school, the first book you remember reading by yourself, the first album you ever bought, the first time you drove a car, the first kiss? How does your memory of these "first" events color your perception of yourself? What kinds of metaphors do they generate for your life story?

Smell

1. Gather articles that you know carry some smell that is evocative for you. One by one, smell them deeply, and then write the images that arise in your mind. Write quickly, allowing the smell to trigger other sensory associations.

2. Which smells in your life are gone for you now? Which ones would you give anything to smell again? Have you ever been "ambushed" by a smell you didn't expect? For example, have you opened a box of clothing from a deceased relative and had the smell of that person's house flood over you? Or, have you walked into a friend's house and smelled a meal exactly like one you remember from childhood? Write a scene about such an incident. If you can't remember anything like that, imagine one. How do these sensory memories differ from memories of the past you'd normally conjure up? Write an essay exploring the idea that your body carries its own dormant memories.

VARIATION FOR A GROUP: Each person brings in an object that carries some kind of strong smell and takes a turn being the leader. Keep the object hidden until it is your turn. The rest of the group members close their eyes while the leader brings this object to each person and asks him or her to smell deeply. After everyone has had a chance, the leader hides the object again. Each person immediately writes the images and associations that smell evoked. Share these writings with each other and see how similarly or differently you reacted to the same odor.

Taste

1. Try to remember the first meal you consciously tasted and enjoyed. Describe this meal in detail; make yourself hungry with these details. Who ate this meal with you? If you can't remember any such meal, imagine one.

2. If you were to write a life history through food, what would be the "touchstone" moments, the meals that represented turning points for you? Which meals have you loved? Which meals have you hated? Which meals marked important transitions in your life?

VARIATION FOR A GROUP: Have "food exploration" days set aside for your group meetings. On these days, one person is responsible for bringing in an item of food for everyone to taste. Try to choose foods that leave strong sensory impressions: a mango, perhaps, or a persimmon. After exploring the sight, textures, and smells, taste it. Describe this food in detail, then go on to whichever images and metaphorical associations arise. In your own life, what is most like a mango? Begin an essay by outlining which people, feelings, events, or memories this food conjures up for you and why.

Touch

1. Take an inventory of the scars or marks on your body. How were they received? How do these external scars relate to any internal "markings" as well?

2. Find an object that you consider a talisman, something you either carry with you or keep in a special place in your home. Hold it in your hand, and, with your eyes closed, feel all its textures. Begin to write, using this tactile description to trigger memories, scenes, and metaphors.

> VARIATION FOR A GROUP: Each person brings in such an object for a "show-and-tell," explaining the story behind the item. Pass these things around the room for everyone to examine, and then write based on *someone else's* talisman. What did it feel like in your hand? How does it trigger memories of your own?

Sound

1. Try re-creating a scene from your childhood using *only* the sense of hearing. What music is playing in the background? Whose voice is on the radio? How loud is the sound of traffic? What do the trees sound like in the wind? Are there insects, birds, animals? A hum from a factory? Rain, rivers, the lapping of a lake? What is the quality of the silence? Try to pick out as many ambient sounds as you can, then begin to amplify the ones you think have the most metaphorical significance. What kind of emotional tone do these sounds give to the piece?

2. Put on a piece of music that you strongly associate with a certain era of your life. Using this music as a soundtrack, zero in on a particular scene that arises in your mind. Try writing the scene *without mentioning the music at all*, but through your word choices and imagery and sentence structure convey the essence of this music's rhythm and beat.

> VARIATION: Do the same thing, but this time use fragments of the lyrics as "scaffolding" for the essay. Give us a few lines, then write part of the memory those lines evoke in you. Give us a few more, and continue with the memory, so that the song plays throughout the entire piece.

VARIATION FOR A GROUP: Each person brings in a tape or CD of instrumental music that evokes some kind of strong emotion. Put on these pieces in turn, and have everybody write for at least five minutes to each track, trying not to describe the music directly but focusing instead on the images and memories the music brings up. Choose a few to read aloud when you're done, but don't mention which piece of music acted as the trigger; have the rest of the group try to guess which music corresponds to which writing.

Sight

1. What do you see when you look in the mirror? Where does your gaze land first? How does this gaze determine your attitude toward yourself and your life? Do you see your younger self beneath the present-day face? Can you determine your future self through this gaze?

2. Using a photograph of yourself, a relative, or a friend, describe every detail of the scene. Then focus in on one object or detail that seems unexpected to you in some way. How does this detail trigger specific memories? Also, imagine what occurred just before and just after this photograph was taken; what is left outside the frame? For instance, write an essay with a title such as "After [Before] My Father Is Photographed on the *U.S.S. Constitution*." (Insert whichever subject is appropriate for the photographs you've chosen.)

VARIATION FOR A GROUP: Repeat the above exercise, but then trade photographs with your neighbor. Which details strike you? How does any part of the scene remind you of scenes from your own life? Perform a number of these trades around the room to see which details leap up from other people's photographs.

2

Writing the Family

One thing that we always assume, wrongly, is that if we write about people honestly they will resent it and become angry. If you come at it for the right reasons and you treat people as you would your fictional characters . . . if you treat them with complexity and compassion, sometimes they will feel as though they've been honored, not because they're presented in some ideal way but because they're presented with understanding.

—KIM BARNES, AUTHOR OF *IN THE*
WILDERNESS AND *HUNGRY FOR THE WORLD*

My brother is swinging the bat and I'm bored in the stands, seven years old. My mother has given me a piece of paper and a pen that doesn't have much ink in it. I've written, "I HAVE TWO BROTHERS. ONE IS A LITTLE ONE. ONE IS A BIG ONE. WE ONLY HAVE TWO GIRLS IN OUR FAMILY. ONE IS ME. ONE IS MY MOTHER." The mothers sit all around me, their straight skirts pulled tight across their knees. My brother is swinging the bat and wiggling his hips on the other side of the mesh. "THE BIG BROTHER IS MEAN. THE LITTLE BROTHER IS SOME-TIMES MEAN." Where is my father? I squint to see him near the dugout, his hands cupped around his mouth. My brother swings the bat, and the ball sails, sails, sails out of sight. Everyone stands up, cheering, but I stay seated long enough to write: "THE BIG BROTHER JUST MADE A HOME RUN AND I THINK THATS ALL I'LL WRITE. GOODBYE." My

brother prances around the bases, casual and grown-up and intelligent, slap-
ping the hands held out in high fives as he trots past third. The catcher
already sulks unmasked against the backstop. My brother casually taps his
foot against home.

On that scrap of paper, I naturally turn toward the people in my life as a
way to begin a description of that life. As a child, it's nearly impossible to think
of myself as an individual separate from my family. And already, as a novice
autobiographer, I see myself spurred by the impulses to document (here is the
world, defined by mother, father, brothers), to explore emotion (oh, the harsh
treatment I receive at my brothers' hands!), and to transcribe events as they
occur (a home run!). In a sense, I'll repeat these impulses over and over
throughout the years as I grow into a writer, hopefully refining them a little
bit along the way.

—BRENDA

Situating Yourself in Relation to Family

From the minute we arrive in the world, we're put at the mercy of the people
who care for us. And we might find the rest of our lives taken up with dual,
contradictory impulses: to be an integral part of this clan and to be a separate
individual, set apart. Our families, however they're configured, provide our
first mirrors, our first definitions of who we are. And they become our first
objects of love, anger, and loyalty. No wonder so much creative nonfiction is
written about family. How can we really get away from these people? How
have they shaped who we are in the world? And how do our particular families reflect issues common to us all?

The most important strategy for dealing with family is learning how you
can approach the big issues by focusing on the smallest details. It's often
tempting, especially when you're dealing with emotionally charged material,
to try and encompass *everything* into one essay. Such a strategy will leave you,
and your readers, numb and exhausted. Ask the small questions. Who was the
family member to come last to the table? Who kept (and perhaps hid) a diary?
Who had the most distinctive laugh? Sometimes these questions are the ones
that lead to the biggest answers. For example, in "Reading History to My

Mother," Robin Hemley spurs a complex essay about his mother by focusing in first on her eyeglasses:

> My mother owns at least half a dozen glasses, and I know I should have sorted through them all by now (we tried once). . . . On her dresser there are parts of various eyeglasses: maimed glasses, the corpses of eyeglasses, a dark orphaned lens here, a frame there, an empty case, and one case with a pair that's whole. This is the one I grab and take out to my mother who is waiting patiently, always patient these days, or perhaps so unnerved and exhausted that it passes for patience.

In this memoir, Hemley will detail the decline of his mother's physical and mental health as she advances in age, and he chronicles his own ambivalent responses to caring for her. This subject will lead into even bigger ideas about how we read history to one another, how we re-create our histories as part of our love for one another. Rather than approach such things head-on, Hemley wisely turns to the small, physical things first—those eyeglasses—as a way to not only create a convincing scene, but also to plant the seeds for the emotional material to come. Those mangled, mixed-up eyeglasses signal the state of mind we'll be invited to enter.

The Biographer

When we're writing about family, sometimes it's helpful to think of ourselves as biographers, rather than autobiographers. This slight shift in perspective just might be enough to create the emotional distance necessary to begin shaping experience into literature on the page. It will also allow you to take a broader view of your subject that encompasses community, culture, and history. It will still be a *subjective* account—all biographies filter through the mind and emotional perspective of a writer—but it will be an account that has managed to take a wider view.

Sometimes it's helpful to imagine our relatives as they must have been before we knew them as mother, father, grandmother, and so forth. In Paisley Rekdal's essay "The Night My Mother Met Bruce Lee," for example, she allows herself to imagine in vivid detail her mother as a sixteen-year-old girl:

Age sixteen, my mother loads up red tubs of noodles, teacups chipped and white-gray as teeth, rice clumps that glue themselves to the plastic tubs' sides or dissolve and turn papery in the weak tea sloshing around the bottom. She's at Diamond Chan's restaurant, where most of her cousins work after school and during summer vacations some of her friends, too. . . . My mother's nails are cracked, kept short by clipping or gnawing, glisten only when varnished with the grease of someone else's leftovers.

We then move from this imaginative scene into a "real" one closer to the present day; the contrast between the two allows for a kind of understanding and character development that would otherwise be impossible.

If you were to take on the mantle of the biographer, how could you begin to see the members of your family differently? How can you combine the objectivity of a researcher with the subjectivity of the biographer? You'll find that even if you haven't written a full-fledged biography, you will have found fresh ways to conceptualize those people who are closest to you.

The Obstacle Course

When we write about family, we set ourselves up for a plethora of ethical, emotional, and technical issues that may hinder us from writing altogether. It's one thing to write about your sister in your diary; it's quite another to write about her in an essay published in a national magazine. And when we set out to write about family, we are naturally going to feel compelled to break long silences that may have kept the family together in the first place. In recent years, many creative nonfiction works have emerged that take on issues of child abuse, incest, alcoholic parents, and other emotionally charged issues. When you sit down to write, you might feel obligated to write about traumas of your family history. You might feel these are the only issues "worth" tackling in literature.

Family is always an enormous subject, and as writers, we must find a way to handle this subject with both aplomb and discretion. If your family history is particularly charged, it will be even more essential for you to find the smaller details—the miniscule anecdotes—that will lead the way into a successful essay. This is not to say that you can't or won't take on the big issues.

But they must arrive on the page less as issues and more as scenes, images, and metaphors that will evoke a strong response from the reader.

Permission to Speak

While drafting your essay, you must instinctively drown out the voices that tell you *not* to write. Your mother, father, sisters, and brothers must all be banished from the room where you sit at your desk and call up potentially painful or embarrassing memories. But once you know you have an essay that is more for public consumption than private venting, you have some difficult decisions to make. How much of this is really your own story to tell?

Writers deal with this dilemma in a variety of ways. Some merely remain in denial, convincing themselves that no one—least of all their families—will ever read their work. Some go to the opposite extreme, confessing to their families about their writing projects and asking permission to divulge certain stories and details, giving them complete veto power. Some, such as Frank McCourt with *Angela's Ashes*, wait until the major players have died so that they can no longer be hurt by the exposure or pass judgment on the writer. Some decide that writing about this material in a nonfiction form is just too risky and decide to present their work as fiction instead. Some writers change the names of their characters—some even go so far as to write under a pseudonym—to protect both themselves and their families.

However you choose to negotiate these tricky issues, remember that your story *is* your story to tell. Yours is not the *only* story or perspective on family or on your community, but it is a perfectly valid voice among the chorus. In her essay "Writing About Family: Is It Worth It?" Mimi Schwartz reminds us that "a memoirist, in particular, must think of truth as having a small 't,' not a big one—as in *my* truth rather than *the* truth." And if you examine this truth with a healthy sense of perspective and with literary skill, you may be surprised at the reactions you evoke among your subjects. They may feel honored to see themselves couched in a work of literature and grateful to discover aspects of you they never realized before.

Here is how Robin Hemley dealt with these issues when he wrote and published "Reading History to My Mother."

I think this is one of the few essays I haven't shown my mother. . . . I don't think that one needs to show everything one writes to those involved—sometimes one can actually do more harm than good with the full-disclosure impulse. Sometimes, one acts more out of one's own need for absolution rather than actually considering the feelings of the person to whom the disclosure is made. . . . We write for many different reasons, and often our best work is dangerous, edgy, and guilt-inducing. Sometimes we feel it's worth sharing with others, whether the reasons are literary or therapeutic, and I don't think we should necessarily engage in self-censorship simply because we might be unwilling to share our work with the person(s) the work deals with. . . . I'd say that my decision was made of equal measures of love and cowardice.

Love and *cowardice* might aptly describe all of us when we find ourselves writing about family or about those close to us in our communities. Complex emotions beset us in this endeavor, and we must remain aware of them before they ambush us altogether.

If we are going to write successfully about family, our motives must be more than simple exposure of family history and secrets. We must have some *perspective* on our experience that spurs the essay beyond our own personal "dirty laundry" and into the realm of literature. (See Chapter 12 for a discussion of the dangers of "revenge prose" and "the therapist's couch.")

Our role as writers can be that of the witness. We continually bear witness to those around us, and sometimes our job is to speak for those who have never spoken for themselves. When we write about our families or take on the mantle of the biographer, we are really writing (and forging) community. As Terry Tempest Williams writes, in her essay "A 'Downwinder' in Hiroshima, Japan": "I think about . . . how much we need to hear the truth of one another's lives. . . . The Japanese have a word, *aware*, which speaks to both the beauty and pain of our lives, that sorrow is not a grief one forgets or recovers from but is a burning, searing illumination of love for the delicacy and strength of our relations."

Think of yourself as a witness and your writing will take on greater weight and urgency. As you write about the other people who populate your memories and life, you will do so with a clearer sense of purpose that will elevate your writing beyond the purely personal.

TRY IT

1. Try to reconstruct the names of your matriarchal or patriarchal lineage. For instance, what is the name of your mother, your mother's mother, your mother's mother's mother, and so forth? How far back can you go? For instance, in Brenda's case, she once started an essay with the line, "I am the daughter of Sandra, the daughter of Beatrice, the daughter of Pearl." Naming them brings them to life and enables you to begin writing about them. Where do the names come from? Does your own name have any "inheritance" attached to it? What are the stories behind the names? Are you adopted? How does this affect how you construct your sense of lineage?

> **VARIATION:** Circle one of the names that intrigues you for whatever reason, then do some research on this person. Find photographs, letters, or birth certificates—whatever might be stored in a family archive. Begin an essay that builds a portrait of this person from the name outward.

2. Describe every member of your family in terms of a part of the body. For instance, describe the hands of your mother, father, siblings, grandparents, and yourself. How are they alike? How are they different? Push this exercise further by going for the smallest images. Look at belly buttons, fingerprints, moles, toenails, or tongues. If necessary, imagine the details. For instance, imagine your grandmother's hands as they were before she was a grandmother. Which traits emerge in your own physical makeup? Which ones do you hate? Which ones do you love? How do you imagine you will look twenty years from now? Forty? Fifty?

3. Begin an essay by imagining the life of someone close to you—a family member, friend, mentor—before you knew them. Use your imagination coupled with your experience of this person. Use any clues that may exist: objects from the past, documents, photographs, and so forth to form a portrait of this person before you were in the picture. Then complete the essay by contrasting this portrait with the person you know today. How are they different or similar?

4. Almost all families have some mythic story about someone meeting a famous person. Try to re-create a relative's encounter with a celebrity.

5. Create a picture of your family based on some simple gesture: the way they sigh, laugh, cry, or kiss. Begin with a vivid, original description of this gesture, then describe your father, your mother, yourself, or any other family members. Try to see how examining these small gestures reveals larger details about the family. (You can track down Bernard Cooper's essay "The Fine Art of Sighing," located in the book *Truth Serum*, as a model if you like.)

6. Write a family story in a voice other than your own. Use the point of view of another family member and see how the story changes or which details now become important.

7. Write a list of the subjects you would "never" write about. What are the silences that can't be broken? Begin each sentence with "I would never write about" or "I am slow to write about." See if this backward maneuver might actually lead you into scenes, details, and memories you *might* be able to handle in a short essay.

3

"Taking Place":
Writing the Physical World

If you live in a place—any place, city or country—long enough and deeply enough you can learn anything, the dynamics and inter-connections that exist in every community, be it plant, human, or animal—you can learn what a writer needs to know.

—Gretel Ehrlich

I am writing about the first place I remember living, casting around for a way to write about it that fits in with what I've learned is acceptable in the literature of place. Elizabeth, New Jersey: people who know the city shudder and mention the rows of smokestacks craning along the side of the New Jersey Turnpike. I spent my early years there, and along with a rickety shore bungalow, it's the place I have the most visceral childhood attachment to. But when I think of the writing of childhood place I think of Vladimir Nabokov's *Speak, Memory*, with the majestic beauty of pre-Revolutionary St. Petersburg; of Annie Dillard's wooded rambles in *An American Child-hood*. How do you write about a vacant lot glinting with glass, where I spent many ecstatic hours as a child, a cemetery where my brother and I played? It was as scary and luminous a childhood as any other. Does place matter only when it carries its own transcendent beauty? How do you memorialize the seemingly unbeautiful?

After many false starts, I begin writing about my early home by reflecting on the city's name. "Elizabeth," I write, "had a Queen's name. Every land's an extension of the monarch's body, a great green I Am of the royal person, and Elizabeth's city showed she'd been gone a long time. It was gassy and bad-smelling as any dead woman."

The Elizabeth of the city, I learned much later, was not Queen Elizabeth, as I'd thought, but some other woman. No matter. It was what I believed at the time of writing, and what I believed, for some reason, as a child. The interest of the place was not in its beauty, its own transcendent qualities, but the way it bounced off my life and the lives of those around me: the character it became.

—SUZANNE

Start Looking

Where are you reading this book? Put it down for a second and look around you; take into account what is both inside and outside the space you're in. In your mind, run over the significance of this place. Are you somewhere that has meaning for you because it is the place you grew up or because it is not? Does this place represent freedom or responsibility? Is it someplace temporary for you or permanent? When you force yourself to look around carefully and openly, do you thrill to the natural beauty or respond to its urban excitement? Or are you somewhere now you feel you could never call home?

Our responses to place are some of the most complex we'll ever experience. Our sense of visual beauty, our psychological drive for comfort and familiarity in our environment, and our complex responses to loaded concepts such as "nature" and "home" embed place with layers of significance. Although fiction writers typically have the importance of location and setting driven into them, it is easy for nonfiction writers to forget that they, too, must be situated physically. We find that an essayist with a wonderful story to tell—a family story, say, of a troubled Vietnam-vet father or of raising an autistic child—will typically leave out the vital backdrop of the story: a supportive small town, a resource-rich city, or a town in which the family's story unfolds against a background of petty bigotry and misunderstanding.

Where We're Writing From

We, Brenda and Suzanne, landed—through various tracks—in the smallish city of Bellingham, Washington, under a volcano called Mt. Baker that is presently giving off steam from under-earth vents called *fumaroles*. On the one hand, our lives are peaceful. We teach classes, write, attend a film or concert now and then, and work on this book. On the other hand, every few years the mountain issues this fleecy reminder that it has more control than we ever give it credit for. Under its crust is enough molten rock to turn our lives into something else entirely.

Environments tend to function as informing elements that we take for granted and edit out of our stories until they act up. We who live here may notice that people become quieter and more lethargic during our gray, rainy winter months, bursting back into exuberant life when the sun returns. Nevertheless, it takes a certain amount of awareness to relate the way our lives unfold to the fact that we live here, in the maritime Northwest, rather than somewhere else. (And in fact, when the first draft of this chapter was written, we experienced the powerful Nisqually earthquake, centered south of Seattle, which sent our computers dancing and our certainties about the ground beneath our feet shaking along with them.)

Before proceeding any further in this chapter, pull out an essay you've already written and check to see if locations and physical settings are established. Can we hear how a key conversation was heightened by the silence of a forest clearing? Do we see and smell the banyan trees of South Florida rather than the cedars of the Northwest? If you write of a town or a city, is its physical location and socioeconomic character clear?

Setting Scenes: Place as Character

In Chapter 13, "The Basics of Good Writing in Any Form," we discuss in depth the techniques of scene-setting and its importance in nonfiction. It seems useful to touch on that topic here as well. Nonfiction writers use place frequently as a primary subject. Even if you never do, however, the place where a story unfolds plays a vital role. In all the elements of setting a scene—character, dialogue, place, action—place can be the easiest one to overlook.

Would *Jane Eyre* have been the same book without her tale unfolding against the backdrop of Thornfield, that gabled mansion with its nests of crows? Would Huckleberry Finn's adventures have had the same resonance without the silvery roil of the Mississippi River? Your own story needs the same depth of field. One useful way to judge your own scene-setting is to think of place as a character unto itself. In the excerpt from the essay "Elizabeth" at the start of this chapter, the city takes on the character of a woman: an aging, decayed figure against which the children's exploits take on an incongruous irony.

Writing About Home

For nonfiction writers, particularly memoirists, the place of childhood has a critical importance. It is the primal map on which we plot life's movements. It is the setting of the rich mythology that is earliest memory (see Chapter 1), the enchanted forest in which our benighted characters wander, looking for breadcrumbs and clues and facing down their demons. If you draw your earliest place of memory—a bedroom, say, or a favorite hiding place in an apartment or a yard—you will, by the highly selective and emotional process of memory, be drawing an emotional landscape of your childhood.

Maybe you remember the deep, sagging chair that attracted and frightened you because it was sacred to your father and he sank into it in the evening, angry from the day's work. Or perhaps you remember the table where your family sat around and ate kimchi, which none of your friends ate and of which you learned to be vaguely ashamed. Maybe you recall the soft woolly smell of your covers at night or the dim blue glow of a nightlight. This is home, the place where the complex person you are came into being. And understanding the concept of home and its physical character is key to understanding the many different individuals you'll write about in your nonfiction.

When Home Is Away

Bharati Mukherjee, an Indian-American writer, says home to her is a place she has never been and that no longer exists in a national sense. At the time of her father's birth, his village was in India. Now it is part of Bangladesh. As a woman of Indian descent, she defines her home patrilineally, making her a citizen of an unknown place, bearing ethnic claims that no longer make any sense. In her essay "A Four-Hundred-Year-Old Woman," she writes:

> I was born into a class that did not live in its native language. I was born
> into a city that feared its future, and trained me for emigration. I attended

a school run by Irish nuns, who regarded our walled-off school compound in Calcutta as a corner (forever green and tropical) of England. My "country"—called in Bengali *desh*, and suggesting more a homeland than a nation of which one is a citizen—I have never seen. It is the ancestral home of my father and is now in Bangladesh. Nevertheless, I speak his dialect of Bengali, and think of myself as "belonging" to Faridpur.

Later, Mukherjee writes that for her, "the all too real Manhattan [her present home] and Faridpur have merged as 'desh.'"

For most Americans, the terms *home* and *native* are probably loaded with connotations we rarely pause to tease out. We—Brenda and Suzanne—for example, celebrate different holidays. We bake our traditional breads—challah and panettone—and mark rites of passage with chopped liver or the dried fish called *baccala* without much awareness of how those foods reflect what was available and affordable in our families' countries of origin, or the poverty and threat reflected in the fact that our not-too-distant forebears came to be here. There are stories in these deeply personal, everyday connections and disconnections in American lives.

Writing About Nature

If we think of place as character, we should add that no "character" comes with as many preconceptions as nature. Drawing energy from early writers like Thoreau, American essayists have always had a particular affinity with nature writing. This country in its present national incarnation is new—the "new country" that creates by being in opposition to the "old country" of the preceding discussion. For much of its life, it has defined itself by its wilderness, by the sense of frontier to be explored and frequently controlled. American nature essayists such as Emerson and Thoreau were called *transcendentalists* because of their belief that nature would allow humans to rise above, or transcend, the limits of civilization. And even as the American wilderness vanishes, literature faces the question of what we have lost with it, along with the buffalo, sequoia, and deep old-growth forests breathing so recently out of our past.

In his classic memoir *Walden; Or, Life in the Woods*, Henry David Thoreau's declarations become a charge to nature writers and nature seekers for generations to come: "I went to the woods because I wished to live deliberately, to front only the essential facts of life, and see if I could not learn what it had to teach, and not, when I came to die, discover that I had not lived." American literature's historic distrust of civilization (think of *Huckleberry Finn*) has created a particular reverence for nature writing in our country. Writers like Thoreau teach us that recording the experiences of the individual removed from society—one on one with the physical world that created him or her—provides an avenue to "live deep and suck out all the marrow of life."

Thoreau's approach to nature—as a way of paring life down to its essentials, finding oneself—continues in the work of writers such as Wendell Berry. In essays like "An Entrance to the Woods," Berry describes how on a hiking trip, "Today, as always when I am afoot in the woods, I feel the possibility, the reasonableness, the practicability of living in the world in a way that would enlarge rather than diminish the hope of life."

To Berry and Thoreau, nature represents life at its most basic—life at the bone. But in the literary world, few subjects are as complex in their symbolic structure as nature. To Wordsworth, it was the ultimate muse, the "anchor of his purest thoughts." To others, it's simply the ultimate power.

What does nature mean to you? For those with a nature-writing bent, it's deceptively simple to wax rhapsodic about the cathedral beauty of old-growth forests or the piercing melodies of the thrush. In other words, we tend to approach nature writing first and foremost as description. While fine description is dandy, it tends to wear thin after a while. Even if your prose about the soft rosy beauty of the alpenglow is first rate, if you don't move beyond that, readers are likely to want to put your writing down and go see for themselves.

What holds readers in the works of writers like Berry and Thoreau is the sense of a *human consciousness* moving through nature, observing it, reacting to it, and ultimately being transformed by it. Thoreau's description of his cottage at Walden Pond is instructive:

> I was seated by the shore of a small pond. . . . I was so low in the woods that the opposite shore, half a mile off, like the rest, covered with wood, was my most distant horizon. For the first week, whenever I looked out on the pond it impressed me like a tarn high up on the side of a mountain, its bottom far above the surface of other lakes, and, as the sun arose, I saw it throwing off its nightly clothing of mist, and here and there, by degrees, its soft ripples or its smooth reflecting surface was revealed, while the mists, like ghosts, were stealthily withdrawing in every direction into the woods.

Notice how Thoreau embeds his basic concept of living in nature as stripping human life bare in this very description. Not only is it beautifully poetic, but we see Walden Pond looming huge in front of him, throwing off its obscuring mists, as a kind of mirror for Thoreau's consciousness, coming clear in nature and throwing off the layer of fog of human convention.

Remember Scott Russell Sanders's essay "Buckeye" from the "Touch" section of Chapter 1? Later in the essay, Sanders describes how his father, a born naturalist, once stripped the husk from a buckeye to show it to his son. "He picked up one, as fat as a lemon, and peeled away the husk to reveal the shiny seed. He laid it in my palm and closed my fist around it so the seed peeped out from the circle formed by my index finger and thumb." Here, the buckeye seems to come alive, almost hatching from the author's hand. It's an image of the life both men find in nature, as well as an image of the father coming alive in the author's memory.

When you think of your feelings about nature, think about Thoreau and Sanders, and the question of how what you see before you embodies larger forces: an aspect of the human condition or the tenderness and toughness of a person you know. Use that larger element as a way into your essay.

Writing About the Environment

In an issue of the literary journal *Granta* devoted to the "new nature writing," editors explained their subject this way: "For as long as people have been writing, they have been writing about nature. But economic migration, overpopulation, and climate change are transforming the natural world into something unfamiliar. As our conception and experience of nature changes, so too does the way we write about it." For instance, critics have coined terms like "superfund Gothic" to describe a natural world in which industrial chemicals interfere with the gender characteristics of fish and wildlife.

In "An Entrance to the Woods," Wendell Berry goes beyond merely describing the woods or the way in which his hiking and camping experience lends perspective to his own human existence. As a nonfiction writer who is constantly pushing himself to examine with the broadest possible lens what exists at the tips of his fingers (which all good nonfiction writers do), he asks himself how he as a human being embodies the larger interaction of human and nature. It's an interrelationship that's become problematic at the beginning of the twenty-first century, as we face global warming and the last century's outpouring of industrial pollution.

While in the woods, Berry hears the roar of a car in the distance and writes, "That roar of the highway is the voice of the American economy; it is sounding also wherever strip mines are being cut in the steep slopes of Appalachia, and wherever cropland is being destroyed to make roads and suburbs. . . ." It is a wonderful moment in the essay, of opening out and refocusing from a simple, enlightening natural experience to a critique of human intervention in the natural order that we've come to label the *ecosystem*.

Typically, a writer sitting down to compose a nature essay such as Berry's would "erase" that car motor from his or her record of this occasion, simply leave it out; it is tempting in nonfiction to pare down our experiences to those sights and sounds that make a unified whole. A passing mention of the noise as an anomaly—out of tone with the peaceful surroundings—would also be a natural move to make. It would be a far less important and less honest tack, though, than Berry's turn, which was to discuss how these woods in the essay exist in uneasy, threatened relationship to the human-dominated world around them.

Travel Writing

Often, a sense of place comes into sharp focus when we travel off our own turf and into lands foreign to us. Our survival instincts take over, and we grow alert as cats, turning our heads at the call of the *muezzin* in the mosque, sniffing out the smell of roasted lamb in the market stall, spying an old man bearing a homemade wooden coffin up the alleyways of a walled city. In the context of travel, "place" begins to seem not so much the land itself, but everything and anything associated with the land: its people, animals, food, music, religion—all the things that make up life itself.

Pico Iyer, a consummate travel writer, sums it up this way: "We travel, initially, to lose ourselves; and we travel, next, to find ourselves. We travel to open our hearts and eyes and learn more about the world than our newspapers will accommodate. . . . And we travel, in essence, to become young fools again—to slow time down and get taken in, and fall in love once more."

Your task, as a good travel writer, is to both pay attention to the details of place—in all their glorious particularities, with all their good points and bad—and to render these details in a voice that is wholly your own. You must situate yourself as both participant and observer, always ready for the unexpected, but armed with the many lenses that enable you to interpret this world for your readers in a way they've never heard before.

This mandate requires you to find a purpose for your writing *above and beyond* the travel experience itself. Otherwise, you will produce a piece of writing akin to those slide shows we all dread: the summons into a friend's living room to view her pictures of last summer's vacation. "And here we are at the Louvre," the hostess quips brightly, while her guests nod off behind her on the couch in the flickering light of the slide projector. If you expect the travels themselves to carry the weight of narrative interest, you will end up with an essay that looks disconcertingly like: "First I went here, then I went here, and look what an amazing/horrible/fascinating/soul-searing time I had!" Eventually, no one will care. They will sneak out your living room the back way, leaving you alone with your out-of-focus slides. The places themselves may be intrinsically fascinating, but if you render them into flat landscapes, you'll be left with the lame protest, "Well, you just had to have been there."

In a way, the demands of travel writing can epitomize the challenges of any kind of creative nonfiction writing. How do you shape or draft the work so that the experience becomes *more* than itself? How do you relinquish the role of the transcriber and take on the mantle of the artist? Critic Paul Fussell answers that question this way: "Successful travel writing mediates between two poles: the individual physical things it describes, on the one hand, and the larger theme that it is 'about' on the other. That is, the particular and the universal."

For instance, to come back to Pico Iyer once more, his books not only describe his travels into places as diverse as the L.A. airport, Burmese temples, and suburban Japan, but they also often become inquiries into the effects of globalization on the world's cultures. Born to Indian parents in England, then living for a long time in California, Iyer brings with him his deep-seated—almost innate—awareness of how modern cultural boundaries have begun to blur. He begins his book *Video Night in Kathmandu* with a description of how Sylvester Stallone's movie character Rambo had infiltrated every cinema in Asia during his visit there in 1985. By using this one specific example as a focus, he sets the tone and purpose for the book. "I went to Asia," he writes a few pages into the first chapter, "not only to see Asia, but also to see America, from a different vantage point and with new eyes. I left one kind of home to find another: to discover what resided in me and where I resided most fully, and so to better appreciate—in both senses of the word—the home I had left."

With this kind of sensibility, Iyer gains the trust of the reader. Here we know we are in the hands of a traveler who has experienced a place not only as a tourist, but as an intellectual, an artist, and a pilgrim. We can read his books, yes, to get tips on how to survive those twelve-hour bus trips, or we can read to enjoy the characters and scenes he re-enacts (his description of the bicycle trishaw driver in Mandalay will stay with you long after the book is done). But these details are held within a much greater context. In this way, he travels with a purpose that allows a sense of place to penetrate him and his readers on many levels at once.

You will find that good travel writers avoid the pitfalls that lead to self-serving or clichéd writing. They not only have a heightened perception, a precise attention to language, and a facility with scene-making, but also a marked *generosity* innate in the writer's stance, a perception that sees the foibles of the world and forgives them. In much of the beginning writing we see about travel, the writer falls into stereotypes about other tourists and the native people; he begins to either make fun of or put down the others he encounters on his travels. Such a stance not only becomes distasteful to the reader, but it betrays an insufficient maturity on the part of the writer to understand what is important and what is not. His attention to place becomes annoyingly myopic, and he becomes a whiner, complaining about "all those tourists" while munching on potato chips in line to the Sistine Chapel, his cameras slung about his neck. He is guilty of just what he is criticizing: the tourist mentality that sees only the surfaces and complains when the place fails to live up to expectations.

The other pitfall in travel writing is for the voice to become too much like a guidebook, commenting heavily on the cleanliness of the bathrooms in a hotel in downtown Istanbul but missing the dawn light on the Blue Mosque. As Fussell puts it: "Guidebooks are not autobiographical but travel books are, and if the personality they reveal is too commonplace and un-eccentric, they will not be very readable." As with any good creative nonfiction, the *self* must be wholly present in the work, a voice that engages us to take this trip along with you, to stand at the windows and gaze out at what you, *and only you*, choose to show us.

Witnesses to Our World

In the last chapter, we discussed the emerging sense of much nonfiction as a literature of *witness*—the sense that, in a world flooded with activity and change and information sources the public growingly distrusts (rightly or wrongly), the individual voice may provide the ultimate record. In the last decades nothing has changed faster than the environment. The world's population has burgeoned, and technology has developed the ability to clear lands, pollute the air, and drive species to extinction in record time. Your life has witnessed the eclipse of hundreds of thousands of species, even if they passed out of this world without your awareness. (The current rate of species extinction is matched only by that of the age of the dinosaurs' demise, sixty-five million years ago.) Your life has also seen the destruction of much natural land and its replacement with man-made habitat, even if this fact too only barely crossed your consciousness.

For instance, if you can remember a time when Rhode Island spent winters buried under several feet of snow—now replaced by light snows and rains—you may be a witness to the phenomenon many would call global warming. Or, if you remember catching salmon or chasing frogs as a child—creatures you now see rarely if at all—you have witnessed the severe recent decline of several indigenous creatures. Perhaps you have simply noticed that where you live, the last decade has contained most of the area's historic high temperatures. There is a reason nature writing has become so urgent in our era—both the need to record what is left and the need to chronicle what we are losing. Take your role as a witness seriously; think of your writing as a way to capture the changes you've lived in the natural world.

TRY IT

1. Isolate a single room or outdoor place that to you forms the most essential place of childhood. Quickly write down every element of the place you can remember with as much detail as possible. What were the patterns of the things you see? Are they old or new? Which odd details do you remember (e.g., a gargoyle-shaped knot in the wood, a gray rug with a dark stain the shape of Brazil, and so forth)? Now fill in an emotional tone for each detail. Did the wallpaper make you feel safe or frightened? What were your favorite things in this place to look at? Your least favorite? Why? What felt "yours" and what felt other? Assemble these specifics into an essay about the emotional landscape of your childhood, moving about the room, letting your essay function as an emotional "camera."

2. Many of us, like Mukherjee, find our sense of "desh" blends real and distant—maybe unseen—places. Is your family one of the many in this country that embodies a divided sense of home? What does "home" mean to you, your siblings, your parents? Many contemporary American families are very transient now. As one of our students, whose father had been transferred multiple times as she grew up, put it, "home is where there's a room for me to unpack my things." Think about whether there's a single place—a physical location—your family defines as "home," or what you do as you move around to bring the sense of home with you. If you're adopted, your birth family, whether you know them or not, may represent another concept of home. Consider writing an essay in which you unpack the complex layers of meaning in the word *home*, with specific references to all the possibilities.

3. Is there an "old country" in your family profile? How does it affect your family culture, traditions, or modes of interacting? Write about the ways your family's country or countries of origin cause you to see yourself as different from others in your area, perhaps straddling several very different cultures.

4. Examine a piece of your writing and scrutinize place as character. Is your setting a developed character? What kind of character is it: positive, nurturing, menacing, indifferent? Imagine the setting of a scene as a silent character, shaping and adding nuance to the action surrounding it.

> VARIATION: Write a biography of a place. Choose a street, a forest, an airport (possibly look at Pico Iyer's essay on the Los Angeles airport, "Where Worlds Collide," for guidance), a shopping center, any place that has character to you, whether positive or negative. Write a profile, a "character study," of that environment.

5. Can you articulate what your own vision of nature is? If the outdoors draws you and brings you a special kind of knowledge or contentment, can you put into words what that connection consists of? What would your metaphor be of the human-nature interaction that is, in many ways, the ground of our lives here on earth? Can you think of a time when you went into a natural setting to make a difficult decision, work something out in your mind, or somehow come to feel more "yourself"? What led you to that place? Did it help you in the way you wanted?

Remember, as you articulate your sense of nature in language, that there's nothing else (besides love, perhaps!) that so easily lends itself to cliché. Tranquil brooks, awesome mountains, trilling birds—these are the stuff of hackneyed authors. Make your description fresh, original, and interesting.

> **VARIATION:** Jennifer Price, who wrote an essay titled "A Brief Natural History of the Plastic Pink Flamingo," writes about *urban nature*, the aspects of nature that thrive in cities—nature stores at malls, even stuffed birds on women's hats. Write about nature without pursuing nature in the traditional sense. Stay in your apartment building or go to a shopping mall and observe the trees, the crow colonies, even the microclimates created by human development.

6. In this era of accelerating change, we ask you to think of your life as a piece of living history. Looking at your life as an intersection of personal history and the environment that surrounds you, to what can you bear witness? Write for about ten minutes, associating freely and spontaneously, about a place of your childhood, a place that for you defines your childhood—the porch of your house, a creek, the fire escape of an apartment, a special place in the woods. What did the place smell, taste, feel like? Include, but don't limit yourself to, the natural elements: air quality and odor, trees, wildlife (including insects).

Now write for ten minutes on what this place is like now, whether from your own current experiences of it or from what you've been told. How has it changed? What is gone now that was there before? What is there now that wasn't there before? Think of yourself as a living history of this place—what changes did you find between the place of your childhood and the place of your adulthood? Do these changes reflect any changes in your own life?

As you compare these two quick writings, see what larger elements emerge. Have you and the place of your childhood changed in tandem or gone in different directions? Are you witness to changes that reflect larger—perhaps dangerous—currents of change in our contemporary world? Think about it: even seemingly small things, like the loss of much of our amphibian life, such as frogs, will alter over time the nature of the planet we live on. Think about your writings in the largest possible sense: often this short exercise unlocks a valuable essay.

7. If you have a travel diary or journal, go back to it now and pull out sections that give highly sensory descriptions of place: the feel of the air, the taste of the food, the sounds, the smells. Type these out in separate sections, then arrange them on a table, seeing if you can find a common theme that may bind an essay together. What can you construe as the greater purpose for your travels? How can you incorporate that purpose into your travel writing? What is the one image that will emerge for metaphorical significance?

8. Take a day to travel your hometown as a tourist. Pretend you've never seen this place before and wander with all your senses heightened. Take a notebook with you and write down your impressions. How can you make the familiar new again?

> **Variation for a group:** As a group, take this trip together. Then compare notes and see how different eyes perceive different things. Take some time at the end of the day, or a few days later, to write together and see where these sensory impressions might lead.

9. Read Annie Dillard's essay "Living Like Weasels" (from her book of essays *Teaching a Stone to Talk*) or Jill Christman's essay "The Sloth" (in the online journal *Brevity*, issue 26). Then think of an encounter you have had with a wild animal that you found personally meaningful. Freewrite on this moment, considering the following questions: How can this creature work as a metaphor for you? How has your encounter with this animal marked you, changed you, or caused you to see yourself differently? How do this creature's actions mirror yours? How are you fundamentally different? What finally haunts you about this moment?

Think of animals we see often, perhaps, with an eye toward reinvigorating our view of them: deer, squirrels, opossums, crows. Use research, if you need more concrete information. Even the creatures we see every day have fascinating aspects to them: opossums are the only North American marsupials. Crows have documented tool use and a sophisticated language.

4

Writing the Spiritual Autobiography

Be patient toward all that is unsolved in your heart and try to love the questions themselves like locked rooms or like books written in a very foreign tongue. Do not now seek the answers, which cannot be given you because you would not be able to live them. . . . Live the questions now. Perhaps you will then gradually, without noticing it, live along some distant day into the answer.

—Rainer Maria Rilke

Before I sit down at my desk, I look out my window and notice the light as it reflects off the bay. I light a candle and a stick of incense, reaching over the small statue of a Buddha sitting on the windowsill. On a shelf above my desk sits a menorah my parents gave me for Hanukkah one year. A St. Christopher medal lies coiled in a small compartment in a drawer of my desk. Photographs of my four great-grandmothers bear witness to all this spiritual paraphernalia, gazing down at me with what I interpret as amused benevolence.

All of these things—the light off the bay, the incense, the meditating Buddha, the menorah, St. Christopher, my ancestors—create an atmosphere of eclectic spirituality that has come to inform much of my writing. From the very beginning, my writing has tended to chronicle the sometimes baffling turns my spiritual path has taken: from acting as the earnest president of my Jewish youth group, to drifting through days of Grateful Dead concerts in the eighties (convinced of the divinity of Jerry Garcia), to backpacking solo in the meadows around Mt. Rainier, to meditating in silence for weeks at a time in California farmhouses. I've settled down a bit in my staid middle age, but I've never lost that sense of spiritual quest driving the trajectory of my life.

Now, writing itself seems to be the deepest spiritual act I can perform. So I sit down at my desk. I light my incense. I look out my window and take a deep breath. I feel the presence of my great-grandmothers cheering me on. I write one word and then another. Who knows where it will lead? What kind of faith can I muster to continue? I don't know. It's a little like prayer, a little like meditation, a little like walking an unknown trail in the high country.

—Brenda

The Tradition of Spiritual Autobiography

Though oftentimes invisible in our lives, spirituality seems to follow us everywhere. From the moment we're born, we're initiated into a world that relies on many different rituals to guide us. Or, if we're born into a family more secular, we become aware of ourselves in opposition to predominant modes of religious belief. Perhaps that is why we've lately noticed a renaissance in memoirs that use either religion or spirituality as a guiding narrative or metaphor.

But the impulse to write spiritual autobiography has been around as long as human consciousness. The form keeps adapting to fit whatever culture and society demand of it. These works range from devotional narratives to science writing that finds spiritual fodder in the cells of the human body, but the basic structure usually wins out. These narratives tend to focus on moments of insight that lead the narrator in a new direction. By their very nature, many spiritual autobiographies appear to mimic or echo classic "conversion" stories found in religious texts: the protagonist is lost and then found, and the narratives hinge on precise moments of "turning," either away or toward points of reference identified as God, Allah, Yahweh, the Great Spirit, and so on.

These conversions may also work the opposite way, especially after defining events such as the Holocaust or the terrorist attacks of September 11, 2001.

The narrator moves from a place of religious or spiritual certainty to one that is more fragmented or full of doubt.

We can call these moments "epiphanies" (sudden insights), but they don't necessarily arrive with the bang the term suggests. They may be quiet moments, barely noticeable until the act of writing magnifies their significance. A turning point can be as subtle as Emily Dickinson's "certain slant of light" into a room, or Virginia Woolf's contemplation of a dying moth in her study.

The Quest Narrative

Full-length spiritual autobiographies essentially take the form of a *quest narrative*, propelled by burning questions, a journey toward an unclear destination. The protagonist sets herself on a path, encounters obstacles and unexpected guides, and is transformed along the way. For example, *The Wizard of Oz* could be the most traditional and metaphoric of spiritual autobiographies. The protagonist, Dorothy, driven by deep, inchoate longing, finds herself on a journey in an unknown country. Essentially alone, she must rely on guidance from unexpected sources to find her way toward a vague, promised land. She encounters many obstacles along the way, many turning points, but finally arrives at Oz, only to find the destination nothing like what she imagines. When she finally returns home, she is the same person but transformed by her quest.

Spirituality does not necessarily need to be contained in religions or places of worship. Nature writer John Muir, rather than turning away or toward an external spiritual figure or destination, includes spirituality in all of nature. In *My First Summer in the Sierra*, Muir writes, "In our best times everything turns into religion, all the world seems a church and the mountains altars." *How interesting everything is*, he muses throughout the book, a good mantra any writer can take to heart.

Personal Renditions of the Sacred

As with any strong work of creative nonfiction, the successful spiritual autobiography hinges on discovery through the writing process itself. The writer does not set out to give us predetermined answers but instead allows us some insight into the questions that drive him. Spiritual autobiographies, in particular, "find interesting" the turns in the road and the roadside attractions; they do not necessarily follow a straight line but proceed more intuitively, meandering from point to point in a way that may seem digressive, but actually forms a clear path in retrospect.

In *Traveling Mercies*, Anne Lamott's wry account of her own spiritual process, she puts it this way:

> My coming to faith did not start with a leap but rather a series of staggers from what seemed like one safe place to another. Like lily pads, round and green, these places summoned and then held me up while I grew. . . . When I look back on some of these early resting places—the boisterous home of the Catholics, the soft armchair of the Christian Science mom, adoption by ardent Jews—I can see how flimsy and indirect a path they made. Yet each step brought me closer to the verdant pad of faith on which I somehow stay afloat today.

If you look on your life as a series of "lily pads," the way Anne Lamott does, you may be able to begin an essay structured around these turning points in your spiritual narrative.

Once you set out to examine your own spiritual inclinations, you will find yourself with a new set of writing dilemmas. Spirituality can be an arena fraught with prefabricated rhetoric and tired clichés. As a writer, your challenge is to find a language and a form so personal that *only you* can give us this rendition of the spiritual life. You must remain aware of how your brand of spirituality has been depicted in the past and find a way to circumvent your reader's expectations and resistance. How do you even begin to discuss spirituality without immediately using language that has lost its meaning from overuse?

As we saw in the last three chapters, powerful writing always emerges from the physical, specific, and sensory details of your experience. If you decide to write about spiritual experience—whether positive or negative—you will want to look closely at the physical elements that make up your spiritual life, whether those include incense in a church, chanting in a synagogue, or the odor of cedar on your daily walk. Beginning there, ask yourself how your sense of spirituality informs your life and the lives of those around you.

You could also approach your spiritual autobiography by becoming a "layperson's expert." Poet Kathleen Norris, author of *The Cloister Walk* and other books on faith, creates a lyrical yet highly researched version of spirituality when she immerses herself in the world of a Benedictine monastery. In *Virgin Time*, Patricia Hampl makes a pilgrimage to the roots of her spirituality and presents a "travelogue" of faith that includes not only her own experience but a great deal of "expert" information.

In contrast to Norris and Hampl, who become friendly experts and guides, Anne Lamott takes on the role of the endearing screwup, a woman who tries her best, often falling short but able to recover. She becomes more of a buddy to the reader, articulating all those weaknesses we thought must be kept hidden. Lamott maintains a sense of irony throughout her writings on faith, a conversational voice that trusts the reader as much as we grow to trust her. One pitfall of spiritual writing is that it can become too heavy and self-absorbed; Lamott provides a good model for an alternative voice, one that claims no perfection in the spiritual life.

What Is Your "Koan"?

In his essay "The Mickey Mantle Koan," memoirist and novelist David James Duncan sets himself a koan, a puzzle or riddle given to Zen students by their masters, the answer to which might lead to spiritual enlightenment. In Duncan's case, the koan takes the form of a signed baseball sent to his dying brother by Mickey Mantle. The brother dies before the baseball arrives, and for more than twenty years it sits on Duncan's shelf—intriguing, puzzling, infuriating. Duncan knows the ball offers some clue to sorting out his grief about his brother's death, but he doesn't really know *how* it will do so.

In the essay, Duncan pushes at this "koan" and works it out before our eyes. He takes a simple, almost mundane object—a signed baseball—and gazes at it until it yields some answers. He approaches spirituality not on the level of the abstract but on a grassy playing field, where dirty old balls "hiss and pop" into the gloves of teenage boys:

From the moment I'd first laid eyes on it, all I'd wanted was to take that immaculate ball out to our corridor on an evening just like this one, to take my place near the apples in the north and find my brother waiting beneath the immense firs to the south. All I'd wanted was to pluck that too-perfect ball off its pedestal and proceed, without speaking, to play catch so long and hard that the grass stains and nicks and the sweat of our palms would finally obliterate every last trace of Mantle's blue ink, till all he would have sent us was a grass-green, earth-brown, beat-up old baseball. Beat-up old balls were all we'd ever had anyhow. They were all we ever needed.

When you set about to write your personal rendition of spirituality, look for the concrete *things* of the world that will help you find your own koan. What are the essential questions these objects trigger in you? These questions will help you move, as a writer, from the abstract to the concrete.

Above all, maintain *honesty*—with yourself and your reader. If it has been said before, don't say it. If you veer into platitude and cliché, veer right out of it again. If you find yourself mired in complaint, laugh your way out of it. Render the spiritual life with the same intuition and intelligence you bring to all your work. Find the details, the tone, the rhythms that will separate your voice from the choir's. Sing a solo. Be brave. Really belt it out.

Writing as a Spiritual Practice

Writing is the only way I know how to pray.

—HELENA MARIA VIRAMONTES

Often writers find that the writing process itself grows akin to spiritual practice. It requires the same kind of patience, ritual, and faith. In her book *The Writing Life*, Annie Dillard compares writing to sitting at a desk thirty feet off the ground. "Your work," she writes, "is to keep cranking the flywheel that turns the gears that spin the belt in the engine of belief that keeps you and your desk in midair." Poet Carolyn Forché has called the writer's stance one of "meditative expectancy." Natalie Goldberg, author of *Writing Down the Bones* and *Wild Mind: Living the Writer's Life*, sees writing as an integral part of her Zen practice: "Jack Kornfield, a Vipassana meditation teacher, said last week up at Lama, 'you meditate by yourself, but not for yourself. You meditate for everyone.' This is how we should write."

When we begin to see our writing in this kind of context, we can more easily maintain the patience and faith necessary for our work to be done. It's a secular practice, available to anyone who feels compelled to put pen to paper. When you write this way, you are "living the questions now" and offering up possible pathways into the ineffable.

TRY IT

1. Describe a religious or semireligious ritual that took place in your childhood with some regularity. Use quotes from this ritual as a frame within which you can describe memory, conflict, pleasure, and pain. Move your reader through this ritual with you. Using present tense and vivid imagery, show the emotion you felt about this particular rite as a child.

> **VARIATION:** Rewrite the scene in the past tense, from an adult perspective. How does your attitude toward this rite change?

2. Try to remember a moment in your childhood when you were first aware of a spiritual presence in your life. This can be anything from a moment within your spiritual tradition, a moment in nature, or a moment when you were alone in your room. Describe this experience from the child's point of view, in the present tense.

> **VARIATION:** Describe a moment when you were aware of the *absence* of a spiritual presence in your life. Where do these different moments lead you?

3. Put on a piece of music that has spiritual connotations for you: Gregorian chants, bamboo flutes, a Verdi opera, whatever puts you in a meditative mood. Write to this music without ever mentioning it at all.

> **VARIATION FOR A GROUP:** Each person brings in a piece of music; do the above, with as many pieces as you can in a writing session.

4. If you have a repeating spiritual ritual, give us one particular *scene* out of this rite. Focus on one day, one morning, or one hour that encapsulates what this ritual means to you. Try not to *tell* us what it means, but show us through the details you choose and the tone you create.

5. Imagine yourself into the mind of one of your spiritual ancestors. Which scene or image provides a turning point in your spiritual life even before you're born?

6. Do some research into your spiritual tradition. What are the controversies? How is it practiced in different parts of the world? Interview an elder, or participate in an intensive retreat. Write as both an observer and a participant.

7. Think about the koans that exist in your own life. Which objects, people, places, or situations have always puzzled you? How do these things represent emotions or ideas that you haven't yet been able to articulate? Begin an essay whose goal is to "push" at these objects until they yield some unexpected answers.

8. For the duration of one or two writing sessions, ban certain words from your vocabulary that already have spiritual connotations (*God*, *Lord*, *Allah*, *soul*, *heart*, scriptural language, and so forth). Often this kind of language becomes a crutch, enabling us to avoid going deeper into our material. Make a list of these words to keep with you. See what moves you have to make to avoid using these words. Which images or scenes arise to take their place?

> **Variation for a group:** Make a group list of such words and promise to abide by the prohibition for whatever duration the group decides. When reading each other's work, make note of when such words arise and their effect.

5

Writing the Arts

Culture is like a magnetic field, a patterned energy shaping history. It is invisible, even unsuspected, until a receiver sensitive enough to pick up its messages can give it a voice.

—Guy Davenport

I've put up a new picture, a photograph bought for me at an Edward Weston exhibit last April. The composition shows a young woman, all in black, posed against a high, white fence. She half turns toward the camera; her right hand lies tentatively across her heart. The shadow of a leafless tree (I imagine it to be a young oak) curves up and over this slight figure. Actually, it does more than curve; the shadow arches behind her in a gesture of protection. Almost a bow of respect.

Why do I like this picture so much? I glance at it every day, and every day it puzzles me. What draws me to those dark, shaded eyes? What holds me transfixed by the movement of gray shadows over the straight white planks, the drape of the black coat, the white hand raised to the breast in a stunned gesture of surprise?

These questions led me to write the first essay I ever published, titled "Prologue to a Sad Spring," after Weston's own title of the photograph I describe. In this essay, the photograph's mysterious title becomes a meditation on what it means to have a "sad spring," on how our lives are full of losses never memorialized in photographs. It's a short essay, with a circular design that leads the reader back to the appeal of black-and-white photography and to this particular photograph that started the rumination in the first place. Though it's a simple piece, with simple ambitions, it remains a favorite essay in my repertoire. It feels almost like a gift, an ephemeral connection between myself and the woman in this photograph, a distant communiqué between a writer and a photographer who would never meet.

—BRENDA

The Visual Arts

With old glass-plate daguerreotypes—the earliest form of photography—if you tilt the plate just slightly, the image disappears and the photograph becomes a mirror, an apt metaphor for how the creative nonfiction writer can approach art. Through a close observation of particular paintings, sculptures, or photographs, you can reveal your own take on the world or find metaphors in line with your obsessions. At the same time, you will elucidate that artwork in such a way that the piece will forever after have a greater significance for your reader.

For example, in the essay "Inventing Peace," art historian and journalist Lawrence Weschler closely analyzes a Vermeer painting to understand what is happening during the Bosnian war crimes tribunal in The Hague. He compares the serene, almost dreamlike settings of Vermeer with the atrocities the judges in The Hague, just minutes from the Vermeer exhibit, hear about every day. One particular painting, *The Head of a Young Girl*, intrigues him. He explicates this painting for us:

> Has the girl just turned toward us or is she just about to turn away? . . . The answer is that she's actually doing both. This is a woman who has just turned toward us and is already about to look away: and the melancholy of the moment, with its impending sense of loss, is transferred from her eyes to the tearlike pearl dangling from her ear. . . . The girl's lips are parted in a sudden intake of breath—much, we suddenly notice, as are our own as we gaze back upon her.

Weschler closely studies this painting, interpreting the details as he unfolds them for us one by one. He creates a *speculative narrative* that brings this painting to life. In a *speculative narrative*, the writer infuses a painting or any situation with a story that arises both from fact and imagination. For instance, it is clear in Weschler's description that the *facts* of the painting exist as he relates them—the parted lips, the pearl earring—but he allows himself to speculate on the *meaning* of those details. He brings his own frame of mind to bear on the portrait; this interpretation sets up the themes for his piece.

Throughout the essay he brings in other voices—art historians, the judges at The Hague, other art patrons, journalists covering the tribunal—until we have a view of Vermeer, and this painting in particular, shaped by Weschler's sensibility and by the context in which he chooses to place the painter. In the end, the image of the girl turning away mirrors an image of one of the war criminals, Dusko Tadic, looking up at a television camera, and then turning away. Both images come to be about loss and the ravages of history:

> Inventing peace: I found myself thinking of Vermeer with his camera obscura—an empty box fronted by a lens through which the chaos of the world might be drawn in and tamed back to a kind of sublime order.

As you can see, though the topic is external to the self, Weschler does not sacrifice personal voice. To the contrary, the "I" remains a guiding force throughout the essay: ruminating, reflecting, and questioning his own fascination.

It's important to remember that while nonfiction work about painting is flourishing right now—such as Terry Tempest Williams's *Leap* or Mark Doty's *Still Life with Oysters and Lemon*—photography, sculpture, and installations are all rich subjects for your writing as well. As Tolstoy wrote, art is a language that communicates "soul to soul," on a level that bypasses the intellect. As a writer turning your gaze to the rich, metaphorical world of art, you enter into this dialogue and add to our understanding of the world and ourselves.

The Moving Image Arts

The term *arts* also refers to the moving image arts—television, film, video. A vital and probably the most visible part of our cultural expression, the moving image arts have been somewhat underrepresented in nonfiction and are due for more serious reflection. Remember that although you can find plenty of top-quality film and TV, the art itself doesn't have to be great to warrant your attention. In a brilliant essay titled "Upon Leaving the Movie Theater," Roland Barthes simply writes about the experience of cinema—the darkness of the theater, the unfolding of a narrative in a giant lighted square—as a way of exploring pleasure and our fascination with images.

Remember Paisley Rekdal's "The Night My Mother Met Bruce Lee," from Chapter 2? The essay invokes pop culture images of the Chinese and the Chinese-American, particularly the narrator's mother, whose school guidance counselor advises her not to go to Smith, "hinting at some limitation my mother would prefer to ignore." At the same time, a cook in the restaurant where the mother works tells her he comes from Hong Kong and hence is "*real* Chinese." Rekdal embeds that sense of cultural limbo—appearing Chinese to a white guidance counselor but an assimilated American to a recent immigrant—in the artifice of kung fu movies. In the essay, mother and daughter bond watching the martial arts film *Enter the Dragon*:

> Bruce Lee narrows his eyes, ripples his chest muscles under his white turtleneck.
>
> "I knew him," my mother tells me. "I worked with him in a restaurant when I was in high school."
>
> "Really?" This is now officially the only cool thing about her. "What was he like?"
>
> "I don't remember. No one liked him, though. All that kung fu stuff; it looked ridiculous. Like a parody."

Rekdal pays close attention to the film itself in this piece; her prose follows the film's use of lighting—the way Lee's chest "seemed outlined in silver," mirroring the way Rekdal's mother's face "twists into something I do not recognize in the television light." It's as if the cultural distortion created by the movie and movies like it distorts the mother even in the eyes of her daughter. Note that Rekdal has been careful to look at the techniques of the films in question and use them throughout her essay—not just the kung fu itself, which becomes picked up by the restaurant chef, but kung fu films' visual style of bright color and exaggerated gesture.

Films can comment on our own lives and on the history surrounding them. And film and television can capture a cultural moment. Think of how at times movies such as *Thelma and Louise* or TV shows such as "Seinfeld" seem to speak for the feelings of large numbers of people in our society, generating catchphrases and images that become embedded in our collective consciousness. These arts define us personally as well, as Rekdal shows.

As you draft an essay using the moving image arts, think of how you can use those artistic techniques for your own purposes. Can you borrow the visual style of the work in question? Can you write an essay that you model on scenes in the work you've viewed?

You can also take a more analytical approach to television and film, exploring what they mean in terms of culture and society. For example, Bill McKibben, in his book *The Age of Missing Information*, performs an experiment in which he has friends record every channel on a Virginia cable network for twenty-four hours, then he goes about analyzing what he sees to create a portrait of the American mind-set: what we learn—and, more importantly, what we *don't* learn—from what surrounds us on TV. McKibben, who doesn't own a television himself, spends several months watching these videotapes of a single day's television programming:

> I began spending eight or ten hour days in front of the VCR—I watched it all, more or less. A few programs repeat endlessly, with half-hour "infomercials" for DiDi 7 spot remover and Liquid Luster car wax leading the list at more than a dozen appearances apiece. Having decided that once or twice was enough to mine their meanings, I would fast-forward through them, though I always slowed down to enjoy the part where the car-wax guy sets fire to the hood of his car.

As you can see, even though McKibben has set himself a huge, intellectual task, he does not sacrifice his personal voice or his sense of humor to do it. He contrasts what one can learn from a day of television to what one can learn from a day in the woods, providing highly specific examples of each mode, and revealing his own personality at the same time. He turns his attention and powers of observation on something as common as television and enables us to perceive its greater meaning.

Music

As we mentioned in Chapter 1, music can key us into powerful memories that define the self. And music can also serve as a medium to channel some of the most vital issues of our time. We still look back at the 1960s antiwar movement by looking at the music that sprang out of it (and what 1960s documentary would be complete without footage of Country Joe and the Fish's "I Feel Like I'm Fixin' to Die Rag"?). Music is a vessel that holds the emotions of its time.

As an example, let's consider David Margolick, Hilton Als, and Ellis Marsalis's book *Strange Fruit: The Biography of a Song*. "Strange Fruit," a song written for blues singer Billie Holiday, tells the horrendous story of Southern lynchings. Through the lens of this song Margolick, Als, and Marsalis weave together the tales of Holiday's short, heroin-addicted life, the white communist sympathizer who wrote the song, the struggle for civil rights, New York café society, even the history of lynching. This single song contains within it a story that branches out and out to speak of two extraordinary human beings as well as the thorniest problem in American history—race.

Another approach might be to mine your obsession with a particular musician or type of music. For example, in his book *But Beautiful*, Geoff Dyer creates improvisational portraits of eight jazz musicians, getting into their heads, using their points of view. His language and prose style take their cue from jazz, running riffs and hitting discordant notes, as he tries to capture the essence of these musicians on paper. As he explains in the introduction: "When I began writing this book I was unsure of the form it should take. This was a great advantage since it meant I had to improvise and so, from the start, the writing was animated by the defining characteristic of its subject." He calls his book "imaginative criticism," and he uses fictional elements along with the facts of these musicians' lives. The result is a speculative narrative, one that roots itself in music and sings itself on the page.

Literature: The "Reading Narrative"

A fascinating subgenre of nonfiction has flourished in the last few years— we've titled these works "reading narratives." These essays show the author in different ways reading another piece of literature and using it as a springboard for his or her own actions and reflections. Like writers who use the visual arts, authors of reading narratives are somehow grappling with another artist's aesthetics as a means of probing deeper into their own. Though reading narratives sound simple, they aren't; in good hands, they present a beautifully counterpointed music of two different lives, aesthetics, and meanings. Phyllis

Rose's book *The Year of Reading Proust* is an excellent example, as the author reads all of Proust's *Remembrance of Things Past* while using it as a means to chronicle her own life, comparing her Key West to Proust's Balbec, the characters inhabiting her life to those in his.

Most of us can remember at least one "eureka" reading moment. That moment may give us permission to do things differently in our own work: use a new voice, dig deeper, or consider new subject matter as potentially ours. These "eureka" writers are our literary mentors, whether we realize that or not. And what we read may spur us on in many different ways—other authors inspire us, give us permission, and also irritate us in ways that stimulate us to try something new. You can try writing a "literary history" of yourself, one that tracks your life through the many different books you've read and loved.

TRY IT

1. Begin an essay by describing a piece of art that has always intrigued you. Feel free to interpret the details, creating a speculative narrative about what is happening in the painting or what was going through the painter's mind. Find other interpretations from art scholars and begin to create an essay that approaches this artwork from several different angles.

2. Write an essay in which you parallel your interpretation of a particular artwork or artist with events going on in the world around you.

3. Write an essay in which you parallel your interpretation of a particular artwork or artist with events unfolding in your own life.

4. Think about a film that you love, that you could watch any number of times. Look closely at the conventions and physical experience of film, and question your obsession. In what ways are you comforted by the artifice of film? Where do you suspend your sense of its unreality and where do you take comfort in it? Where did you first see the film, and what has it represented to the larger culture? If you like, you can substitute something from television, but for this exercise you should go for a quality piece.

5. Think about television commercials that stick with you. How do they define the eras they appear in? How have they shaped you, perhaps in terms of social relationships, signs of status, body image?

6. Write a review of a film or a television show, using specific details that reveal your own voice and vision and that place the show in a larger context.

7. Write an essay that uses popular television or radio shows to establish the time and place of your piece. What were the shows you watched as a child? How did they establish the routine of your day? Why do you think those particular shows hooked you?

8. This prompt expands on uses of music presented in Chapter 1. Identify the piece of music that's been most important to you in your life. First, try to write down why it means so much to you, and when and where you can remember hearing it. If there are lyrics, write down all you can remember, and list adjectives that describe the melody.

Now try tracing all of the cultural connections of the song, as the authors of *Strange Fruit* did. This may or may not take a little bit of research.

9. Try to imagine your way into the head of a musician you love. Create a speculative narrative that combines fact and fiction to bring that person's music to life on the page.

10. Think about your reading life. What piece of writing has "taken the top of your head off," to use Emily Dickinson's phrase? Write a reading narrative in which you enter into dialogue with this writing—feel free to quote it. How has this reading experience changed you and helped you to redefine your life and your mission as a writer?

11. Write a history of your life through the books you've read. What was your favorite book at age five? Age ten? Age sixteen? Age twenty? Write these out in sections, rendering in specific, sensory detail the memories these books inspire in you.

6

Gathering the Threads of History

Everyone has his own story, and everyone could arouse interest in the romance of his life if he but comprehended it.
—George Sand

History is nothing more than a thin thread of what is remembered stretched out over an ocean of what has been forgotten.
—Milan Kundera

I am working on a short essay about a strange summer I had when my brother worked for the New Jersey Department of Environmental Protection, running tests on water samples that had been held up for years. He drives a tiny, two-seater Fiat Spider, the car of choice that year. My start: "It's my brother's Spider summer. Not dog days but spider days. My brother has a blue Fiat Spider. It has no backseat but I ride in the back anyway, rolled up in the ten inches or so under the rear window. Spiders aren't much more than human-sized tins so this is risky but it doesn't matter. Let me be a bottle rocket."

What follows is the revised beginning, after a quick search on major events of the year (1974) and surrounding years. I did this search primarily on the Internet, on Historycentral.com's "this year in history" service: "It's my brother's Spider summer. Not dog days but spider days. It's 1974 and things have been crashing. Nixon's resigned or is going to and a few years ago Apollo 13 crash-landed when an oxygen tank blew. (Astronauts in there like Spam in a can, Chuck Yeager said.) Karen Silkwood's about to crash. My brother has a blue Fiat Spider. It has no backseat but I ride in the back anyway, rolled up in the ten inches or so under the rear window. Spiders aren't much more than

55

human-sized tins so this is risky but it doesn't matter. I am a lost person. Let me be a bottle rocket."

When I add these historical details—the space program, the death of Karen Silkwood—my story becomes enriched and begins to expand outward: connections move back and forth, between the closeness of the car and of space capsules, the sense of questing and uncovering and yet danger that marked that time. The reference to Karen Silkwood adds a reference to those who ask difficult questions, particularly environmental ones, as this book goes on to do. The imminent resignation of President Nixon captures the sense of chaos and rebellion, embodied in these teenagers, so prevalent in our country at that time.

—SUZANNE

✓ Our Historical, Universal Selves

As the preceding experience shows, each of us exists in both a private and a public way. We're all at once son or daughter, lover, sister, brother, neighbor—the person who must have chocolate cereal in the morning and who absently puts the milky bowl down for the cat to lick. We're also pieces of history. We have created digital culture, with all the implications of lives lived in virtual games, social network postings, and tweets. We are also the people who have lived through economic downturns and Mideast wars.

To look at what it means to exist and be human—and who we are as a species—we must look at history. That historical frame is one that may simply enrich your story. Or—as the Kundera quote shows—writing creative nonfiction focused on history might have a deep ethical implication. Sometimes using our own experience of history is a way of preventing that destructive forgetfulness that Kundera describes. Leslie Brody sums up her reasons for writing her book *Red Star Sister*, a memoir of her anti–Vietnam War activism, when she simply said, "You have a responsibility to tell history because people forget history."

✓ What Will Be Your Stories?

Consider yourself as you exist in this historical moment. Doing so will involve acknowledging what historical and social changes—as well as intractable problems—you have witnessed.

We all have those moments when we think, "This is what I will tell my grandchildren about," whether what we've experienced is large and grim, like serving in a war or witnessing an act of terrorism, or smaller. In "The Hazing of Swans" (included as a sample reading at the end of this book), Suzanne's experience of seeing threatened trumpeter swans ambling around at the side of a highway becomes a meditation on whether such a casual pleasure will happen again in the future.

History has occasions that are joyful as well as somber. Such an occasion can be as simple as the widespread celebration that occurred in many places at the election of the United States' first African-American president. Your historical moments don't have to carry weight beyond what they reflect about society at this time and even what they say about our popular culture. Suzanne once turned a corner in New York City and saw the Rolling Stones filming a music video in front of a crowd of gaping fans (with whom they did not interact!). While this event is hardly newsworthy in the sense a presidential election is, it speaks volumes about contemporary celebrity culture.

First Actors

As creative nonfiction writers, we occupy the ticklish position of being both the authors and, much of the time, the subjects of our own work. We are shaper and protagonist—from the Greek *protos* (first) and *agonistes* (actor), i.e., the person who generates the action of a drama—and we must learn to assess ourselves as protagonists with all the objectivity we can muster. Everyone who sits down to write is, in some sense, a *privileged observer*—a writer who has had experiences and witnessed events any reader would be fascinated by, if the writer can learn to uncover and record them.

The French memoirist and novelist George Sand wrote, "Everyone has his own story, and everyone could arouse interest in the romance of his life if he but comprehended it." Any of you could write a book that would be treasured in two hundred years, as we treasure the best pioneer diaries, if we could all learn, as those authors did, really to *see*.

We take many things about ourselves for granted—and take for granted too their societal implications. Gender, race, religion, class, ethnicity, sexual orientation— these aspects of ourselves govern our social interactions in ways that are unique to our moment in history. There have been many past cultures in which race mattered little, for instance, but gender determined your every movement, even what—and how—you could eat and what cutlery you used. There have also been cultures in which classes were fairly fixed—if your father was a blacksmith and you were a male, that fact would determine your life. These ways of being, of course, are no longer true in Western cultures, but we have our own "givens" about the many facets of ourselves.

It can be helpful to make a list of *all* the elements that make up your social self—the part of yourself that is always historically determined. List very basic things, such as race, religion, sexual orientation, and so on, along with all the other small—or not so small—items that make you you. Did you go to religious school? Have you lived in a commune? Do you have children? Are you from a minority group in any way? What assumptions about you do others leap to based on these simple facts of your life? The aspects of yourself that have led to the greatest challenges, even discrimination, can be among the most rewarding to put under the lens of your nonfiction writer's scrutiny.

In Sui Sin Far's 1909 essay "Leaves from the Mental Portfolio of a Eurasian," which is available on our website, Sin Far describes becoming aware of her status as a biracial child in an intolerant United States. In one scene, a man examines her at a party:

> [A] white-haired old man has his attention called to me by the hostess. He adjusts his eyeglasses and surveys me critically. "Ah, indeed!" he exclaims. "Who would have thought it at first glance? Yet now I see the difference between her and other children. What a peculiar coloring! Her mother's eyes and hair and her father's features, I presume. Very interesting little creature!"
>
> I had been called from play for the purpose of inspection. I do not return to it.

The power of Sin Far's description lies in how skillfully she lets the story tell itself: the man who examines her, adjusting his glasses as if looking at a laboratory specimen. He discusses her as she stands there, as if Sin Far's race renders her beneath comprehension. Sin Far's dry comment that she does "not return" to her play makes it clear how devastating her awareness of herself as racially different becomes.

An essay published in 2010, Jenny Boully's "A Short Essay on Being," also on our website, describes a similar encounter:

Two older, white women are sitting on chairs in front of us and ask where we are from. We say we're from Valley-Hi, because that's the section of San Antonio where we live. No, they say, what's your nationality? We had never heard that word before, and although we had never heard that word before, we answered that we were Thai, although our nationality was American.

Again, through a simple but meticulous description of the encounter, Boully gives her readers a vivid sense of the dislocation it created in her as a child. The fact that the questioning women used "where are you from?" as a veiled way of asking the author her race—and that they could not accept her answer—shows how deeply race mattered to these women.

You do not have to be a product of activism, be biracial, or have witnessed a world-changing event to have a historical perspective. Unless you exist alone on an uncharted island—and are never discovered!—the elements of your life are reverberant with historical significance because you live in a communal group whose attitudes and choices are historically shaped. We've all experienced meeting someone who claimed to be ordinary while finally slipping into the conversation that he or she had sung opera as a child or—like one person we remember—come of age living inside the Statue of Liberty with his Park Service father. The world he grew into, literally seen through the eyes of the Statue of Liberty, is not the same world the rest of us know.

It's important for you as a writer, particularly a nonfiction writer, to think through what is different and important in your world, and what historical events formed the canvas for the fine brushstrokes of your own life. You can easily check the highlights of particular dates and years by using resources like Historycentral.com on the web or reference books such as *The New York Times Book of Chronologies*.

The "When" in Addition to the "What"

Here is the opening of James Baldwin's famous essay about racism and family, "Notes of a Native Son":

On the twenty-ninth of July, in 1943, my father died. On the same day, a few hours later, his last child was born. Over a month before this, while all our energies were concentrated in waiting for these events, there had been, in Detroit, one of the bloodiest race riots of the century. . . . On the morning of the third of August, we drove my father to the graveyard through a wilderness of smashed plate glass.

Notice that the author's attention operates like a moving camera, panning between familial and national tragedy. Family events come first; then, as if his gaze is forced away, Baldwin takes in the larger chaos of the country's rioting. Right at the start of the essay Baldwin carefully states the season and the year; it's a hot summer month during World War II. Part of the race frustration building up to the riots described here arose from black GIs risking their lives overseas and coming home to face the same old racism, a fact that would have been clear to Baldwin's contemporary audience. By the end of the paragraph, the rioters' smashed glass has become a "wilderness," as if that landscape equals the natural landscape about to close over Baldwin's father's body. The essay accomplishes an unforgettable weaving of personal tragedy with the period that spawned it.

✔ Always keep in mind the extent to which history is the individual writ large, and the individual life is history writ small. Understanding what shapes how you perceive the world—and how you are perceived—is critical to using your own experiences to create strong nonfiction.

TRY IT

You will likely be the last person to recognize what's fascinating—and deeply significant—about you. Your friends will see it, and if you're lucky your family will too. If you're normal, you will brush off their interest, tell them it really wasn't so different—you just don't see what all the fuss is about that last night on board the *Titanic*.

Here's a tool to help you along: a checklist to start yourself off with, whether you choose to answer on paper, in a journal, or in the privacy of your own head. This checklist is designed to elicit a greater awareness of the historical events that have shaped your life, and also a greater awareness of your *social self*—you as conservative or liberal, member of a disadvantaged group, Buddhist, activist, Rosicrucian. While considering these questions, it's important to remember that this social self *always* functions in a cultural and historical context.

1. Many of us vividly remember the events of September 11, 2001. There are also hundreds of other historical milestones you may remember particularly well: the election of Barack Obama, acts of global terrorism, the Arab Spring when many nations rose up demanding fairer government—in the case of Egypt, with the help of Facebook. Which event of national or world importance do you remember most clearly? How did you hear of it, and what did you hear? What were other people around you doing? What was going on in your own life that this event bounced off of, resonated with, or formed a strange contrast to? Use all of your senses to re-create this memory.

2. Which aspects of your life do people around you consistently find most interesting? What questions do they ask you? What can you tell them that satisfies/ dissatisfies them?

3. At a writer's conference, Leslie Brody talked about living through an unpleasant divorce while the royal wedding of Diana Spencer to the Prince of Wales dominated the news. She talked of the ironies of seeing the two events juxtaposed, and how the memories came to interfuse: the painful sundering of a marriage, the artificial romance of the royal wedding. Which news events formed a backdrop to the most emotional moments of your life? How do the two stories intersect?

4. Try to imagine your own life as someone five hundred years from now might view it. What about your life—the place you live in and the historical unfoldings you've witnessed—do you believe that person would find most interesting? (Hint: what do you find most interesting about life in the past?) How are you a privileged observer?

5. Get in the habit of thinking of yourself in the third person—seeing yourself move through the world as a protagonist—at least once a day. Narrate your daily story to yourself in the third person. As an objective listener (and, to some extent, you can be one), what interests you?

Dating a Significant Event
This is the exercise that helped Suzanne expand her description of the summer of 1974.

1. For the first part, write a description of several paragraphs about a scene or event you consider critical in your life. It should date from at least a few years in your past and can be from childhood. As in most writing exercises, write quickly and do not censor yourself. Be as specific and detailed as possible, using all your senses.

2. Now use a list of chronologies, possibly a simple one printed from an Internet site such as Historycentral.com, to date your experience with a corresponding national or world event. Don't worry if you feel you weren't thinking about the event at the time; your obliviousness to it may be part of what makes the essay fascinating.

3. Once you find a historical corollary, write as many connections, real or metaphoric, as you can. (Suzanne might have written "secrets, cover-ups, crashing, underground corruption, apathy.") In an essay, draw together the two links to show how a critical moment in your life unfolded against a corresponding moment in history. Don't feel the need to justify to yourself immediately why something feels important. If your gut tells you it's important, then surely it is.

7

Writing the Larger World

Like Flemish miniaturists who reveal the essence of humankind within the confines of a tiny frame, McPhee once again demonstrates that the smallest topic is replete with history, significance, and consequence.

—From a review of John
McPhee's *Oranges*

The first nonfiction book I remember reading and going back to read again was Lewis Thomas's *The Lives of a Cell*. I read it while sitting in my little rented room in Arcata, California; I was a senior in college, a nascent Buddhist brimming with questions about the world and my place in it. Thomas had me thinking about mitochondria—mitochondria!—and the topic had called into question every perception I thought was sound. No longer was I a separate organism, contained within my skin, but a mere continuance of a single cell that erupted eons ago in the primordial soup.

What got to me about these "Notes of a Biology Watcher" was not the information itself (had I read the same information in the encyclopedia I doubt it would have affected me so), but *how* that information was presented. Thomas was no mere biologist, but a philosopher and a poet; his sensibility permeated the information and made it real, made it personable. As I became more and more interested in creative nonfiction, I found this same kind of voice in many of the writers I loved: E. B. White, John McPhee, Tom Wolfe, Joan Didion, to name just a few. These authors brought their "I" to the world, without becoming self-centered; their focus often remained determinedly outward without sacrificing the voice that made their work unique.

There's been a recent spate of nonfiction books that focus on topics one might not expect to find interesting: orchids, tulips, mosquitoes, clouds, ether, and something as diminutive and common as dust. People are reading these books on the bus, at the beach, in a chair by the window; they're coming to the breakfast table and saying to their loved ones, "Did you know about . . . ?"

—BRENDA

Turning Outward: Finding Your Material Outside the Self

Your own private world—if you inhabit it long enough—will become claustrophobic, not only for yourself but also for your readers. In Chapters 5 and 6, we showed how placing yourself in the contexts of art or history can help diffuse some of the inward focus of creative nonfiction. In this chapter, we encourage you to direct your gaze outward, not leaving the self behind but perhaps sublimating the self to newly discover the subjects the world has to offer.

Lee Gutkind, founder and editor of the journal *Creative Nonfiction*, believes that one of the genre's essential missions is "to gather and present information, to teach readers about a person, place, idea or situation combining the creativity of the artistic experience with . . . research. . . . Read the books and essays of the most renowned nonfiction writers in this century and you will read about a writer engaged in a quest for information and discovery."

In the Renaissance, the concept of the "Renaissance man" reflected the ideal of the citizen who brought together knowledge of literature, science, theology, and invention. Contemporary nonfiction writers, too, can embody that ideal, considering the deepest levels of what the natural world, the arts, spirituality, and the mechanical world have to teach us.

A good creative nonfiction writer will be attuned to the things of the world that beckon for examination. In this chapter, we've broken down the categories into a few that interest us, but as with all the prompts we provide in this book, these are mere gateways for your own creative instincts.

Science

Albert Einstein wrote, "The most beautiful experience we can have is the mysterious. It is the fundamental emotion that stands at the cradle of true art and true science. Whoever does not know it and can no longer wonder, no longer marvel, is as good as dead, and his eyes are dimmed" (from "The World as I See It," on our website). The sense of the mysterious visits us daily, if we are open to it.

A friend said recently that every time he opens up a newspaper these days he reads something that hits his view of the world with a thunderbolt: Stephen Hawking announces that we must use genetic engineering to evolve faster or computers will make us extinct; there may be infinite parallel universes; a religious group is working to clone human beings. In her book *The Immortal Life of Henrietta Lacks*, Rebecca Skloot tells the story of one ordinary woman whose unusually vital cells have become a priceless medical commodity for cancer and other research, even as her family lives in poverty.

When you write about science in creative nonfiction, it becomes much more than a recitation or analysis of facts; it is a means of probing the deepest levels of our common existence. Right now we live steeped in startling scientific and technological advances. These changes signal more than quirky facts to recite; they invade our deepest assumptions about who we are. Here's where literary nonfiction writers become almost essential for our very survival.

Lewis Thomas helps us take in the infinite complexities science has found in cell behavior. A mysterious particle called the Higgs-Boson, so important it is dubbed the "God particle," is theorized to be the reason physical bodies—like yours—can contain mass. Oliver Sacks, writing books like *The Man Who Mistook His Wife for a Hat*, teaches us how humans cope and remain whole while a myriad of neurological forces buffet them. Michael Pollan, in *The Botany of Desire*, plants genetically modified potatoes in his garden and maps out the exact nature of genetic modification and its implications for agriculture, as well as how it feels to grow these potatoes, classified by the EPA as "pesticides," not food. (Hint: he doesn't eat them.) Writer-scientists like Stephen Hawking take us by the hand through a changing cosmos that barely makes sense to physicists now.

The Layperson's Approach. Many personal essayists, such as Annie Dillard, draw heavily on scientific knowledge without being classified as science writers, per se. These authors may flesh out a personal experience with facts that enrich the narrative and that may also be alive with metaphoric significance. Dillard's well-known essay "Total Eclipse" begins with the bald declaration, "It had been like dying, that sliding down the mountain pass." She approaches this experience with a voice that is personal and vulnerable. She writes of the experience of a total eclipse as something that continually threatens to overwhelm her and the other onlookers. The intensity of her reactions ("God save our life," "the last sane moment I remember") continues to emphasize that vulnerability. This passion is matched by that of the cosmos she constantly fits herself into, one in which light and darkness exist in a constant dance of existence and extinguishing.

> The Ring Nebula, in the constellation Lyra, looks, through binoculars, like a smoke ring. It is a star in the process of exploding. Light from its explosion first reached the earth in 1054; it was a supernova then, and so bright it shone in the daytime. Now it is not so bright, but it is still exploding.

Because Dillard insists on switching back to the world of cosmic activity from the world of human activity, we see her sense of being "obliterated" by the eclipse as a coherent response to a cosmos where darkness can signal an ultimate end. Hers becomes a thinking reaction to the universe we're tied to so intimately.

The Expert's Approach. Richard Selzer's perspective is different. He is an essayist and also a practicing surgeon, and rather than recording his own vulnerability in his essay "The Knife," he records the fearful power his practitioner's skills give him. Selzer implies again and again that perhaps no human is fully equipped to have the life-and-death power of the surgeon: "A stillness settles in my heart and is carried to my hand. It is the quietude of resolve layered over fear." As he operates, he records the following: "Deeper still. The peritoneum, pink and gleaming and membranous, bulges into the wound. It is grasped with forceps, and opened. For the first time we can see into the cavity of the abdomen. Such a primitive place."

Selzer performs a matching "surgery" on his own emotions, delving deeper and deeper into the emotional and philosophical aspects of his role. "Here is man as microcosm, representing in all his parts the earth, perhaps the universe." Or: "And if the surgeon is like a poet, then the scars you have made on countless bodies are like verses."

You don't have to be a veteran of the surgical theater to have a topic you can approach as an informed voice. If you have mastered computer technology, been part of a field camp, dissected something, or learned to fix a car, you have a subject you can write about with both expertise and poetry.

Sports Writing

It is astonishing how much we reveal about ourselves, personally and as a society, through sports. Think of the social implications of being a "tomboy" or a "klutz," then think of the way sports figures embody our cultural idealizations. There's a reason a great basketball player or Olympic gymnast can use his or her image to sell almost any product going. Reflecting about sports has yielded much great writing on the topics of our societal concepts of success and failure, masculinity and femininity, and race, as well as a way of experiencing through words one of life's great visceral excitements.

David Halberstam, one of the editors of *The Best American Sports Writing of the Century*, described the sports writing he presented as a portrait "of the nation itself during the explosive period" of the twentieth century. His coeditor Glenn Stout called ours a "golden age" of sports writing. Both editors—seasoned writers themselves—credited the upsurge in this form to authors like Gay Talese and Tom Wolfe, who refused to sacrifice breadth and literary flair in their sports journalism. As Stout put it, describing the Best American Sports Writing series, "at least once or twice in every edition it was proven, unquestionably, that the best 'sports writing' was . . . just good writing that happened to be about sports." Keep this in mind as you go through the exercises at the end of this chapter. Think about how your own sports obsessions reflect yourself and your culture and what larger questions—of race, violence, and gender—come into play in the sport you choose to write about.

Joyce Carol Oates's book *On Boxing* uses the sport to reflect on larger questions. Sports writing is a field still dominated by men; it's a little surprising to see a woman writing about sports, especially such a traditionally masculine sport as boxing. She begins the essay by complicating this kind of masculinity:

No sport is more physical, more direct, than boxing. No sport appears more powerfully homoerotic: the confrontation in the ring—the disrobing—the sweaty heated combat that is part dance, courtship, coupling—the frequent urgent pursuit by one boxer of the other in the fight's natural and violent movement toward the "knockout."

Oates punctures most readers' basic beliefs about boxing, using specific observations of movements in the ring—movements mirrored by her jumpy, fragmented writing—to do so. She observes the embrace the fighters exchange after the fight and goes on to ask, "Are men privileged to embrace with love only after having fought?" Oates makes the bold statement that this proves man's greatest passion "is for war, not peace." You might disagree with her conclusions, but the essay uses a close observation of a sport Oates loves to ask questions about gender roles, the nature of love and intimacy, and our human instincts.

TRY IT

1. Scientific facts are often rich in metaphor, as is scientific language. Great science writing draws the material facts of the universe into the process of reflection on the human experience. How would it inform your writing to know that doctors call the two coverings of the brain the "hard mother" (dura mater) and the "tender mother" (pia mater)? How does it change your sense of your own experience to know that physicists believe there may be an infinite number of parallel universes, containing what ours contains, in somewhat different form?

To speed you in the process of exploring the metaphorical value of scientific facts, do a twenty-minute freewrite on any of the following bits of information. Write whatever associations or suggestions come into your head. Which of your own experiences crop up when you think of these facts?

- The human body contains a vestigial tailbone.
- Our galaxy contains a black hole into which our solar system, including earth, will ultimately collapse.
- Stephen Hawking has said that if humans don't begin to use genetic engineering to modify themselves—including incorporating computer technology—computers will evolve past us and possibly cause our extinction.

- Clones are, for little-known reasons, abnormally large.
- A recently discovered jellyfish, *Turritopsis nutricula*, does not "die" but merely returns to its formative state (the sexually immature polyp) and starts life over, much as if you returned to the stem-cell fetal state and began again rather than dying.
- Ozzie Osbourne has had his genome sequenced and was found to have an unusually large share of Neanderthal genes.

Before you begin your freewriting session, whether in a class or a writing group or alone, add to this list any facts that have stuck in your mind as sugges- tive, fascinating, or just bizarre.

After your freewriting session, assuming the material interests you, try expanding it into an essay this way: use a human story (it can be your own or someone else's) to intersperse with the scientific material. At some point in the essay, you must expand on the science, but promise yourself it will not dominate.

2. Write an essay modeled on the style of Einstein's "The World as I See It." What particulars of the world do you, through your own experiences and areas of expertise, view especially clearly? What fundamental beliefs do these lead you to have?

3. Identify an area of expertise you have. (We *all* have them!) Detail that work, as Richard Selzer does so carefully in "The Knife." Examine your role and the larger significance of it, as well as the role this specialized activity plays in human culture and your own life. Think of how it makes you feel, what aspect of your humanity it accentuates.

4. Examine a sport in terms of the imagery of its body movements, dress, rituals, and rules. Do any of these seem to defy our stereotypes of this sport? What social significance can you draw from what you see? How do you connect to this sport emotionally?

5. Think of a way in which a sport has had significance in your own life or that of someone close to you. Are there ways in which this personal experience and the sport, or a sports player's career, have run parallel? How? Can you think of a time when a sporting event had an emotional impact on an important event in your own life?

6. Freewrite a list of things you deal with on a daily basis and don't think about very much. Don't be choosy; jot down whatever pops into your head: paper, fluorescent lighting, mosquitoes, slugs, flush toilets. Then select one item from your list.

What are the larger metaphysical (that is, dealing with the properties of the universe at large) connotations of your item? Look at it if you can. Let's say you have chosen a piece of white paper. What does your paper suggest? What are the implications of its smoothness and whiteness? Of writing on pressed trees? Of writing within a square frame? Don't censor yourself but simply go with your impulses. Be weird. Be funny. Find the universe in the particular "grain of sand" in front of you.

Next, uncover a few facts about your item. They may be things you already know, or that classmates or group members can tell you (having a group discussion can really launch a great freewrite here; we trivia buffs are many!) or that you can look up quickly on the Internet. (See Chapter 8, "Using Research to Expand Your Perspective," if you're stymied.) Then do a second freewrite, focusing on details about your item that feel interesting or suggestive. Again, don't censor yourself. Feel free to be silly, and to be broad.

7. Make a list of the abstract concepts on which you have some opinions: racism, politics, gender wars, and so forth. Now circle one of these, and come up with a list of some specific examples from your own experience that elucidate these abstract concepts in a concrete way. How can you gain *authority* to talk about these issues? How can you demonstrate to the reader that you have firsthand knowledge of these topics?

8

Using Research to Expand Your Perspective

Facts in all their glorious complexity make possible creativity. The best nonfiction writers are first-rate reporters, reliable eyewitnesses focused on the world, not themselves, and relentless researchers with the imagination to understand the implications of their discoveries.

—Philip Gerard

Working on a book that combined memoir with environmental writing, I found in many areas I was overwhelmed with information. Pesticide research, industrial waste, radiation, and the course of the Cold War: books, papers, old newspapers piled up and slid off my desk, defying all attempts at organization. In other ways, though, I found questions that had no answers: questions about the root causes of environmentally related disease, family stories that were irreconcilably different in everyone's telling. It was an enormous relief to sit at my desk one day and realize that the lack of answers—the evasions, the uncertainties, the whole process—was a story in itself. I continued to research as doggedly as I could, but when I came up blank again and again, I began asking that emptiness whether it had a story to tell. One day I conclude the tale of a particularly frustrating phone call with these words: "I make telephone calls, hour after hour. Mostly I listen to message machines. EPA sends me to DEP, which sends me to ATSDR, which sends me to the County Board of Health, which says it has no records."

By the time I wrote this passage, I had tried to write around what I couldn't uncover, in many awkward and unsuccessful ways. I avoided subjects I needed to confront, or I tried to fake a knowledge I didn't have. I finally realized—with a liberating shock—that the reader needed to confront my own frustrations and uncertainties just as I had, in order to understand this story. The reader needed to hear and see the whole inquiry, even the phone calls that petered out into more avenues of possibility without certainty.

—SUZANNE

The Myriad Things Around Us

Can you imagine writing an entire book about a color? The writing of the *Oxford English Dictionary*? The flight path of a single type of butterfly? How about those clingy grains you thoughtlessly shake off your feet at the beach? Lovely, profound, and popular books have been published in the last few years about such seemingly small things. We call this subgenre *topical nonfiction*— essays that draw from particular, concrete topics.

Poet Theodore Roethke wrote, "All finite things reveal infinitude." William Blake wrote "To see a world in a grain of sand, / and heaven in a wild flower." These thoughts are not just poets' ideas but philosophical truths nonfiction writers have been among the most successful at plumbing. On the one hand, Annie Dillard's *For the Time Being* is a book about everything, and, on the other hand, a book about—sand. At least sand—a solid substance that flows and functions like water—forms a starting point for her long theological look at the flux of the world, Hasidism, and God.

OK, you might say, perhaps sand is interesting, but color? As Simon Garfield, author of *Mauve: How One Man Invented a Color That Changed the World*, discovers, mauve had a lasting impact on the culture of its day (and ours). The color was discovered by an eighteen-year-old chemistry student, who found it in a test tube in the course of trying out something else. The first synthetic color, mauve soon became a status symbol flaunted by royals, including Queen Victoria. (Contemporaries decried the aristocratic passion for mauve by describing streets pocked by wearers as having a case of "mauve measles.") And, naturally, the invention of synthetic color changed the textile industry and the economies of the day.

Hindus speak reverently of "Indra's net"—a web of interconnectedness with a jewel at each intersection that can be used to embody the interconnectedness of the world. Gifted writers like Dillard and Garfield find the "webs" attached to the subjects that draw them—the flowing and flux suggested by sand, the accident of a test-tube residue changing the fashions and industry of a nineteenth-century imperial power.

As a writer, once you begin to look closely at what's around you—recognizing both the closest details and the larger ways each thing fits into the "Indra's net" that holds us all together—nothing will seem less than a fruitful subject for your writing.

Porosity

Perhaps we can equate openness to research with openness to incorporating the world around us and its events into our own life meditations, a kind of artistic *porosity* to the world around us. Porous materials, such as fabrics, absorb what comes in contact with them. The best nonfiction writers have a special porosity to what is around them; they're unable to ignore even a moth they happen to notice.

Not everyone will want to do full-blown investigative journalism. It's worth remembering that sometimes the best research we can do involves going somewhere we wouldn't normally go and talking to people we wouldn't normally talk to—and of course, really listening. Are you writing an essay about someone who lifts weights? Get a day pass to a gym and absorb the culture of weight lifting—how lifters push themselves, how muscle curves out of itself when flexed. Imaginatively, see your subject there.

If you want to write about your childhood, don't settle for your memories but look at all the media that shaped your world. Check out magazines from the early years of your life from a library; watch Nickelodeon reruns from that period on television; or go to Historycentral.com and look up the key songs, plays, films, and news events of those years. Confront primary sources, such as documents, photos, films, newspapers, even gravestones; you will often find discrepancies between stories people tell you and the facts you uncover, discrepancies that reveal a lot about your stories and your subjects.

If you are writing about your parents, think about them as human beings at that earlier time—what messages were they hearing? How did those messages help shape them into the people they were?

Using Fact as Metaphor

Factual research will most often be used for what it is: fact. Water may contain a certain complex of chemicals; weight lifting may have such-and-such an effect on the body. These facts can become the basis of an essay that explores the physical wonders and limitations of our world. At times, however, fact will also function as metaphor, informing the essay both on its own terms—information about the physical world the reader may need or find interesting—and as a basis for comparison for a more intangible part of the piece.

One novice writer, Jen Whetham, wrote an essay, "Swimming Pool Hedonist," chronicling how swimming and swimming pools have defined her and held her milestones: learning to trust, early sports success, even a first sexual encounter. The first draft of the essay began by saying "My earliest memory is at a swimming pool," and included a passing reference to the odor of chlorine. That odor turned up again and again, and so Jen researched the chemistry of chlorine; she came up with this section in her final version:

> My skin has always smelled like chlorine. . . .
>
> Chlorine is missing one electron from its outer shell: this makes it highly attractive to other molecules. Chlorine's extreme reactivity makes it a powerful disinfectant: it bonds with the outer surfaces of bacteria and viruses and destroys them. When it kills the natural flora on human skin, the reaction creates the stuffy, cloudy smell we associate with chlorine.
>
> Chlorine marks us in ways we cannot see.

The essay goes on to use the touchstone of chlorine—odorless, changing forever what it contacts—as a metaphor for all the invisible ways life touches and changes us, and how we touch and change one another. It is a subtle and nuanced use of fact as fact and fact as metaphor.

Researching a Key Fact or Detail

Peter Balakian set out to write a family memoir in his book *Black Dog of Fate*. Yet, as he probed memories of life with his immigrant family in New Jersey—communal meals, days spent at his grandmother's helping her as she baked—he began to notice that the real story of his family lay in a subject they did *not* discuss: their homeland of Armenia, including the fate of family members who had remained there. Finally, by asking questions of his family and doing his own historical research, Balakian came to grips with the real story haunting him: the massacre of the Armenians by the Turks early in the twentieth century. The massacre was so successful it gave Hitler the confidence to conceive of the Holocaust.

In Terry Tempest Williams's "The Clan of One-Breasted Women," the close of her book *Refuge*, Williams begins to examine the larger forces that may be contributing to her family's high breast cancer rate. In the following excerpt, you can see her seamless and organic movement from personal history into researched analysis. She has, as this dialogue begins, told her father of a recurring dream she has of a flash of light in the desert.

> "You did see it," he said.
>
> "Saw what?"
>
> "The bomb. The cloud. We were driving home from Riverside, California. You were sitting on Diane's lap. She was pregnant. . . . We pulled over and suddenly, rising from the desert floor, we saw it, clearly, this golden-stemmed cloud, the mushroom. The sky seemed to vibrate with an eerie pink glow. Within a few minutes, a light ash was raining on the car. . . ."

Williams goes on to tell us that "above ground atomic testing in Nevada took place from January 27, 1951, through July 11, 1962." Williams provides an analysis of the political climate of the period—the growth of McCarthyism and the Korean War—summarizes litigation stemming from the tests, and returns seamlessly to her own story. She clearly researches the dates of the bomb testing as well as the wind patterns during those years, but she weaves those facts unobtrusively into her own narrative.

Working with Immersion

Immersion refers to the technique of actually living an experience—usually briefly—to write about it. The late George Plimpton, who was a writer and the editor of the *Paris Review*, lived for a while as a football player to research the book *Paper Lion*. Lee Gutkind, a writer and editor of the journal *Creative Nonfiction*, has done a great deal of immersion writing: he has lived as a circus clown and has followed transplant doctors and umpires on their rounds. Several years ago Robert Sullivan lived for months with the Makah Indian tribe and observed their hunt for gray whales in his book *A Whale Hunt*.

Writers differ in their approaches to immersion research. Gutkind writes of the writer's need to become invisible, almost a piece of furniture in the room with the subject(s): "I like to compare myself to a rather undistinguished and utilitarian end table in a living room or office," he writes. Didion, on the other hand, is always a presence in her research, one whose shy, questioning self forms another character in the piece.

Several years ago a woman we know read about an adult nightclub in Seattle; it was one of the only such clubs in the United States owned and run entirely by women, with a woman-friendly and safe atmosphere. She visited the club, whose dancers were mainly college women and single mothers. Her immersion experience resulted in an essay uncovering a fascinating side of a business generally viewed as exploiting and degrading to women.

Developing Interview Skills

You'll find as many interview styles as there are writers in this world. Writer Gay Talese's polished assurance invites confidence. On the other side of the spectrum are writers like Joan Didion and John McPhee, both of whom describe themselves (or are described by others) as so shy and unsure that interviewees tend to underrate them. It's important to remember artistically as well as ethically that when you conduct research and interview people, their words may ultimately be used in ways they won't like. Didion puts it bluntly, "Writers are always selling somebody out."

Regardless of your style, there are some tips that will help any interview go more productively. Most researchers ask a few "throw-off" questions—those with simple and unimportant answers—to relax their subjects before moving on to more difficult questions. And, as far as that goes, the toughest questions should be saved for last. If someone shuts down because you asked why he or she supported the Iraqi War, for example, you don't want that confrontation to ruin the entire interview. Begin with the simplest and least emotional information, and move forward from there.

Always begin an interview with a list of questions you want to ask; a prepared list will prevent you from forgetting to ask something important because of nerves or simple absentmindedness. Also, end interviews with an open-ended question that will direct you to your next research source. For example, "What do you think is the best place to go for information about the war?" "Are there other people I should speak to about this subject?"

Philip Gerard advises that you always strive to use interviews to find primary sources. "An interview may be a great start," he says, "but will that person also let you read his or her diary, letters, business correspondence?" Gerard tells the story of an F. Scott Fitzgerald scholar who found the most valuable document in studying Fitzgerald turned out to be the writer's tax returns, chronicling his inflated lifestyle and his debt.

Above all, put your questions out there, pause, and really listen. Have your list of questions ready, but be prepared to change course when you get an answer—or a partial answer—that intrigues you. If your subject says casually, "Well, of course John wasn't around then because he was in jail for a while," follow up on that point right away; don't continue with your checklist. You may forget to come back to it, or the person you're speaking to may regret having let it slip. Listen carefully, and follow up on what you hear.

Developing Print Research Skills

Here, we'll explore three commonly used and easily accessed print research sources—the library, the Internet, and primary sources, such as legal documents and statistics.

The Library

The best thing about libraries, we think, is reference librarians. The smallest library contains an overwhelming wealth of information. There are newspapers from all over, going back many years; reference books from the obvious, World Book–type books to dictionaries of chronologies and disasters; specialized encyclopedias; works on microfilm; and tapes and videos. When you know just what you want, the computer or card catalogue will steer you to it. When you don't—say you have a general question about molecular physics or weather or genealogical research—reference librarians will point you to the right sources and help you find what you need.

We went to several of our favorite librarians for advice on how to use the library's resources most effectively. Western Washington University's Paul

Piper's first tip was to develop a relationship with your research librarian—introduce yourself, and try to keep working with the same person. He or she will get a sense of what you want and keep a lookout for materials you can use. Piper also recommends spending time articulating to yourself what you're really looking for. He remembers well a patron who asked for books on dogs, then, after wasting quite a bit of time in the dog section, complained she couldn't find anything about the life cycle of the flea there! Dogs are dogs; fleas are fleas. Articulate your interest to yourself as clearly as you can.

Al Cordle, a reference librarian in Portland, Oregon, gave us this piece of advice: "I have a favorite technique for locating books in my library. I always go to the online catalogue and type in one or two keywords to describe my topic and the word *dictionary* or *encyclopedia*. Almost without fail I find specialized reference books devoted to my research topics." Cordle notes that keyword searches, as opposed to subject searches, can be more successful because the search engines operate more flexibly with keywords. Keyword searching should be an option offered by any library computer's toolbar. "So, for example," says Cordle, "if I type *encyclopedia* and *Native Americans*, I may come up with *Encyclopedia of Minorities in American Politics*, *Native Americans: An Encyclopedia of History, Culture, and Peoples*, and *The Encyclopedia of North American Indians*."

Even without the help of a reference librarian, libraries are not hard to navigate if you keep in mind that most print information can be tracked through master sources found in the library's reference section. To begin, articulate to yourself as specifically as you can what information you're looking for. If you had to ask one question to move forward on this writing project, what would it be? Once you have that specific question (or questions) in mind, identify the major reference works that might help you.

If you delve deeply into reference sources covering books and periodical literature, you will come across print sources that sound tantalizingly perfect for your research but that your library does not hold and aren't available on online archives either. Go to the information desk and inquire about your library's interlibrary loan policy. Almost anything, including out-of-print books and old newspapers on microfilm, can be borrowed through interlibrary loan. You may have to wait a few weeks for the text to appear and do a lot of reading rather quickly once it arrives, as these items generally can only be kept for several weeks. But knowing you've solved a puzzle or put together information no one else has by tracking little-known sources is part of the thrill of research.

The Internet

The Internet offers access to trillions of pages of material at the touch of a finger. This massive access also forms the Internet's biggest drawback: the large volume of unsorted material it turns up. Still, it's one of the best quick sources of information available now, especially for facts that don't hold too much ambiguity. If you want to know the migration habits of the gray whale, a quick search will get this information for you, along with maps and sound that will enable you to hear the grays making their way along the coast. This is quite a large payoff for very little effort.

An enormous amount of material is posted on the web in its entirety—Environmental Protection Agency reports, NASA documents, much literature that is out of copyright. Numerous specialty search engines can put you in touch with articles on particular topics—Medline, for instance, houses medical papers, and PsycINFO has professional works of psychology. If you are writing about an illness or a psychological issue, it may give you a fascinating new perspective on your subject to read what medical journals have to say about research in the field, possible avenues of treatment, and so on.

A number of search engines track what's published in thousands of print sources, and many offer summaries of the articles—some offer complete copies. Check your library for its list of online resources to see what specialized search engines you can use there if the right engines aren't available on your home computer. While many recommend avoiding Wikipedia, which can include incorrect information, it can be a useful place to start—remember that anything you see there that feels useful to you needs to be corroborated, and linger carefully over the footnotes to the articles, which often provide the best sources for your subject. Google Scholar is an excellent search tool for specialty searches. If only an expert will do, try posting a question to Yahoo Answers. Tens of millions of users bring their expertise to posted questions, and it's free.

If you can think of an institution that would house information you need, consider checking its website. Museums, government organizations, the Library of Congress, all offer immense amounts of information on the web. You might, for instance, wonder what the Smithsonian Institution in Washington, D.C., a premier science source, could tell you about eclipses. Use a search engine to access the Smithsonian's site, then follow its navigation instructions to access its online resources. You can often figure out web addresses even without search engines; if you want information on nuclear energy, you might start with the U.S. Department of Energy. Put their abbreviation (DOE), with the .gov suffix used by all government agencies, after the basic World Wide Web address of www, and voila—there it is.

You can begin playing with Internet research—assuming you haven't done this already—by choosing a good browser and search engine and typing in key words or phrases that capture your interest. Give this process a dry run just to see how it feels—choose a subject that has either interested you for a long time, or something you take absolutely for granted, maybe "the molecular structure of DNA" or "the electoral college." (We don't think much of the vagaries of how we vote, we just do it.)

Learn to scrutinize both the search engine summaries and the sites themselves for clues to how useful or downright flaky they are. The suffixes .edu and .gov, for instance, indicate sites run by educational institutions (edu) and the U.S. government (gov). A number of sites run by leading-edge universities like MIT have pages on the molecular structure of DNA, as does the World Book online (worldbookonline.com); the identities of these sources are clear from their URLs, or web addresses. Several government sites, denoted by their .gov suffix, have good explanations of the electoral college. Lots of sites will also come up that you'll probably want to give a pass—sites not relevant to your question, personal online diaries, even stories about alien DNA! Or maybe these are another essay altogether.

Remember that computers are literal creatures. The woman searching for information on fleas can stumble through an explanation by looking for dog books, however much time she may lose approaching the subject that way. No search engine, however, can intuit the leap from "dog" to "flea." Phrase your search as precisely as you can without narrowing it down too much. "AIDS in Africa" will result in hundreds of thousands of sites; "AIDS in unwed mothers between the ages of twenty-eight and twenty in the lower Volta delta" probably won't yield any. And try alternative terms to see if you uncover more or better results—both "FBI" and "Federal Bureau of Investigation," for example.

Primary Sources

One writer we know wanted to research a point in family history about which he'd heard conflicting stories—his grandparents' marriage and the birth of his mother. Visiting the courthouse in the county where the marriage took place, he requested his grandmother's marriage license and was handed a license to a marriage other than the one to his grandfather. Intrigued, he recovered copies of both marriage licenses, wedding announcements that ran in the newspapers of the time, and his mother's birth certificate—and discovered his grandmother had been pregnant and just divorcing when she married his grandfather. Back in the 1930s both events would have prompted a great deal of scandal. Tensions in family relationships suddenly fell into place.

You may not discover anything quite so interesting, or you may find something far more interesting, but the fact is, courthouses keep records of births, adoptions, marriages, divorces, deaths, and more. Anyone can request copies; you visit the courthouse in the proper town or county, ask to see the directory of records, and request copies of what you want. Or you can register with an online service like Courtlink (lexisnexis.com/courtlink), which, for a fairly low fee, can generally obtain legal documents on file anywhere in the country. If you're researching a topic in a particular town, you might want to try the historical society; most towns have them, and they keep all sorts of documents, including deeds of sale, photographs, and frequently, diaries and old publications. Old newspapers, too, teem with information, and are kept in local libraries on microfilm. You may want to back up your family interviews with research into what really happened.

There are so many other print sources of information they're hard to list here. The Government Printing Office, for example, has reports and statistics available on everything imaginable, from congressional testimony to government-sponsored research. The Television Archives housed at Vanderbilt University contain tapes of television broadcasts, including news broadcasts as well as programs, going back to the earliest days of television. You can also request written transcripts of old broadcasts. It's possible, through intelligent research, to immerse yourself completely in another place and time.

Ethnographic Research

Ethnography as a field concerns itself with examining cultures, and ethnographic inquiry can be multifaceted and lively. In autobiographical ethnography, you might mull over the books, films, television programs, and music that appeal to you and consider the specific communities to which these connect you. Think of yourself as an anthropologist studying the world you inhabit. Conduct an interview with yourself, listing elements such as your age, gender, passions, relationship status, sexual orientation, and so on.

We take these basic aspects of our lives very much for granted, but, as described in Chapter 6, "Gathering the Threads of History," each connects you with a specific population—it is very different to be a Generation Xer than a baby boomer, for instance—and, within those connections, you can either fit in with overall trends or be the exception that proves the rule. Even those parts of your biography that feel most different link you with some cultural subgroup; being raised in a commune, for instance, might join you with children of parents or grandparents who matured during the idealistic 1960s. This self-examination can turn into an essay or a way of exploring your world that will enrich your future writings—not *why* are but *how* are you *you*?

Once you have turned your ethnographic lens on yourself, consider generating essays by conducting ethnographic "fieldwork" in the communities you inhabit. While such research may overlap with immersion writing, the point of ethnographic fieldwork is to examine cultural groups in which you feel comfortable. These cultural communities could share a classroom, a workplace, a sport, or another passion, like gaming. Keep a journal or notebook and pen with you to collect *field notes*—notes on what you observe and what you think about what you see as it happens. Be aware that the act of taking notes may change the behavior of those you observe! Ask the hard questions: not just how these communities form and define themselves but whom they exclude.

For any research project, begin the process with lists of places you would most like to visit to complete the research, documents you would most like to see, people you would want to interview. Push yourself by writing down one or more "wish list" items—a place it would intimidate you to go to, a person it sounds impossible to actually speak to, or a document that feels too hard to obtain. Then challenge yourself to do it. Well-known people, politicians and the like, have publicists who may decide to put your call through. Almost anything you might want to know exists in the form of a document somewhere: divorce decrees, military records, and other documents can be rich sources of information you can obtain with determined calling.

Turning Your Research into an Essay

Research can be overwhelming as well as exhilarating. We find nothing can get you quite so stuck as sitting at your desk—or wherever you write—with slipping piles of notes and documents and no obvious way to begin. The easiest way to create a situation in which you won't feel stymied is to choose a subject that you love—what poet Emily Dickinson would call a "flood subject," one you find endlessly fascinating. Given that you are passionate about your topic, however, you can still feel overwhelmed by needing a focus when surrounded by piles of information. Here are some ideas for using research to generate a powerful essay.

With many personal essays, intuition might guide you to a strong start and innovative structure. With a research-informed essay, it can be easier to do some prewriting to guide your structure. Remind yourself why this subject appeals to you, what caught your attention in the first place. This prewriting may include jotting down anecdotes and personal experience; in Suzanne's essay "The Hazing of Swans" (see page 223), the anecdote of seeing the trumpeter swans with a friend while their boys played together might be in this list.

Expand on the immediate and anecdotal by writing down the larger issues this essay, and the research behind it, calls upon: in the swan piece, this would include the environment and its degradation that have led to the swan die-off, the violence invoked by the lead bullets the swans eat, and the conspicuous consumption represented by swan slaughter for cosmetic and millinery purposes. Write connections, such as the connection between the cosmetic slaughter of the swans long ago and the careless consumption of modern celebrities. Jot down the overarching metaphors of your idea; in Suzanne's piece these metaphors would include the idea of the uncanny, suggested by dead species returning to life; resurrection; and the image of ourselves as final recorders of many species' existence.

Once you have your prewriting list finished, write down possible writing strategies. If you have identified more than one thread in your essay, you may want to try braiding your work, as Suzanne does in the swan essay, enabling the piece to contain the history of swan endangerment, the concept of Sigmund Freud's uncanny, and the interview material on the swan die-off. If the research you did proves heavily metaphoric, you may want to position the research to clearly illuminate the more personal story to follow.

Lee Martin's essay "Paper Wasps," published in *Brevity*, uses research on the lives of these wasps to contrast with the story of his earlier life trying to help the deeply disadvantaged and his depression as he discovered he could not. Though the wasps, "frantic at the crape myrtle," superficially resemble his former clients, in the end the "industrious, persistent" wasps represent a self the author mourns never finding, and a cohesive society his clients suffered without. In "Paper Wasps," the wasps serve largely as metaphor rather than main subject, though Martin makes the decision to lead with the wasps to create a foundation with which to read and understand the story that follows. Think, as you generate ideas, of where you want your research to go, and how it will guide the reader through your essay.

TRY IT

1. Pull out an essay you've been working on, one that has promise but doesn't feel quite finished yet. Make a list of facts that inform this piece—none of these facts needs to be present in the work but can be implied, either through location, time, action, or characters. Here's a sample opening paragraph, and the list it generates.

> *It is 1963 and I am watching, for what seems like the hundredth time, Lee Harvey Oswald collapse as he is shot by Jack Ruby. I am wearing my Winnie the Pooh pajamas and listening to the ice clink in my mother's glass as she drinks another gin in the kitchen. I've told her I'm watching "Rocky & Bullwinkle" but by this time of night she's too far gone to pay attention.*

This is a very promising start: emotional without any trace of self-indulgence, nicely detailed. Here's a list of possible research areas:

- Kennedy assassination: political climate of the time? Bay of Pigs?
- Media in the early 1960s
- Postwar Midwest (unstated in the opening, but this is the location)
- Alcoholism, particularly during this period. What was the medical view of alcoholism? The social view? How was alcohol portrayed in the media of the time?

Going down the list, the author decides that alcoholism is the most promising avenue for further study. She begins by looking at advertisements and films from the period, seeing how alcohol is portrayed: as an everyday diversion, the province of sophisticates and James Bond–types. She explores medical textbooks dating from the 1960s to probe how alcohol dependence was viewed then. She finds it a much more character-driven view, less a disease model, than today. Finally, she browses Alcoholics Anonymous literature to see how a sense of the disease of alcoholism has evolved.

The final step is highlighting information worth using and then working it into the author's story without a change of voice: it's important not to sound textbook-y, as if another author has come in to serve as newscaster. Compare two moves this author could make next, given below:

In 1963, more than half of Americans, current experts agree, use alcohol to excess, and 75 percent of films show characters drinking alcoholic drinks.

Or:

Everybody is in love with James Bond this year, who drinks martini after martini in his movies without any change in behavior. James Bond has made "shaken, not stirred" a mantra for this martini-smitten culture. My mother simply eliminates the vermouth.

2. The next time a strange fact grabs your attention write it down or, if it appears in a newspaper or magazine, cut out the source. Ask yourself why this fact seems to demand your attention. Write an essay based on this fact, using additional research if necessary. If you're trolling for odd facts, try almanacs or *Harper's Index*, which holds a plethora of bizarre tidbits, like the fact that the Pentagon spends $100 a minute on Viagra.

3. Chances are you've already had at least one terrific immersion experience, even if you didn't call it that: maybe it was the wedding you attended where the bride and groom were Goths who married in black robes with white talcum on their faces. Maybe it was the time your uncle dragged you along to a meeting of the local Elks Club. Fascinating immersion experiences exist all over. Do you

live near a hospital? A casino? A group of Wiccans? A Society for Creative Anach-
ronism? Ask them if they would mind you observing them a while for an essay.
Keep notes, use a tape recorder, or both.

Decide, before you begin your immersion experience, how you see your role.
Will you take the approach of Didion and acknowledge your presence in the
events you write about, or, like Gutkind, try to keep yourself out of the narrative? Adjust your presence accordingly.

4. To hone your interview skills and create a body of information you'll almost
certainly want to come back to, try family interviews. These interviews are generally far less intimidating than tracking down your local physicist to ask questions about the implications of the Big Bang. Families also tend to be repositories
of fascinating hidden information—uncles who had more money than they
should have, cousins who disappeared in disgrace.

Start with a question you have always wanted to get an answer—or a clearer
answer—to. It may be the life story of the family scapegrace, an immigration
story, or a detailed picture of a parent's early years. Make a list of questions;
keep them fairly simple. If you're pursuing the story of a family member in legal
trouble, your questions might include what year that trouble first occurred, full
details of it, how family members responded, and so forth.

Ask your questions of two or three different family members—preferably
including several generations, such as a cousin, a parent, a grandparent—and
make note of the discrepancies between their versions of events. Unless your
family is very different from most, there will be plenty. Follow up on your initial
interviews with further questions, to see if you can explain differing versions of
the story.

This second round of questions will tell you a lot about the person/event
you're researching, and it will also tell you a lot—maybe even more—about the
structure of your family. Typically, families have keepers-of-the-family-name
types, who minimize or dismiss what seems "improper." They also have tell-all
types—those who collect stories and relish relating them. You may want to
meditate on who plays these roles in your family (does the answer surprise you?)
and, of course, who you are in the hierarchy of things.

PART 2

THE MANY FORMS OF CREATIVE NONFICTION

The best work speaks intimately to you even though it has been consciously made to speak intimately to thousands of others. The bad writer believes that sincerity of feeling will be enough, and pins her faith on the power of experience. The true writer knows that feeling must give way to form. It is through the form, not in spite of, or accidental to it, that the most powerful emotions are let loose over the greatest number of people.

—JEANETTE WINTERSON

9

The Tradition of the Personal Essay

After a time, some of us learn (and some more slowly than others) that life comes down to some simple things. How we love, how alert we are, how curious we are. Love, attention, curiosity. . . . One way we learn this lesson is by listening to others tell us true stories of their own struggles to come to a way of understanding. It is sometimes comforting to know that others seem to fail as often and as oddly as we do. . . . And it is even more comforting to have such stories told to us with *style*, the way a writer has found to an individual expression of a personal truth.

—Scott Walker, editor,
Essays, Memoirs & Reflections

I am a young woman in college, beginning to write. One day I pick up Annie Dillard's book *Pilgrim at Tinker Creek*. A book-length, meditative personal essay, *Pilgrim* documents the speaker's observations of the natural world around her home in Virginia. It is at once deeply individual, as she looks at the "rosy, complex" light that fills her kitchen in June, and deeply philosophical, as she draws everything into relationship with the galaxy that is "careening" around her. It is a bold book, drawing on the seemingly small in order to embrace the entire world. More important to me at the time, the speaker is a young woman in her twenties, the author herself. She's not speaking with the authoritative male voice I have come to associate with the essay. She speaks as Annie Dillard, with only the authority of our shared human experience.

I was fascinated to learn later that Annie Dillard originally began *Pilgrim at Tinker Creek* in the voice of a middle-aged male academic, a metaphysician. She didn't trust her own young woman's voice to engage and convince her audience. Other writers persuaded her to trust her voice and abandon the constructed one, and the book won the Pulitzer Prize, proving that the personal essay form is a broad one. It only requires that you be alert, perceptive and human.

—SUZANNE

Find Your Form—Find Your Slant

We began this book with a nod to Emily Dickinson and her mandate to "tell all the truth but tell it slant." Part 1, we hope, has helped you find out just what kinds of "truths" you may have to offer. Now your job is to find a way to "tell it slant," to find the forms that will contain these truths in the most effective and interesting ways. As a writer of creative nonfiction, you must continually make artistic choices that will finesse life's experience into art that will have lasting meaning for others.

Through a careful attention to form, you will be able to create art out of your own experience. Understanding *how* we are structuring our experience forces us to be concrete and vivid. Ironically, the more particular you make your own experience—with sensory details, compelling metaphors, and luscious rhythms—the more fully a reader will feel the personal story along with you. By experiencing it, the reader begins to *care* about it, because your experience has now become his own.

We hope that you will come to find that form is your friend; that by placing your allegiance to artifact over experience, the material becomes just that: raw material that you will use to fashion art, rather than the intractable stuff of memory and experience. To come back to our friend Emily Dickinson, in a letter to Thomas Higginson, she said, rather cryptically, "My business is circumference." By this she means perhaps that she circled her life, encompassing every hummingbird, every fly, every bit of bread into her art. All creative nonfiction writers should take heed. Observe your life from every angle—cocking your head, squinting your eyes—then fashion what you see through a voice that is yours and yours alone. Tell us the truth, but shape it in a way that wakes us from our doldrums and startles us into a new grasp of our strange and remarkable lives.

The Personal Essay Tradition

The personal essay is "the way a writer has found to an individual expression of a personal truth." When Scott Walker wrote those words in 1986, the personal essay was making a comeback. The reading public seemed hungry for a form that engages us the way fiction does but that also teaches us something about the way real life works. While the phrase "creative nonfiction" had not yet come into popular use, "personal essay" seemed adequate to convey that sense of combining a personal voice with a factual story.

In the West, scholars often date the essay tradition back to the sixteenth-century French writer Michel de Montaigne. *Essays*, composed in Montaigne's retirement, lay much of the groundwork for what we now think of as the essay style: informal, frank (often bawdy), and associative. His book moves easily from a consideration of the classical author Virgil to pieces like "Of Thumbs." His title *Essays*, playing on the French verb meaning "to try," gives us the term we now use routinely in nonfiction writing. The essay writer "tries out" various approaches to the subject, offering tentative forays into an arena where "truth" can be open for debate.

Phillip Lopate, editor of the historically astute anthology *The Art of the Personal Essay*, puts it this way: "The essayist attempts to surround a something—a subject, a mood, a problematic irritation—by coming at it from all angles, wheeling and diving like a hawk, each seemingly digressive spiral actually taking us closer to the heart of the matter."

Prior to Montaigne, as Lopate's anthology illustrates, plenty of writers worked in what we would now consider a personal essay mode. Just a few examples include Sei Shonagon, a tenth-century Japanese courtesan who created elaborately detailed lists that revealed much about herself and her place in the Japanese court; the Japanese monk Kenko's meditative ruminations translated as *Essays in Idleness*; or Roman emperor Marcus Aurelius, whose book *Meditations* embodies an aphoristic essay style, creating pithy "slogans" as advice to those who will succeed him. The Stoic philosopher

Seneca the Younger and the Greek biographer Plutarch both wrote "essays in disguise" in the form of letters that ruminated on a range of subjects, from noise in the marketplace to the proper comportment to maintain in the face of grief.

After Montaigne, British essayists such as Charles Lamb and William Hazlitt made the essay form their own. According to Lopate, "it was the English, rather than Montaigne's own countrymen, who took up his challenge and extended, refined, and cultivated the essay." Lamb wrote about intensely personal material. (His sister killed their mother and wounded their father; Lamb, himself, suffered a nervous breakdown.) But, he used a fictional persona that gave him some distance from his subject. Hazlitt wrote more in the style of Montaigne, creating essays with titles such as "On Going a Journey" and "On the Pleasure of Hating." At the same time in America, Thoreau was writing his journals and *Walden*, works that would form the foundation of American nature writing taken up by writers such as Edward Abbey and Annie Dillard.

Women left an indelible mark on the essay too. Just a few examples include Maria Edgeworth, a memoirist and feminist from the Romantic period; Isabella Bird, a nineteenth-century travel writer who died in her seventies with her bags packed; and Nellie Bly, another nineteenth-century woman writer who pushed her way into the male world of journalism, famously practicing immersion in sweatshops and institutions.

As an essayist, you should take it upon yourself to study the tradition, not only for general knowledge but to situate yourself within that literary lineup. How does your own writing work with or against the stylistic tendencies of a Joan Didion, say, who in turn has a voice that emerges in direct dialogue with the voice of essayists such as George Orwell? Lopate's *The Art of the Personal Essay* is a good place to start, but also look at works of your contemporaries to see how the essay is evolving in your own generation. The literary magazine *Fourth Genre: Explorations in Nonfiction* publishes some of the best contemporary writers in the form, as do the journals *Creative Nonfiction* and *River Teeth: A Journal of Nonfiction Narrative*. You should also avail yourself of the Best American Essays series. The editor, Robert Atwan, culls a selection of the strongest essays published by American magazines in each year, and a guest editor pares those down further to a select few. While we will all have our own definitions of *best*, it is useful to read these anthologies to see what your contemporaries are up to. John D'Agata's anthology, *The Next American Essay*, plays off this concept of "best," and he includes more experimental work that could be overlooked by mainstream media. Another useful anthology is *The Touchstone Anthology of Contemporary Creative Nonfiction*, edited by Michael Martone and Lex Williford. By reading widely, you will learn not only what is possible, but what has still to be discovered.

You may find, as Lopate has, that "at the core of the essay is the supposition that there is a certain unity to human experience." The personal essay carries the implication that the personal, properly rendered, is universally significant or should be. Montaigne echoes this. "Every man has within himself the entire human condition." At the same time, Lopate writes that "the hallmark of the personal essay is its intimacy. The writer seems to be speaking directly into your ear, confiding everything from gossip to wisdom." These two poles—intimacy of voice and universality of significance—go to the heart of the personal essay tradition. The essay speaks confidingly, as a whispering friend, and these whispers must be made meaningful in a larger context—capturing a piece of larger human experience within the amber of your own.

The Way Essays Work

What makes an essay an essay? How can you recognize one when you see it? When we study fiction writing or poetry, certain elements of form are easy enough to identify, such as plot or character development in short stories or lineation and rhythm in poems. Essays can be analyzed the same way, but the task is complicated by the wide variety of styles and forms encompassed by the term *personal essay*. Many of these forms overlap with content, and perhaps you've already experienced several of them in the first section of this book. You've already been writing memoir, for example, when you focus on selected memories for a particular metaphorical or narrative effect. You've already started a nature essay when you described some aspect of the environment around you. Perhaps you've already tried the travel piece or a biographical sketch of someone close to you. Perhaps you've sidled up to the spiritual autobiography or the topical essay. All of these are forms, defined more by content than craft.

When we turn our attention to craft, we can begin to see some stylistic qualities that help to define the essay form. In his essay "A Boundary Zone," Douglas Hesse describes the difference between essays and short stories in terms of movement. In any narrative prose piece, some sense of forward movement emerges. Visualized as a horizontal line, this line keeps the story moving forward. Some essays read almost like short stories. For example, in the well-known essay "The Fourth State of Matter" by Jo Ann Beard, the horizontal line is a shooting at the author's workplace at the University of Iowa. She begins the piece before the shooting and continues through the event and its emotional aftermath. Three other strands also propel the essay forward: a dying collie, a divorce, and squirrels inhabiting her attic. All these form miniplots, very much like a short story. She uses dialogue freely and re-creates scene with vivid, specific details. And the essay itself reads like a short story because of the present-tense voice (a narrator), and the sense of horizontal story lines unfolding and intersecting at the same time.

In contrast, a more essaylike narrative might have a stronger vertical line to it, the reflective voice that comments upon the scenes it re-creates. David James Duncan often works in this mode. In "The Mickey Mantle Koan," for example, the forward, horizontal line of the narrative—the brother's death— is interrupted, or balanced, by his ruminations on the arrival of a signed baseball after his brother's death. This reflective voice runs underneath the horizontal line, creating a sense of movement that delves below the surface of narrative.

Once you begin seeing essays in terms of their movement, you can decide how your own work might fit or work against the categories of personal essay. At one extreme, we have the short-story style that engages us with plot, sub-plots, and scenes. At the other extreme is the analytic meditation that engages us through the power of the writer's interior voice. Where do you fall on this grid? How can you expand your talents and write essays that create their own definitions?

Traditional Forms of the Personal Essay

Remember, most essays use elements of different literary approaches. For instance, one piece by John McPhee might contain within it nature writing, science writing, and memoir. But for purposes of scrutinizing our own work and understanding our traditions, we can discuss nonfiction in terms of categories, bearing in mind all the while that we don't want to allow ourselves or the writers we admire to be limited by those categories.

Memoir

A nonfiction category strongly linked with the personal essay is memoir. *Memoir* comes from the French word for *memory*; no writer of any stripe is prescient enough to put everything he or she wants to record into notes, therefore drawing on memory is an essential part of what we all do. Some readers confuse anything written with a first-person "I" that draws on personal experience with memoir, though new journalists like Joan Didion and Tom Wolfe indulge freely in both without necessarily being memoirists. And some writers, reacting to criticism that the form has become overly confessional and overly prevalent, avoid the term *memoir* when that's exactly what they're writing.

To be memoir, the writing must derive its energy, its narrative drive, from exploration of the past. Its lens may be a lifetime, or it may be a few hours. In "Total Eclipse," Annie Dillard recollects a past event, but her narrative drive—the punch of the piece—is metaphysical meditation, not memoir. On the other hand, in his "Afternoon of an American Boy," E. B. White writes a piece of pure memoir. His lens is small; he recalls a period in his teenage years when he first got up the courage to ask a girl out to dance—"that precious, brief moment in life before love's pages, through constant reference, had become dog-eared."

William Zinsser, who edited *Inventing the Truth: The Art and Craft of Memoir*, says, "Unlike autobiography, which moves in a dutiful line from birth to fame, memoir narrows the lens, focusing on a time in the writer's life that was unusually vivid, such as childhood or adolescence, or that was framed by war or travel or public service or some other special circumstance." In other words, memoirists need not have had fascinating lives, worth recounting in every detail. (Those kinds of books, as Zinsser notes, are generally considered autobiography.)

Memoir mines the past, examining it for shape and meaning, in the belief that from that act a larger, communal meaning can emerge. Memoir can heal, it can warn, and it can provide spiritual direction. Spiritual memoir—like the writings of Kathleen Norris and Andre Dubus, among others—falls in the last category. Memoir can open societal lines of communication on subjects previously held taboo. For example, Richard Hoffman's memoir of child sexual abuse, *Half the House*, eventually led to the prosecution of a child molester.

In his essay "Backtalk," Hoffman provides a defense of the surge of memoir as a corrective to a culture that has accepted the verb *to spin* to mean deliberate distortion of our news. "The ascendance of memoir . . . may be a kind of cultural corrective to the sheer amount of fictional distortion that has accumulated in [our] society." For those of you interested in the memoir form, Hoffman's words may provide a useful starting point; think of yourself as an "unspinner," a voice striving to undo some of the cultural distortion you see around you.

Though memoir is the nonfiction form most closely associated with an "I," it can be written in second or third person; Judith Kitchen uses third person in her brief memoir "Things of This Life," for instance. She begins:

> Consider the child idly browsing in the curio shop. She's been on vacation in the Adirondacks, and her family has (over the past week) canoed the width of the lake and up a small, meandering river to where the beaver dams have made passage impossible; found a stable and spent an afternoon on horseback; cooked pancakes and hot dogs and beef stew over a campfire; and spent each evening lying stretched on their backs on a canvas tarp, hoping to catch sight of the meteor showers as the darkness deepens. So why, as she sifts through boxes of fake arrowheads made into key chains, passes down the long rows of rubber tomahawks, dyed rabbits' feet, salt shakers with the words "Indian Lake" painted in gold, beaded moccasins made of what could only in the imagination be called leather, is she happier than any time during the past week?

We understand, intuitively, that "the child" is the author, herself. We are allowed to gaze back in the past with her, observing the younger self. A little later in the essay, she travels through time and begins a new paragraph this way:

> Now consider the woman who was that child. Today she wakes up in her untidy bedroom with sunlight slanting through the panes where she has recently adjusted the blinds. Outside, there is snow and for some reason that

makes the sunlight brighter, sadder. There has been too much snow this winter and she is tired of it, tired of stepping out of the passenger seat of the car into a wall of snow that filters into her shoes, tired of keeping the porch steps swept for the mailman, tired of the way everyone talks about nothing but weather.

By using the third-person point of view, Kitchen is able to "consider" both herself and her memories in a detailed way that carries a great deal of perspective. She is able to show how this memoir-like essay is focused not really on memories of "things" themselves, but how contemplation of these things allows her to come to an understanding of the gap between the childlike self, full of wonder, and the more adult self, who, at this moment, is tired of the world. This is one way a memoir essay transcends the personal: by examining small concrete details to approach larger, more universal themes.

These kinds of techniques—experiments with point of view, use of different tenses (past, present, future), finding just the right metaphorical image to anchor the piece—all serve to help the memoir elevate itself out of self-centered rumination and into the arena of art. As Adam Gopnick wrote in his Introduction to *The Best American Essays, 2008*: "Memoir essays move us not because they are self-indulgent, but because they are other-indulgent, and the other they indulge is us, with our own parallel inner stories of loss and confusion and mixed emotions."

Literary or New Journalism

In 1972, for an article in *New York* magazine, Tom Wolfe announced "The Birth of the 'New Journalism.'" This new nonfiction form, Wolfe claimed, would supplant the novel. It allowed writers the luxury of a first-person voice and the use of literary devices—scene, imagery, and so forth—in the service of reporting. In other words, Wolfe's new journalism marries traditional journalism with the personal essay. Wolfe cited such new journalists as Hunter S. Thompson, then writing a first-person account of his travels among the Hell's Angels.

Wolfe emerged as one of the leaders of New Journalism, along with other writers such as Joan Didion, Gay Talese, and Norman Mailer. Wolfe rode buses with LSD guru Ken Kesey and his Merry Pranksters to write *The Elec-*

tric Kool-Aid Acid Test, all the while using his first-person voice liberally and appearing in his trademark starched high collars and white suits, a character in his own right. Wolfe's insistence on the primacy of his own experience in the act of reporting comes through even in his titles, like this one of an essay about Las Vegas (surely one of the loudest cities in the country): "Las Vegas (What?) Las Vegas (Can't Hear You! Too Noisy) Las Vegas!!!!" New journalism does stress the act of reporting; its practitioners have done some of the most intense reporting in the nonfiction world. But they also avail themselves of literary techniques and a personal voice.

As research becomes more crucial even to very personal nonfiction, such as Terry Tempest Williams's *Refuge* or Andrew Solomon's *The Noonday Demon* (a heavily researched but intimate look at depression), the lines between other forms of nonfiction and new journalism blur. And, in the age of instant information on the Internet, traditional journalism becomes more interpretive and less formulaic. Think of it as a healthy blurring of the categories that can sometimes stifle the evolution of forms.

David Foster Wallace—both a novelist and a nonfiction writer—provided some of the most exciting new writing in this form. He once said, "Writing-wise, fiction is scarier but nonfiction is harder—because nonfiction's based in reality, and today's felt reality is overwhelmingly, circuit-blowingly huge and complex." He deals with this complexity through innovative uses of form: his writing often combines immersion research with a fiction writer's sensibility, and the resultant work exhibits his unique voice and playfulness. For instance, in his essay "Consider the Lobster," he travels to the Maine Lobster Festival, where he observes:

> . . . lobster rolls, lobster turnovers, lobster sauté, Down East lobster salad, lobster bisque, lobster ravioli, and deep-fried lobster dumplings. . . . There are lobster T-shirts and lobster bobblehead dolls and inflatable lobster pool toys and clamp-on lobster hats with big scarlet claws that wobble on springs.

These list-like observations are a hallmark of Wallace's work, and he intersperses direct observation with in-depth information gleaned from many sources. Throughout the essay, footnotes give interesting "factoids" as well as his running commentary on what he is learning and observing about the humble lobster. These techniques allow us to learn a great deal about lobsters, certainly, but more important we also learn about Wallace and his own sensibilities. The essay ends up debating the moral issues involved with cooking live lobsters. "I am concerned," he writes, after bringing up these issues, "not to come off as shrill or preachy when what I really am is more like confused, uneasy." We probably wouldn't be all that interested in lobsters and the moral issues they raise if Wallace didn't show them to us with this self-revealing, and highly entertaining, voice.

The Meditative Essay

Composing his essays, Montaigne referred to himself as an "accidental philosopher." The term *essay* carries a double meaning of both *trying* and *proving* or *testing*. To essay an action means to attempt it; to essay a substance, particularly a metal, means to test it, weigh it, and try to determine its composition. The essay itself enfolds this dual nature of the term—essays typically approach their subjects tentatively, allow readers the luxury of seeing the author roll ideas around in his or her mind, *test* conclusions rather than presenting them.

The essay form lends itself to tentative, meditative movement, and the meditative essay derives its power from careful deliberation on a subject, often but not always an abstract one. Some meditative essays announce their approach in their title, like Abraham Cowley's *Of Greatness*. In "Total Eclipse," Annie Dillard recalls the event of the eclipse in great detail before switching to her true subject, a metaphysical meditation on our relationship to the universe:

> The mind wants to live forever, or to learn a very good reason why not. The mind wants the world to return its love, or its awareness; the mind wants to know all the world, and all eternity, and God. The mind's sidekick [the body], however, will settle for two eggs over easy.

Another example of the meditative essay is Richard Bausch's "So Long Ago." Bausch's meditative intent comes through in the essay's opening, where he addresses the reader in a conversational tone that both engages us and signals that he's about to take us step by step through his thoughts:

Indulge me, a moment.

I have often said glibly that the thing which separates the young from the old is the knowledge of what Time really is; not just how fast, but how illusive and arbitrary and mutable it is. When you are twenty, the idea of twenty years is only barely conceivable, and since that amount of time makes up one's whole life, it seems an enormous thing—a vast, roomy expanse, going on into indefiniteness.

Time—and how we perceive it—is an abstract and slippery subject. Bausch's confiding voice, leading us into his meditation as if we're going into a difficult but rewarding conversation, engages us from the outset. He weaves memories, notably a funeral, among his meditations on the larger importance of time and history. "We come from the chaos of ourselves to the world, and we yearn to know what happened to all the others who came before us. So we impose Time on the flow of events, and call it history."

Without specific events, it's hard to imagine such an abstract meditation holding our interest. The best meditative essayists instinctively make this technique their own. They probe concrete events until they yield up the deeper meanings that lie buried below the surface.

The Essay of Ideas

Strongly connected to the meditative essay is the essay of ideas. The essay has long been *the* form for exploring the workings of the human intellect. Running the gamut from argument to rumination, authors have always used the essay as a vehicle for both developing and expressing ideas, holding political debates, and delving into personal philosophy. Many of us have bad memories of writing "themes" in high school, the five-paragraph essay that rigidly prescribed the way an intellectual essay could work: thesis, three supporting paragraphs, and a tepid conclusion. Here, in the realm of creative nonfiction, you can redeem the essay of ideas and return it to its rightful place in the literary arts.

As with all good creative nonfiction, it's important to make the essay specific to you and your particular voice. Writing about abstract concepts does not need to be dull or dry; on the contrary, here is an opportunity for you to use the techniques of vivid writing to illuminate difficult and obscure topics.

You will seek to uncover the scenes, the details, the images, and the metaphors that make for a memorable essay.

For example, in the essay "The Semiotics of Sex," Jeanette Winterson begins a highly complex discussion of aesthetics, art, and ideology with a scene in a bookstore:

> I was in a bookshop recently when a young woman approached me.
>
> She told me she was writing an essay on my work and that of Radclyffe Hall. Could I help?
>
> "Yes," I said. "Our work has nothing in common."
>
> "I thought you were a lesbian," she said.

With this brief scene, Winterson provides a compelling example that whole-heartedly admits the "I" into the intellectual discussion to follow. Rather than dryly elucidate her thesis in the first paragraph, *then* provide a support for that thesis, she does the opposite; she finds a scene that encapsulates her argument and she renders that scene in a way that reveals her personality, her voice, and her concerns.

It is the combination of a personal urgency with intellectual musings that makes the essay of ideas thrive. Remember "Notes of a Native Son" from Chapter 6? Baldwin focuses on the death of his father, but issues of race and violence pulse through the essay, creating a political argument much more effective than any pundit's analysis.

Paradoxically, when you write about abstract concepts—ideas—it is even more important to pay attention to the concrete details that make such things comprehensible. The good essay of ideas will be a mix of argument and reflection—knowledge and experience—so that in the end the reader has gained some insight into both the ideas and the mind behind them.

The Sketch or Portrait

One of the most popular essay forms of the nineteenth century, the sketch or portrait held ground partly because of the lack of other forms of communication—the average person traveled little and, even after the invention of photography, saw far fewer photos than we see today. Writers like Dickens stepped into the breach, offering verbal snapshots of cities, foreign countries, and people.

Today we have newspapers, TV, even the Internet, but the power of language to provide not just verbal pictures but emotional ones keeps the portrait an important form. Immediately after the September 11th attacks on the World Trade Center and the Pentagon, the *New Yorker* magazine commissioned a handful of writers to capture that day in short verbal portraits, collectively titled "First Reactions." The editors realized something crucial about that world-changing event: photos may best hold the searing image of the buildings, but a writer can also capture the reality of "stumbling out of the smoke into a different world" (Jonathan Franzen).

The character sketch is also an integral part of the portrait form. Originally a kind of verbal photograph, portraits still can capture individuals in a way visual forms cannot, using imagery and description to leap from someone's surface to their essence. Maxine Hong Kingston's "No Name Woman" forms at once a largely imaginary portrait of the author's disgraced aunt and a portrait of her very real mother:

> If I want to learn what clothes my aunt wore, whether flashy or ordinary, I would have to begin, "Remember Father's drowned-in-the-well sister?" I cannot ask that. My mother has told me once and for all the useful parts. She will add nothing unless powered by Necessity, a riverbank that guides her life. She plants vegetable gardens rather than lawns; she carries the odd-shaped tomatoes home from the fields and eats food left for the gods.

What a world of information is packed into this formidable portrait! We see Kingston's mother sketched before us in terms of telling actions—choosing the practical over the ornamental, refusing to waste food, even for presumably religious reasons. We're prepared by this sketch for the tension mother and daughter experience over the suppression of the aunt's story, and the way that story reflects their own uncommunicative relationship.

Humor

Of all the audience responses writers may want to elicit, none is harder to gauge than humor. It's hard to argue about the sentimental value of people falling in love or the tragedy of war, but we all tend to have a comedy vocabulary peculiarly our own. Emily Dickinson, who lends our book its title, had a peculiar habit of roaring with laughter over the obituaries every day.

In *How to Write*, Stephen Leacock said, "Humor may be defined as the kindly contemplation of the incongruities of life and the artistic expression thereof." The juxtaposition of odd or unexpected things makes up a lot of what we find comic.

In his essay "The Drama Bug," humorist David Sedaris falls in love with theater and affects a Shakespearean speech that becomes hilarious in juxtaposition with the ordinary events occupying his teenage years. Over a chicken dinner with family, he proclaims, "Methinks, kind sir, most gentle lady, fellow siblings all, that this barnyard fowl be most tasty and succulent." Humor writers like Sedaris are constantly mining their lives for incongruities to use in their work.

Patrick McManus, author of *The Deer on a Bicycle: Excursions into Writing Humor*, offers a wonderful piece of advice: write humor out of your bad experiences, not your good ones. Think about it. Which would make a better essay, your best family car trip, with snacks and singing "Kumbaya," or the worst, with your father muttering oaths over a flat tire while your little sister screams for a bathroom or else? What was awful then is probably hilarious now. Some of life's most irritating things—telemarketers, computerized voice answering systems, HMOs—yield some of its most reliable humor.

Exaggeration, or hyperbole, is also a classic American form of humor, dear to practitioners like Mark Twain, who once swore that in a tour of Europe he'd seen the equivalent of a "barrelful" of nails from the True Cross. While the exaggeration is evident, Twain's comment makes a point about the number of false religious relics on display in Europe at the time. Sedaris clearly exaggerates in the long-winded pseudo-Elizabethan speeches he delivers in "The Drama Bug"; no one could remember their own monologues that precisely. (And surely his family would have swatted him with the barnyard fowl before listening to all of that!) Writer Anne Lamott is another comic exaggerator. It's a device she uses again and again to great effect, as when she describes a reading in which "I had jet lag, the self esteem of a prawn, and to top it off, I had stopped breathing. I sounded just like the English patient."

One characteristic that Sedaris and Lamott have in common is the self-puncturing qualities of the authors. They laugh at themselves so freely we feel encouraged to laugh with them—and, if we're honest with ourselves, we all have a gold mine of material in self-deprecation. No one knows our foibles better than we do. If you look at the Lamott quote—the "self-esteem of a prawn. . . . I sounded just like the English patient"—you'll note that she's laughing above all at how seriously she took herself at the time of this bookstore reading. Humor writers laugh at themselves and encourage us to laugh at those qualities in them, and in the process, at the whole human condition.

TRY IT

1. Write a short piece of memoir using a particular event. Write quickly and then examine the piece in light of the distinctions between the intimate and the universal. Where do you speak as though the reader is a friend, listening at your side? Do you need to reveal more of yourself, of your feelings? And where is the universality of your experience? You may want to trade with a partner to uncover the answers to these questions. You can seek out E. B. White's "Afternoon of an American Boy" as a model for this prompt.

> **VARIATION:** With Richard Hoffman's comments in mind, write a memoir of an event that seeks to "unspin" some kind of official version of it.

2. Try writing about a small childhood memory from the third-person point of view, as Judith Kitchen does in "Things of This Life." You could even imitate her sentence structure, using the phrase "Consider the child . . ." as a way to begin. See if this technique enables you to view yourself as a character and unearth more details.

3. Write a journalistic story, perhaps about a colorful place nearby or an event in your community (a protest? a festival?) that uses reportorial style to capture the story but also includes your own presence as a character. Use literary devices to describe the people you see; use metaphor to paint their lives. Take advantage of literary devices, while respecting the factuality of journalism.

4. Write a sketch of a person or a place. Focus on keeping your work vivid and simple—a language portrait. Think of it as being intended for someone who cannot meet this person or visit this area.

5. Write an essay titled "On _____." Fill in the blank yourself and use the title as a way to explore an abstract concept in a personal and concrete way. All of us have abstract questions we would secretly love to write about. Why are we here? What does it mean to love a child? Why does society exist in the form it does?

6. Write down the abstract question you would most like to explore. Then free-write a group of events you somehow associate with that question: a brush with death, giving birth, living in a different culture. Meditate on the question, alternating your meditations with the actual event.

7. Practice writing deliberate incongruities, twists, exaggerations, and under-statements. What is the strangest sight you've seen over the last year? Was it a Hare Krishna at an airport talking on a cell phone? A Santa Claus withdrawing money from an ATM? What experience in your own life led to the most unexpected sight?

8. What irritates you? Write a few paragraphs on the most constant irritants in your life, whether it's telemarketers, the fact that you have almost the same phone number as the local pizzeria, whatever. Write dialogue and scene; strive to be funny. At the same time, think, as previously, of larger subjects this irritant suggests.

9. Actor Billy Bob Thornton constantly pokes fun at himself for his phobias and obsessions, notably a fear of flying and of antique furniture (!). True or not, these self-lampoons are extremely funny. What are your most humorous foibles? What do friends and family lampoon you about? What do these foibles say about you, and our human aspirations?

10

Playing with Form:
The Lyric Essay and Mixed Media

> I go out of my way, but rather by license than carelessness. My ideas
> follow one another, but sometimes it is from a distance, and look at
> each other, but with a sidelong glance . . . I love the poetic gait, by
> leaps and gambols.
>
> —MICHEL DE MONTAIGNE

I find myself thumbing through an encyclopedia of Jewish religion I happened to pick up at the library. As I turn the pages of this marvelous book,
I'm struck by how little I, a Jewish woman who went to Hebrew school for
most of my formative years, know about my own religion. I start writing
down the quotes that interest me most, facts about the Kaballah and ritual
baths and dybbuks and the Tree of Life. I've also started noodling around
with some other stories: a recent trip to Portugal and the news I received
there of my mother's emergency hysterectomy; notes on the volunteer work
I perform at the local children's hospital; and musings about my on-again,
off-again yoga practice. As I keep all these windows open on my computer,
the voice of the encyclopedia emerges as an odd, binding thread, holding
together these disparate stories in a way that seems organic. I begin to fragment the stories and to move these fragments around, finding the images
that resonate against one another in juxtaposition.

I feel like a poet, creating stanzas and listening for the rhythms of the
sentence, using white space, reading aloud to determine when another quote
from the encyclopedia is necessary to balance out my personal story. Sometimes I have to throw out whole sections that no longer fit, but this editing

leaves room for new segments, new phrases, new images that build and transform over the course of the essay, weaving in and out, but always grounded on the thread of prayer and the body. It takes some time, this shuffling gait, but finally I have an essay, "Basha Leah": a spiritual self-portrait in the form of a complex braid.

This lyric essay allows for the moments of pause, the gaps, the silence. The fragmentation feels correct to the piece: it allows for the moments of "not knowing," the unspoken words that seem truer than anything I could ever say aloud.

—BRENDA

What Is the Lyric Essay?

Lyric. Essay. How do these two terms fit together? At first these words may seem diametrically opposed. *Lyric* implies a poetic sensibility concerned more with language, imagery, sound, and rhythm over the more linear demands of narrative. *Essay*, on the other hand, implies a more logical frame of mind, one concerned with a well-wrought story, or a finely tuned argument, over the demands of language. When we put the two together, we come up with a hybrid form that allows for the best of both genres.

To put it simply, lyric essays do not necessarily follow a straight narrative line. The root of the word *lyric* is the lyre, a musical instrument that accompanied ancient song. Lyric poetry and essays are songlike in that they hinge on the inherent rhythms of language and sound. Lyric essays favor fragmentation and imagery; they use white space and juxtaposition as structural elements. They are as attuned to silences as they are to utterance. In its thirtieth-anniversary issue devoted to lyric essays, the *Seneca Review* characterized them as having "this built-in mechanism for provoking meditation. They require us to complete their meaning."

The writer of the lyric essay brings the reader into an arena where questions are asked; it is up to the reader to piece together possible answers and interpretations. Fragmentation allows for this type of reader interaction because the writer, by surrendering to the fragmented form, declines a foregone conclusion. Writer and literary theorist Rebecca Faery notes, "In the essays that have in recent years compelled me most, I am summoned, called upon. These essays are choral, polyphonic; there are pauses, rests. . . . The rests in these essays are spaces inviting me in, inviting response."

The lyric essay requires an allegiance to intuition. Because we are no longer tied to a logical, linear narrative or argument, we must surrender to the writing process itself to show us the essay's intent. In so doing, we reveal ourselves in a roundabout way. When we write in the mode of the lyric essay, we create not only prose pieces but a portrait of our subconscious selves, the part of us that speaks in riddles or in brief, imagistic flashes.

Part of the fun of the lyric essay will be making up your own form as you go along. But, for the sake of argument, we will break the lyric essay down into four main categories that seem to encapsulate the lyric essays we see most often: prose poem (or flash nonfiction), collage, the braided essay, and a form we've dubbed the "hermit crab."

Prose Poem or Flash Nonfiction

For the introduction to their anthology *The Party Train: A Collection of North American Prose Poetry*, the editors begin with this piece by S. C. Hahn called "If My Father Were to Ask":

> "What's a prose poem?" I would turn my face and look into the distance away from our farm house, into a wild copse of trees which runs from the road's edge and on up the hill to the far fields. Box elder, green ash, and black locust tangle in a net of branches, tied together by thorny greenbrier. I know of a coyote den beneath one old box elder tree, on the edge of a gully cutting through the copse. If I were to stick my hand into the hole, I could feel cool wet air and perhaps the playful teeth of pups.
>
> "Remember when you plowed the fields in the spring," I say to my father, "and the air behind you filled suddenly with sea gulls?" I can see him inhale the aroma of memory: the green and yellow tractor, the motor exhaust and dust, steel blades of the plow sinking into the earth and turning it, the smell all sexual and holy, worms and grubs uncovered into sunlight, then an unexpected slash of white as the gulls materialize behind the plow, a thousand miles and more from any ocean.

What is a prose poem? Well, maybe it's the feeling you get when you're standing in a landscape you know well and love, a landscape where you can imagine what lies hidden behind the trees or beneath the ground. Maybe the prose poem is the "aroma of memory" and all the sensual details it evokes. Or maybe the signature of the prose poem is the unexpected surprise at the end, the improbable appearance of sea birds above the plowed fields of the heartland.

Maybe the prose poem is all these things, but most importantly, the prose poem speaks to the heart rather than the head. The prose poem is about what is possible, not necessarily what has already occurred. Even the title, "If My Father Were to Ask," privileges imagination over experience. The father has not asked the question, but what if he did?

In this way, the terms *prose poem* and *flash nonfiction* could be nearly interchangeable. Flash nonfiction is a brief essay—usually less than a thousand words—that focuses on one particular image. It is tightly focused, with no extraneous words, and it mines its central image in ways that create metaphorical significance. The language is fresh, lyrically surprising, hinged on the workings of the imagination.

This form is fun to both write and read. The popular online magazine *Brevity* "publishes concise literary nonfiction of 750 words or less focusing on detail and scene over thought and opinion." This journal is an excellent place to find scores of diverse examples of the short-short form—some that read more like compressed narrative, and others that blur the line between prose and poetry. One such piece is A. Papatya Bucak's very short essay "I Cannot Explain My Fear." In it, Bucak lists fears, sometimes expanding for a line or two, but remaining in the rhythm of a list. It begins:

> Fear of bears, fear of ladders, fear of freezing. Once, in the Sonoran Desert, I woke with ice on my sleeping bag. Fear of a cancerous thyroid; fear of eating poisonous fish from Japan; fear of sharks, overly large seals and sea lice, too. Fear that my glasses are radioactive because the first time I had a nuclear scan the technician didn't tell me to remove them, but the second time he did. Fear of swimming to the bottom of the pool because people get suctioned to the filter and drown.

Bucak continues in this rhythm until the end, as the piece slows down, takes some breaths, begins new ways of listing, and approaches things that the narrator does *not* fear:

Once I saw a coyote standing on the stump of a tree in a farmer's field. Once I saw three bald eagles at once. Once I saw a snake with the leg of a frog sticking out of its mouth.

Words don't scare me.

I am quiet, but that is not the same as afraid.

For other examples of flash nonfiction you can look to the several collections that have come out in recent years. W. W. Norton has issued three volumes of short nonfiction, edited by Judith Kitchen and Mary Paumier Jones, called *In Short: A Collection of Brief Creative Nonfiction*, *In Brief: Short Takes on the Personal*, and *Short Takes: Brief Encounters with Contemporary Nonfiction* (edited by Kitchen alone). In the introduction to *In Short*, Bernard Cooper elucidates the stance of the lyric essayist working in the flash nonfiction form: "To write short nonfiction requires an alertness to detail, a quickening of the senses, a focusing of the literary lens, so to speak, until one has magnified some small aspect of what it means to be human."

Collage

Do you remember, as a child, making collages out of photographs, images cut from magazines, bits and pieces of text gathered from ticket stubs, documents, or newspaper headlines? Often, these mosaics represented the self in a way that no other form could quite accomplish. Our teachers gazed down at us lovingly as we showed them these renderings, our selves displayed in fragments made beautiful by their juxtapositions.

The collage essay works in the same way. It brings together many different fragments and assembles them so they create something wholly new. *Juxtaposition* becomes the key craft element here. One cannot simply throw these pieces down haphazardly; they must be carefully selected because of how they will resonate off one another. In this way, you act as a painter might, scrutinizing how this particular blue will shimmer against this particular yellow. You must listen for the echoes, the repetitions, the way one image organically suggests the next.

The writer must also provide some kind of grounding structure for the reader to hold onto. Going back to those collages you made as a child, they would be useless collections of fragments without the poster board and glue used to hold the pieces in place. The supporting architecture for a collage essay can take the form of numbered sections, or it can be subtitles that guide the reader along. Or the structure may be as subtle as asterisks delineating the white space between sections. The title, subtitles, or an epigraph (opening quote) can provide a hint of direction for the reader.

For example, in his essay "The Son of Mr. Green Jeans: A Meditation on Fathers," Dinty Moore uses an alphabetical structure—sometimes called an "acrostic"—to hold together a collage that does exactly what its title telegraphs: meditate on his own father, as well as the television fathers that influenced his generation's perception of fatherhood. He goes from "Allen, Tim" to "Zappa" as his twenty-six subtitles (yes, he does find something for X!) in order to contain what might otherwise seem a random collection of thoughts.

Closely related to the collage essay is the "found essay." In these pieces, the author might not use any words of his or her own, but instead cobbles together text that is found in other media. For example, David Shields wrote an essay, "Life Story," completely made up of bumper sticker slogans. These slogans take us "from the crib to the grave," as one reviewer put it, showing how life progresses in platitudes:

First things first.

You're only young once, but you can be immature forever. I may grow old, but I'll never grow up. Too fast to live, too young to die. Life's a beach.

Eat dessert first; life is uncertain. Why be normal?

Don't follow me; I'm lost, too. Wherever you are, be there. No matter where you go, there you are. Bloom where you are planted.

The found essay is, of course, closely related to the found poem, a form that reconfigures the words of others in poetic techniques. Some good examples of this can be found in Annie Dillard's *Morning Like This: Found Poems*, which creates poems out of sources as diverse as Van Gogh's diary and *Prehospital Emergency Care and Crisis Intervention, 1989*.

In this age of information, you can find many sources that would be ripe for this kind of experimentation. Even a series of e-mail or text messages could make for a profound narrative that tells a story all on its own, without the benefit of the author's interpretation. It's not as easy as it looks, however. You can't just slap together random words and call it good; you must carefully select and use your skills of juxtaposition, just as you would with any good lyric essay.

Collages work through repetition but not in a monotonous way. You must *transform* your recurring motifs from beginning to end. You must make transitions but not in the conventional way. In the collage essay, transitions occur through the strategic placement of images, stories, and phrases. How does one story lead to the next? Which image can you pick up from the last section to begin the next? Which phrase can act as a repeating and variable mantra throughout the piece? You must trust yourself and your readers to make sense and meaning out of the gaps between steps, the pauses between words, but you must also act as a guide on this pilgrimage, a pathfinder who directs with a touch we barely notice.

The Braided Essay

On the Jewish Sabbath, we eat a bread called challah, a braided egg bread that gleams on its special platter. The braided strands weave in and out of one another, creating a pattern that is both beautiful and appetizing. We eat a special bread on the Sabbath because this day has been set aside as sacred; the smallest acts must be differentiated from everyday motions.

The braided challah is a fitting symbol for an essay form closely allied with collage: the braided essay. In this form, you fragment your piece into separate strands that repeat and continue throughout the essay. There is more of a sense of weaving about it, of interruption and continuation, like the braiding of bread, or of hair. (See "A Braided Heart: Shaping the Lyric Essay" by Brenda Miller on page 233 and "Basha Leah" on the *Tell It Slant* website.)

For example, in his braided essay "Kissing," Anthony Farrington braids in quotes and information from sources as diverse as *The Sensuous Woman* and the New Testament with his own history of kissing. He begins:

This is a story about the mouth and the tongue, about conversations of one kind and another. This is the story about the first girl who ever kissed me. Her name was Lulu, and we were in the second grade.

That first line—with its poetic rhythm and imagery—alerts the reader that we are in for a more "lyric" examination of this particular topic. Farrington's personal story proceeds in a chronological spiral, with the story of his failed first marriage acting as a narrative thread that interweaves with many different voices and forms. He makes up his own advice column with whimsical answers ("*Question:* My partner won't kiss me. All he wants is sex. It's the same routine. *Answer:* Only kiss the irresistible. Small children, for example, or aging grand-mothers. Or men who love you."); he drops in definitions and lists of rules; he quotes personal ads. The actual form of the piece mirrors his style, with blocks of text interspersed with traditional typesetting to create a montage effect. As a reader, we are invited to interact with this essay, creating it as we go along, since there is no one way to read it. This, too, is one of the joys of lyric forms: they often invite the reader in as cocreator. Farrington explodes his prose to put it together again in a new pattern that is inordinately pleasurable.

The braided form allows a way for research and outside voices to intertwine with your own voice and experience. When you write a braided essay, find at least one outside voice that will shadow your own; in this way the essay gains texture and substance.

The "Hermit Crab" Essay

Where we—Suzanne and Brenda—live, in the Pacific Northwest, there's a beautiful place called Deception Pass. Deception Pass is prone to extreme tides, and in the tide pools you can often find hermit crabs skulking about. They look a little like cartoon characters, hiding inside a shell, lifting up that shell to take it with them when they go for cover. They move a few inches, then crouch down and stop, become only a shell again.

A hermit crab is a strange animal, born without the armor to protect its soft, exposed abdomen. And so it spends its life occupying the empty, often beautiful, shells left behind by snails or other mollusks. It reanimates these shells, making of them a strange, new hybrid creature that has its own particu-lar beauty, its own way of moving through the tide pools and among the rocks. Each one will be slightly different, depending on the type of shell it decides to inhabit.

In honor of these wonderful creatures, we've dubbed a particular form of lyric essay the "hermit crab" essay. This kind of essay appropriates existing forms as an outer covering, to protect its soft, vulnerable underbelly. It is an essay that deals with material that seems born without its own carapace—material that is soft, exposed, and tender, and must look elsewhere to find the form that will best contain it.

The "shells" come where you can find them, anywhere out in the world. They may borrow from fiction and poetry, but they also don't hesitate to armor themselves in more mundane structures, such as the descriptions in a mail-order catalog or the entries in a checkbook register.

For example, in her short story "How to Become a Writer," Lorrie Moore appropriates the form of the how-to article to tell a personal narrative. The voice of the narrator catches the cadence of instructional manuals, but at the same time winks at the reader. Of course these are not impersonal instructions but a way of telling her own story. And by using the literary second person, the reader is unwittingly drawn along into the place of the narrator and a natural interaction develops:

> First, try to be something, anything, else. A movie star/astronaut. A movie star/missionary. A movie star/kindergarten teacher. President of the World. Fail miserably. It is best if you fail at an early age—say, fourteen. Early, critical disillusionment is necessary so that at fifteen you can write long haiku sequences about thwarted desire.

Though "How to Become a Writer" is presented as fiction, the story can act as a fine model for innovative lyric essays in the how-to mode. What are the aspects of your life that you could render in how-to form? How will the second-person address enable you to achieve some distance from the material and thus some perspective? These types of essays can be quite fun to write; the voice takes over and creates its own momentum.

In his essay "Primary Sources," Rick Moody appropriates the form of a footnoted bibliography to write an autobiography. In "Nine Beginnings," Margaret Atwood takes on two different forms; ostensibly it is a question/answer piece with only one persistent, annoying question. But the title also suggests the form of crumpled first drafts, fished out of the wastebasket. Nancy Willard has written an essay called "The Friendship Tarot" that begins with a sketch of a tarot card layout; she then goes on to insert her autobiographical story into the interpretation of that layout. Several writers have fashioned essays in the form of "to-do" lists. Sei Shonagon has written her lists of "Depressing Things," "Adorable Things," and so forth. The possibilities are endless.

In a hermit crab essay, you can decide how deeply you want to use the form. On one end of the spectrum, you can fully inhabit the voice of the form, as Moore does in her story, or you could simply use the form as a way to structure your piece (a more formal way of making a collage or braided essay). For example, in her essay "The Pain Scale," Eula Biss uses the form of the pain scale—which attempts to measure one's pain on a scale of 0 to 10— as a way to structure a highly complex piece that explores not only the nature of pain, but the many different ways we try to measure the immeasurable.

In this way, the form itself adds meaning to the piece. It becomes part of the metaphorical significance. Even in "How to Become a Writer," the "how to" is ironic: there really is no one way to become a writer, so the attempt to put this story in that form adds meaning; it highlights the desire to be taught what cannot really be taught, that yearning for finding the "right way" to do something that simply must be experienced on our own. The hermit crab essay allows for these kinds of subtle inferences, the form providing meaning without the writer having to say a word.

Often when you write in these forms, you'll find yourself writing about memories and topics you never thought you would approach. It can often be a way to break through resistance, because your conscious mind will be occupied with the form itself. You might even be having some fun. The form can then lead to what we like to call "inadvertent revelations," where it feels like the *essay* is revealing unexpected insights, not the writer.

For example, one of our students had trouble writing about growing up with a mother who suffered from a hoarding disorder. This student grew up in complete chaos, and her writing had been too chaotic to make sense. When she decided to write her story in the form of a real estate ad—with the chipper voice of the ad revealing the horrifying state of the house—she created a powerful story with a great deal of compassionate perspective. Another student wrote her essay in the form of a crossword puzzle, complete with clues that sometimes had no answer (a form also used in Jane Jeong Trenka's memoir, *The Language of Blood*). Our student thought she was writing about her fascination with the true crime genre, but the form led her to drop "clues" about an abusive childhood—a subject that truly did not have definitive answers that would hold still.

Look around you. The world is brimming with forms that await transformation. A recipe for making soup, handed down by your grandmother, can form the architecture for an essay that fragments a family narrative into the directions for creating something good to eat. An address book that shows the many different places you or your family has lived can begin to shape the material of memory and history. A table of contents, an index, an itinerary, a playlist—all these speak with recognizable voices that might work as the right container for your elusive material.

By taking on the voice of an exterior form for your internal story, you automatically begin the process of creating an artifact out of experience. The form, while it may seem restrictive, actually allows you a great deal of possibility. Suddenly the second-person voice or the third-person perspective is available to you. You're able to take a step back and view your experience through a new lens. Often the form itself will lead to new material you never even suspected.

Think in terms of *transformation*. The word itself means to move across forms, to be changed. Think of the hermit crab and his soft, exposed abdomen. Think of the experiences you have that are too raw, too dangerous to write about. What if you found the right shell, the right armor? How could you be transformed?

Thinking Beyond the Page

Sometimes, words alone just won't cut it. You find yourself with a topic, or a memory, whose complexity demands a form that is more three-dimensional. In mixed-media works, the relationship between form and content becomes even more symbiotic than purely written works, as the form becomes both a highly visible architectural component of the piece *and* an artistic statement in itself.

It can be a little daunting to think beyond the page in creative nonfiction. Writing can be hard enough; why add any other medium to complicate it?

But what our students have found, over and over, is that the opportunity to expand the means of creative expression becomes quite exhilarating. With mixed-media projects, the text becomes tactile, and the work takes on layers that lend new meaning to the prose. Rarely do we *feel* our work in such a concrete way, with bits of it sticking to our fingers. Suddenly we're allowed entry into the realm of the visual artist, who appears at the end of her workday splattered with paint, a visual testament to the work she's accomplished.

Combining Text and Other Media

In his book *A Postcard Memoir* (see a sample on the *Tell It Slant* website), Lawrence Sutin juxtaposes images from his extensive postcard collection with the brief, vivid reminiscences and ruminations these images inspire in him. Sutin uses fragmentation and interplay between image and text to powerful effect. For example, in his piece "Boy and Man," Sutin uses an old black-and-white portrait of an anonymous father and son to ruminate on the nature of his relationship to his own father. He sees in this photograph not just the figures of a man and a boy, but the emotional underpinnings and connection implied by the placement of a hand on a leg, the identical smiles, the way man and boy imperceptibly lean toward one another. Sutin does not spend time describing the photograph; in fact, the prose itself hardly refers to it. Rather, his own story arises from the image, and the details he chooses enable us to look at this photograph through his eyes. In this way, the reader becomes a participant in the creative process. As Sutin remarked in an interview with the *Bellingham Review*:

> The interplay of text and images was very important, and I think it allows the readers to jump off to consider their own lives because the images are sort of shared islands between us. The reader can float along with the image in their own way, too, because it's clear that these aren't real photographs of my life, so there's a *shared* quality to them.

By using the form of postcards to tell his own story, Sutin automatically gives himself parameters that both contain and liberate his personal history. The images lead him into memories he may not have expected. "In some cases," Sutin says, "the response to the postcard allowed me to see more clearly what my life meant, more than I knew in advance." The form of the postcard also necessitated brief vignettes, rather than drawn out narratives, he explains:

Obviously many, if not all, of my pieces are longer than you could fit on the back of a postcard, even if you had very spidery, tiny handwriting. But the idea of the postcard being a brief recollection, and in my mind, an intense recollection was something that I used. . . . I suppose the typical postcard message is, "Hi, we're having a great time, wish you were here," and I was going totally beyond that. Something about the brevity of the message, and the fixed, chosen quality of the image to represent the time or place, those things were important to me.

The postcard medium also carries within itself, intrinsically, the intent of communication—an intimate yet public communication between writer and reader. After all, a postcard is meant only for the recipient, but in the course of its journey can be read by many eyes. By working in the genre of the postcard, Sutin automatically brings these philosophical issues to bear on his writing, and so he is able to craft a voice that is intimate and public at the same time.

This mix of image and text is a relatively simple example of how a writer can use other media in her work. But such projects can be as simple or complex as the material demands and in accord with the artistic skills of the writer. For example, book artist Susan King created a piece entitled *Treading the Maze: An Artist's Book of Daze* (you can find samples of her work at http://www.susanking.info/Susan_King_Site/work/Pages/Artists_Books.html#25). King had spent several months traveling in Europe and was then diagnosed with breast cancer on her return. The book that came out of these two experiences charts her travels through these two different types of terrain. "The artwork that resulted from these two journeys," King writes, "uses the maze at Chartres Cathedral in France as the structure of the book. It places the reader/viewer in the role of a pilgrim, confronted with unexpected images, stories that look back and forth in time, and a sense of what it means to walk into the maze of illness and back again."

Our students, though generally not trained as artists, have found the mixed-media project both a challenge and a delight. They've created a plethora of artifacts incorporating written texts, visual arts, photographs, and whatever other medium the student finds appropriate. We've had students incorporate their own music into their presentations, or create a website for their final projects. One student printed her essay on strips of paper baked into fortune cookies, and another brought to class a planter full of specimens from an arboretum, each with its own fragment of a nature essay attached. In this last case, the student, Anna, asked her classmates to choose the pieces at random and read the fragments aloud. We all got our fingers covered in dirt, and in so doing collaborated with Anna in creating the shape of the final essay. Another student enlisted the help of her family to sew a quilt that had fragments of her essay (all about family) embedded within.

The possibilities are endless, and one of the side effects of such work is that it so wholly depends on the viewer's participation in order for the project to come to fulfillment. In this way, perhaps, mixed-media works are the perfect vessel for creative nonfiction because you connect with your reader in such a concrete way. The use of different media in your creative nonfiction work also allows you to discover new sources of creativity within yourself. Too often, we get bogged down in habitual ways of writing; the requirement to use other media forces us to approach writing from a fresh perspective, and it adds a wonderfully tactile quality to our personal expressions.

The Graphic Memoir

Making a strong emergence in recent years, the graphic memoir is one of the most popular and engaging forms in which creative nonfiction writers combine words with images. Writers create these memoirs, also called "autobiographical comics," in comic book panels, a form that allows us to read on many different levels. The visual story often complements the written story, but can also contradict it or comment upon it in original ways.

For example, the Pulitzer Prize–winning books *Maus I* and *Maus II*, by Art Spiegelman, took on the challenging material of Holocaust survival and framed it in the images of Jews as mice, Germans as cats, and Poles as pigs. Throughout, we see the narrator, Artie, struggling with how to portray his father's story as a Holocaust survivor, while at the same time telling his own story of what it's like to be the child of a survivor. This "meta"narrative—the writing behind the writing—threads throughout the books, with images breaking through their frames, being erased and re-envisioned as new information comes to light.

More recently, Alison Bechdel's *Fun Home: A Family Tragicomic* tells the story of the author's complex relationship to her father, a relationship that was mired in secrets. This graphic memoir made many of the "Best Books of

2006" lists, and *Salon* magazine said of it, "Bechdel's years of drawing a serial comic strip have honed her ability to convey oceans of feeling in a single image, and the feelings are never simple; *Fun Home* shimmers with regret, compassion, annoyance, frustration, pity and love." The graphic elements become crucial in understanding not only the story, but the narrator's evolving perspective and point of view.

In another award-winning graphic memoir, *Tangles: A Story About Alzheimer's, My Mother and Me*, Sarah Leavitt deals with the story of her mother's illness and death by combining straightforward, even humorous, prose with simple line drawings that convey strong emotion succinctly and powerfully. As one reviewer put it, "Sarah Leavitt uses the medium of comics to tell her story with more economy and power than either words or pictures could muster by themselves." It is the synergy between word and image that can make graphic memoir so appealing to readers.

While we don't all have the talent and training to write a graphic memoir, it could be useful to look to this form as a model for how we might be able to "convey an ocean of feeling in a single image." You could envision a traditional narrative as a comic strip and allow this visualization to help you hone in on the key details, scenes, and gestures that are necessary to bring your story to life. You can try inserting even a primitive drawing or sketch within a traditional narrative to see how it disrupts and deepens the piece. Or you might collaborate with a talented artist who could envision even a small part of your work in the complexities of visual language.

The Radio Essay

The ancient art of oral storytelling underlies the impulse of much contemporary creative nonfiction. We once told stories as a way not only to pass the time, but also to pass along our familial and cultural heritage. Think about how much you loved to hear stories as a child; the spoken voice engages you and brings a narrative to life. When we attend readings by talented authors, we hope to gain more of a sense of the human being behind the prose.

Radio shows have always embraced storytelling as a mainstay of their offerings; in the days when radio provided the primary form of entertainment, people gathered to listen intently to their favorite narratives spun out in familiar voices. These days, with so many (too many!) entertainment options available to us, oral stories still have a powerful draw, and there are many ways to hear them and learn from them about how to tell our own stories.

Magazine-style radio shows, such as *This American Life* and *A Prairie Home Companion*, led the way in their field. Garrison Keillor's monologues in *A Prairie Home Companion* give an entertaining glimpse into small-town life; while fictional, they still provide an excellent model for how to bring characters into three-dimensional existence with just a few well-placed brush strokes, and how to build momentum in a simple narrative. Ira Glass, host of *This American Life*, chooses a theme for each week's show, and then several segments elucidate that theme through true stories. Sometimes the story may be a personal narrative, and often the stories are research pieces with a twist. For instance, in one wildly popular episode, called "Act V," the entire show follows the story of prison inmates in a high-security prison, many of them incarcerated for murder, as they prepare to perform Act V of Hamlet. The men—many of whom have little education—give startling insights into the Shakespearean characters they portray, while the narrator of the piece shows the complexities involved in putting on a show in the prison environment.

Other magazine shows include *To the Best of Our Knowledge*, a program that also chooses a theme and interviews several authors or experts on that topic, and *On Being*, a program that explores faith and spirituality from eclectic viewpoints. Both of these shows not only demonstrate how to interview effectively, they also provide the listener with fascinating facts and stories that could be quite useful for essays of your own.

Some popular radio shows have more affinity with spoken word or slam poetry, as the narrators tell their true stories to an audience. *The Moth: True Stories Told Live* broadcasts live performances from stages in New York and around the country, with the rule that the narrator cannot use notes, so the pieces have the quality of spontaneity and vibrant energy. Often these stories are funny, but just as often they are infused with powerful emotion. For instance in one show titled "It Wasn't Enough," Charlene Strong tells us what it was like to experience the death of her partner while not being allowed in her hospital room. She went on to become a gay rights activist who was instrumental in change.

In *Snap Judgment*, hosted by Glynn Washington, the storytellers sometimes perform before a live audience, and sometimes in the studio. In both cases these true stories are often accompanied by music or other sound effects to underscore the narratives. As with other shows, the producers choose a theme and the stories gathered for that episode all approach that theme in different and unexpected ways. For instance, in one show titled "Wild Kingdom," storyteller Scott Kravitz describes how he acquired a dog he never wanted, named Anne, and how this relationship grew to the point that he "stole" her back from her rightful owner, who was homeless. He ends up changing his life—buying a house, moving to the suburbs—because of this creature that showed up in his life. Other shows in this mode include *The Tobolowsky Files*, where actor Stephen Tobolowsky quietly tells true stories that can break your heart.

All of these shows can be accessed via their websites and by podcast, so you can listen whenever you like, and perhaps use these shows as a way to prepare for your own writing. If you're a teacher or leader of a writing group, bringing in an occasional radio show to share with your students can be an excellent way to vary the routine, and many students are able to immediately recognize the elements of good storytelling when they hear them; these elements can then be translated to the page. The shows also have blogs and other features on their sites that encourage you to tell your own story and share it with the world.

TRY IT

1. Go back to one of your own pieces and turn it into fragments. Take a pair of scissors to it and cut it up into at least three different sections. Move these around, eliminating what no longer fits, juxtaposing the different sections in various ways. How can you make use of white space? How can you let the images do the talking for you?

2. Wander the streets of your town looking for random objects. Gather as many of these as you like, then bring them back to your desk and start arranging them in a way that is artistically pleasing. Then write for several minutes on each object and see if you can create a fragmented essay that juxtaposes these elements in the same way.

VARIATION FOR A GROUP: Go out and gather objects individually, but come back together as a group to sift through the pile. Use each other's objects to create three-dimensional collages. Then write for one hour to create a collage essay using these objects as a guide.

3. Write an essay that has fewer than five hundred words. Give yourself a time limit—a half-hour, say—and write about one image that comes to mind or an image that has stayed in your memory from the last couple of days. Use vivid, concrete details. Do not explain the image to us but allow it to evolve into metaphor. If you are stuck, open a book of poetry and write down the first line you see as an epigraph (an opening quote). Write an essay using the epigraph as a starting point for either form or content or imagery. If you write more than five hundred words (about two pages), you must trim and cut to stay under the limit. Find what is essential.

VARIATION FOR A GROUP: Each person should bring in a line of poetry as an epigraph and offer it to a partner. Write for fifteen minutes, and then pass this epigraph to the next person. Write again for fifteen minutes. Continue this process for as long as you like. Try shaping one of these experiments into a complete essay of fewer than five hundred words.

4. Begin a piece by imitating Bucak's "I Cannot Explain My Fear." You can list fears, or loves, or jealousies, or any kind of emotion at all, transforming that emotion into a concrete list that reveals some narrative about your life. Try to do this in three hundred words.

5. Structure an essay around a journey of some sort, using brief, discrete sections to build a collage. This can be a journey to somewhere as commonplace as the mall, or it can be more romantic. What kind of purposeful journey can you imagine taking, such as a pilgrimage to a sacred place?

6. Choose at least three distinctly separate time periods in your life. Begin each section with "I am _____ years old," and freewrite from there. Stay in the present tense. After reading what you've written, see if you can start finding any thematic connections or common images that would link the sections together.

7. Experiment with transitions and juxtaposition. Find one image to repeat in the essay from start to finish, but transform this image in some way so that it has taken on new characteristics by the end of the collage essay.

8. As David Shields did in "Life Story," try writing a found essay made up entirely of others' words. You can find material in text messages, Facebook updates, T-shirt slogans, bumper stickers, e-mail subject lines (spam can be wonderful for this!). You can also seek out unfamiliar material, such as an old etiquette manual from the 1950s. You can try looking at advertising jingles, or anything else that is ubiquitous in our culture, as a way of making a broader statement beyond the personal. Another way to approach this is to "borrow" language from other literature, as Ander Monson does in chapters he labels "assembloirs" in his memoir *Vanishing Point*.

9. Go back to an essay that's been giving you problems. Look for the one image that seems to encapsulate the abstract ideas or concepts you're trying to develop. Find at least one outside source that will provide new information and details for you. Explode the essay into at least three different strands, each focused on different aspects of that image, and begin weaving.

10. Write an essay in the form of a how-to guide using the second-person voice. You can turn anything into a how-to. In Lorrie Moore's book *Self-Help*, she has stories titled "How to Talk to Your Mother" and "How to Be the Other Woman."

11. Choose a field guide to the natural world as your model ("A Field Guide to Desert Wildflowers," for example, or "A Field Guide to the Atmosphere"). Write an essay in the form of a field guide, inserting your own experience in this format.

12. Write an essay in the form of an interview or as a series of letters.

13. Brainstorm a list of all the forms in the outer world that you could use as a hermit crab essay model. We've done this with groups that have come up with lists of sixty entries and more! The possibilities are endless. Examples of what they came up with include crossword puzzle clues, horoscopes, fortune cookies, letters to the editor, and missing kids flyers. Choose one of these forms and begin an essay, using your own material to flesh out the "shell." Let the word choices and tone of your shell dictate your own approach to your topic. How would the vague cheeriness of fortune-cookie fortunes or horoscopes inform your family or relationship tale?

14. Write a list of the topics/issues in your life that are "forbidden" to speak about, the things you could never write. Choose one of these, and then begin to write about it in a hermit crab form.

15. Study a painting or a photograph that you have looked at often. What is it about this image that appeals to you so much? Begin a short essay, fewer than five hundred words, that focuses on some unexpected detail that catches your eye in this artwork. Explore this detail for metaphorical significance.

> **Variation for a group:** Each person brings in a postcard of an artwork; these are all set on a table in the front of the room. Each person browses these postcards and chooses one that appeals to him or her on an intuitive level. Begin writing. You can do this as many times as you like until an image sparks a piece of writing that interests you.

16. Create a mixed-media piece that uses other kinds of documents and images along with your own prose. Make several photocopies of these documents so that you can cut them up and experiment. Create collages, paying attention to the kinds of textures you create with these elements.

17. Collaborate with a photographer, a musician, a painter, a sculptor, or a graphic artist to create a mixed-media work for presentation to an audience.

18. Consider recording your stories to tell before an audience and see how that process affects your structure, your content, and your written voice. Look at the websites for radio shows and give yourself a goal of submitting a story to them.

11

Writing Online: Hypertext and Social Media

Technology is neither *good* nor *bad*, nor even *neutral*. Technology is one part of the complex of relationships that people form with each other and the world around them.

—SAMUEL COLLINS

Think of hypermedia as a collection of elastic messages that can stretch and shrink in accordance with the reader's actions. Ideas can be opened and analyzed at multiple levels of detail. The best paper equivalent I can think of is an Advent calendar. But when you open the little electronic (versus paper) doors, you may see a different story line depending on the situation or, like barbershop mirrors, an image within an image within an image.

—SVEN BIRKERTS

Over the past few years I have been asked to write guest blogs for different websites. The sites' topics varied from feminist to theological, but one aspect of blogging that I found, regardless of the subject, was the sense of community evoked by these writings. In print books and essays, though I often receive mail about my work, the slow speed of publishing, then receiving letters and answering them, works against a sense of dialogue. With blog ging, I discovered the responses were many and immediate when the blog was posted—sharp comments deepening points I had only touched on, thoughtful questions, invitations to continue the dialogue. I ended up feeling I had not just put thoughts of mine out there, but created a small community mulling over the points I made, taking ideas farther than I would have thought possible.

Similarly, with hypertext and hypermedia, the classroom experience becomes communal, even as we read as individuals who will navigate the links in the work very differently. I have students write down how they moved through a piece like Shelley Jackson's "My Body: A Wunderkammer"; responses reflect who we are at our core (most interested in the mind? the body? sexuality?) and the way experiences of the work cocreate a text that is then shared with and by the group. In the end we—and it—are changed.

—SUZANNE

Hypertext and Hypermedia

A book is not an isolated entity; it is a narration, an axis of innumerable narrations.

—JORGE LUIS BORGES

Are you surprised to see a writer like Jorge Luis Borges supplying a quote that provides context for web-based writing? The Argentinean author came along before much on the web existed. Yet he—and writers like Emily Dickinson, who left her unpublished poems behind in small groupings called fascicles, with words placed so many options existed for putting her lines together—are authors of what we call *forerunner texts* of hypertextual writing. Borges's story "The Garden of Forking Paths," for example, presents the concept of a lost book and a labyrinth that are one and the same—a book that would function with many facets of intersection and ways of moving through it, much like work on the web. Dickinson's fascicles offer multiplicities of form for each of her poems.

Hypertext and hypermedia feel natural in our age. We do more and more of our reading online—much of it accompanied by image and video—and virtually every library has web-accessed computers patrons can use. Much of the room in cyberspace is still largely devoted to print, taking the form of millions of websites—clusters of images and documents.

The existence of cyberspace means that anyone learning a fairly simple coding program can post on the World Wide Web his or her own essays, diaries, and artwork, or create a sophisticated literary journal, without the cost of paper and printing. The accessibility and low cost of web access, compared to other forms of publishing, has led to an explosion of literary experimentation.

What Is Hypertext and Hypermedia?

Technically speaking, anything written on the web is *hypertext* or *hypermedia*. But for literary purposes these terms are typically used to mean writing that uses a "link-node" organization, or an organization somehow similar to link-node movements. This means that embedded in the literary work—which much of the time will incorporate visual elements, such as photos, artwork, and streaming video in addition to text—will be hyperlinks that, once activated by the click of the mouse or some other action by the reader, move the reader to another screen. Each screen is a new chunk, or "node," of the work. Chunks of text in hypertext are called *lexia*. One of the goals of hypertext and hypermedia is to get away from page-bound thinking and embrace the possibilities of digital art and digital culture.

There are, of course, infinite possibilities when contemplating online literature: links can be stored in lexia or elsewhere; texts can be self-contained or networked, meaning they can incorporate other sites on the web; they can be open to manipulation by outside users, thus becoming truly cocreated works of art.

When a hypertext uses more than a nominal amount of visual material, either driving or supporting it, it is known as *hypermedia*. Hypermedia can use image, video, audio, film, Flash animation, and a host of other visual components. Visual elements can be navigation devices, directed by the viewer's choices, or not. As most hypertext now is presented with some visual element, the distinctions between the two can be blurry. In this chapter, as we are focusing on creating the text or lexia of a digital work, we will lean toward using the term *hypertext*, with the understanding that the text you create may be intended for hypermedia applications.

In a traditional hypertext site designed to be navigated easily, linking words are highlighted—blued—so the viewer can immediately move to the word or phrase of interest, such as *This week's events*, click on it, and be done. Early literary hypertexts generally worked through the same kind of highlighting links, and many still do, to great effect—you may read an essay and use links to follow a particular story line or learn more about a character that appeals to you. As hypertext has grown in sophistication, however, authors use many alternatives to traditional blued linking: different colors or highlights can be used to link, but links can also be embedded in artwork (as we'll see later on in this chapter), made invisible until the cursor hits them and changes shape, or taken out of the viewer's control—he may find himself swept off the page at the end of a sentence, or fooled by links that do not lead further.

To compose hypertext and hypermedia, you must gain some mastery of an HTML (hypertext markup language) program. These have evolved from cumbersome hand-inserted codes to programs that function much like straight word processing programs. Many computers have basic HTML programs, such as Dreamweaver, bundled into the software they come with. If you are interested in working in hypertext and not familiar with an HTML program, the programs are not difficult to learn. Many users teach themselves; many have skilled friends happy to do some tutoring. One way to begin digital composition, if you are fortunate enough to be in a writing group or a classroom, is to identify the more computer literate among you and have those folks take the lead on helping you design your own works.

Hypertext and Nonfiction

At first, as writers explored the implications of the World Wide Web and web publishing, they tended to reproduce the page on the screen. But it soon became clear that reading in cyberspace is a new experience. Even in the most leaping lyric essay, the printed page has, by its spatial presence, a top-to-bottom organization; there are few forms so successfully experimental that you don't read from the top down.

Hypertext is spatial in every direction, truly nonsequential—nothing follows by necessity anything else in the essay. You can read screen by screen, or read only the first few words of the first screen, and so on. You may come to the screen that describes a wedding and only navigate the links that lead to the engagement much later, mixing up chronology. Link-node hypertext branches out, and allows choice to the reader, who creates the text through interaction. It offers different reading and viewing paths, and so it isn't a closed, fixed work but one in a constant process of shifting and revision.

Though links in hypertext were originally compared to footnotes—words that could be followed out of the text to another place, at the end of the chapter or bottom of the page—it's a false comparison. With footnotes, a clear primary text exists. With hypertext, it often does not: the reader interacts with the work and can make her own primary text, possibly following only the sports links in an essay, or only ones having to do with horticulture, or surfing a little of everything all the way through.

The branching, associational, and inherently lyric quality of hypertext writing forms a natural fit with much nonfiction, particularly the type of nonfiction we describe in Chapter 10, "Playing with Form: The Lyric Essay and Mixed Media." If you tend to braid your work, with different strands of writing moving between each other, or jump via association, hypertext might be an apt form for you. Hypermedia offers a natural way to use visual images, with text or on screens of its own, and other media as well: music, chanting, nature sounds. There are few limits on what elements you can weave into your nonfiction.

In hypertext you can make your leaps optional, creating a main text or *anchor* readers can stay with or return to as they navigate. Authors and critics of hypertext use the term *decentered*—it can (though doesn't necessarily) become impossible to say where the core of a hypertext work lies. French critics Gilles Deleuze and Félix Guattari compare this writing strategy more poetically to the branching systems of rhizomatic plants such as mints and strawberries, plants spreading via a loose root system that establishes nodes for new plants but has no base: "any point on a rhizome can be connected with any other, and must be. This is very different from a tree or root, which fixes a point and thus an order." Vannevar Bush, a midcentury thinker who anticipated the development of the World Wide Web, pointed out that such a writing system comes much closer to the way we think and learn: nonsequentially, interactively, working off association.

If you find yourself drawn to the use of visual elements in your writing, and consider the use of interactivity and decentering exciting aesthetic possibilities, you may want to investigate hypertext. There are myriad online journals eagerly looking for well-crafted hypertext works (see Chapter 16, "Publishing Your Creative Nonfiction"). One side benefit of this mode of composition is that visual elements become much easier to publish; if you can present your work to an interested editor in the proper format (this will vary with the publication), the editor, barring copyright problems, can use them. With print publications, the limits of the page can be daunting for visual imagery.

Exploring a Nonfiction Hypertext

To help you see what can be done with hypertext, we are going to show you samples from two of our favorite hypertext essays: Shelley Jackson's "My Body—a Wunderkammer" and Dinty Moore's "Mr. Plimpton's Revenge: A Google Map Essay," both available on our website. Of course, viewing these works on the web, as hypertext, is an irreproducible experience, but this discussion will give you an idea of the form.

Though most of "My Body" consists of words, we enter the essay with an overwhelming visual statement: a woman's body, boxed and fragmented, except for the head. The architecture of this image, as we stated in the earlier discussion of mixed media, has already shaped our responses to the words. Next to the drawing of the author are words for the various boxed parts: "arms," "stomach," etc. The hand-drawn, crosshatched script ties the words directly to the crosshatched drawing, making it clear there's no distinction here between word and image (indeed, she bears on her arm a tattoo of an ampersand, a typographical mark). Image is text: text, image. The words and body are further drawn together by the fact that the boxed arm and word *arms* are both links to the same screen—a screen in which viewers see a close-up of the illustration beside text in which the author explores, in memoir form, that part of her body.

At twelve I did more chin-ups than anyone else in my class, and the boys came running jubilantly across the playground and caught me up like a sports hero. The girls were exhorted to manage one chin-up. That was considered sufficient. I looked at the other girls' arms and knew I was a different animal.

Within these nodes of text and illustration are more hyperlinks, indicated by bluing. These may lead to screens of writing that further elaborate on themes from the lead-in screens, often with a more philosophical and conceptual approach. Or, just as often, they jump the reader to other body parts. The link on "I looked at the other girls' arms" leads to the "hand" screen. The reader is invited to share the intricate connections Jackson makes within her body, to make her own connections, to see the body as inextricably interlinked. The navigation of this long work is a work in itself.

Dinty Moore's "Mr. Plimpton's Revenge: A Google Maps Essay" is also anchored, by a Google map of Pennsylvania. The essay tells the story of the author as an intimidated—and stoned—college student tapped to drive author George Plimpton around when Plimpton visited the University of Pittsburgh. Later in life, the author has several more run-ins with Plimpton, episodes delivered in short, witty bursts headed by subtitles like "The word 'stalker' was not much in use in those days."

"Mr. Plimpton's Revenge" is a networked piece. Not only is it built on a Google map, it also enables the user to access outside material on the web: viewers can see the hotel where Plimpton stayed during the visit, and even read user reviews of it. The viewer's stumbling through an unfamiliar road map, following links and resorting to the back button to return, reflects the young Moore's fumbling through a disorderly life and intimidating job, as well as reflecting ironically on the coming "intersections" with the famed writer.

Blogs and Social Media

As many of us experience daily, online writing takes many forms. There are the complex forms of hypermedia, and then there are the common genres of blogs, Facebook and other social networking sites, and Twitter missives that form the basis for a good percentage of the reading we do today. At the same time, these writings also embed themselves within a linked community conversation, branching out and growing.

For those of us born in the dark ages before 1970, writing was most often conceived of as a private, solitary activity. We wrote our work alone, and ventured to share it only when it had been mulled over, edited a bit, and shaped up for the public eye. When we entered into a conversation about our writing, it was usually face-to-face, or via long letters. But in the last decade, we have seen a grand shift in that perception: with the prevalence of social media, certain kinds of writing are becoming a public act, with more writing coming across our desktops—literal and virtual—than ever before.

In these online modes, writing becomes part of a larger community conversation that can be linked in many directions. As such, they are a good fit for creative nonfiction, for these forms allow more interaction between writer and reader, and blog posts have an air of spontaneity, of working things out, of "essaying" a topic to see where it leads and what memories or stories it might jog in others.

When blogs first began to be in use on the web, they were generally web diaries with a self-centered, generalized focus; the term *blog* was coined in the late nineties as a shortened version of *weblog*. Since then, the word has also turned into a verb, "to blog," and there are blogs specific to nearly every sector of human society. Even fictional characters on television shows have their own blogs, with legions of avid followers.

Blog as Writing Practice

At its most basic, a simple blog can be a way to focus and structure your own writing practice, giving you deadlines and some measure of accountability. You can make your blog as public or as private as you like, and now blogging programs—such as Blogger, WordPress, and others—make it very easy to create your own blog. Facebook Notes—and other journaling programs in social network sites such as Google Plus—have also become quite popular as a way of blogging instantly: notes are longer than a status update, but still quite short, snapshots into what the writer is thinking about at the time. Commentary on the notes often extends the conversation, and they can be a way to capture and catalog those fleeting thoughts that can disappear.

The blog form lends itself to writing practice because the posts can be short, "occasional" (that is, tied to a particular occasion, or trigger for the thought), and are usually fairly informal while retaining a sense of craft. They could be a way to discipline yourself to work through a particular topic you've had on your mind, with more structure than a paper journal entry, but with the same sense of spontaneity and intimacy.

For example, one writer we know set herself a goal of writing fifty blog entries, under the title "Fifty Ways to be a Brilliant Mom Without Having a Baby." She chose this topic because, as she puts it, "It could be that I'm a poet with a secret desire to be an advice columnist. So when I couldn't find any good sites about becoming a stepmom, or having an eccentric elderly mom for a friend, I started this blog." At first it was to be a private blog, but she wanted the accountability that came with having it available to the public. And by choosing a finite number, fifty, she had a concrete goal and was able to narrow down an overwhelming task to a workable routine. As a result, she wrote her fifty entries, attracted a small but solid group of followers, and now has the foundation for a strong book of creative nonfiction around this topic.

There are as many different types of blogs as there are people; according to some sources, there are over a million blogs in active use in the world today, and the number keeps growing incrementally. Why are blogs so popular? The exact reasons are elusive, but we can speculate that they exemplify the way readers are now hungry for authentic stories from real life; they also serve to bond communities together, as well as expand our circle of associations.

You can focus your blog on a particular topic—this gives you the best chance for your blog to be read—or have it be a more generalized, quotidian (everyday) blog that records your activities or the activities of your community. These generalized blogs function more like the traditional almanacs of frontier communities or villages, recording the happenings of the day for future generations.

Some of the most popular categories of successful topical blogs are: food; politics; technology; science; lifestyle (such as those recording the process of building a house, or living off the grid); literature (including the writing life, or "what I'm reading right now"); how-to or advice (training a dog, home decoration, gardening, etc.); or specific demographic groups ("new mom" blog, adoption, marriage, etc.).

Some successful blogs take on the form of "the year of living _____" in which the writer takes on the task of doing a specific activity or living a certain way for a year (or any amount of time) and then recording it. For example, one writer, Teresa Jordan, has written a blog called "The Year of Living Virtuously (Weekends Off)." In it, she commits to musing on, and trying to follow, the virtues elucidated by Benjamin Franklin. She writes, "I begin this year-long meditation organized, at least to start, around Franklin's thirteen virtues and peppered with attention to another archetypal list, the seven deadly sins. I expect to veer from that form as time goes on: I have never been able to use a recipe a second time around without amendment, and there are a panoply of attributes Franklin left out of his charts (though not out of his life) that intrigue me, such as gratitude, generosity, courage and forgiveness. I expect this blog, like life itself, to surprise me."

The moderated blog has also become immensely popular. In this case, the blogger chooses a topic, and then allows others to submit photos, video, or text on that topic. For example, one such blog—The "Blog" of "Unnecessary" Quotation Marks—airs the author's irritation at the random and incorrect use of quotation marks, but it is almost entirely made up of photos and commentary submitted by others. It became so popular that Chronicle Books contracted with the moderator to create a book based on this concept.

From Blog to Book

There is a growing trend for successful blogs to be turned into books. One of the most publicized is the book and movie of the same name: *Julie and Julia*, where blogger Julie Powell set herself the task of making every recipe in Julia Child's *Mastering the Art of French Cooking* in one year. Since the form leant itself to dramatization (would she be able to do it? what trials and tribulations would get in her way?), the blog gained a dramatic following, which got her noticed by agents and publishers. As with any good creative nonfiction, the writing had to be strong on many levels: it couldn't just be a dry recitation of the recipes and how she made them; there needed to be scene, story, sub-text, and emotional investment in the topic.

Another example, again from the food world (yes, we're foodies, we admit it!) is Molly Wizenberg's *A Homemade Life*. In this case, her blog, "Orangette," was not focused on a specific activity like Powell's, but featured recipes she liked to make, along with stories about these recipes and quality photographs. Her writing was so engaging that her blog gained an enormous following, and a conversation developed in the comments section that was vibrant and ranged beyond food to life itself. Her blog earned her a writing column with *Bon Appétit* magazine, and eventually a book deal. When her book was published, there was already an eager community of readers ready to devour it. On her website, Wizenberg has this advice for new bloggers: "Are you having fun with your blog? Because if you're not, it's not worth doing—or reading. Above all, write about what you want to write about. It sounds simplistic, but I mean it. Write about *what moves you*, whether it is chocolate, contemporary art, or hardcore punk. If you're passionate about something, and if you write about it *honestly* and *clearly* and *thoughtfully*, chances are, someone else will be interested too. Also, look closely at your favorite blogs. Study them. What do you like about them? What do they do well? And how can you bring elements of that into your site, while still making it your own?"

Another popular blog and book is *The Daily Coyote: A Story of Love, Survival, and Trust in the Wilds of Wyoming*, by Shreve Stockton. The blog started as daily postings of pictures of an orphaned coyote Stockton had taken in, and the blog then expanded to include details of her life in a very small community in Wyoming. The photographs created a narrative all their own. Since it was a daily posting, her blog audience made this site a part of their daily lives; they loved getting this glimpse of a world that was so far away from their own and yet contained so many universal elements (as her book title suggests: love, survival, trust). And, as with *A Homemade Life*, the community Stockton created with her blog guaranteed her an eager audience once the book was released.

As all these examples show, you don't need to be a special or famous person to write a blog that people will want to read. You just need to be passionate about something, and to hone the writing skills to bring that passion to life on the page. You can use what you've learned in previous chapters of this book: an awareness of the senses, for example, vivid creation of place and character, pleasing rhythms to your sentences. You need to hook your readers with the first line, drawing them into the conversation. The nature of the blog is short sections, so you can keep studying short-short forms to see how to contain your thoughts in the best way possible. Many blog writers post first-draft writings, but just as many let their posts "rest" before posting and do a substantial amount of editing, especially for concision.

You also need the commitment and discipline to focus on the blog and keep it active and alive, posting at least once a week (ideally more) so that the space doesn't grow stagnant. By doing so, you also train your writing muscles to keep at it, no matter what. If a life event is making it difficult to write, you can share that with your readers, creating even more intimacy and trust, while at the same time training your mind that you *can* write, even under trying circumstances.

Getting Your Blog Read

Since blogging is so popular (by the time you read this, who knows how many millions of blog sites will be out there), your readership is glutted with choices, information, and voices vying for attention. So it can be hard to make your own writing stand out. There are many sites on the web with tips for successful blogging, if public attention to your blog is what you're after (you may want to keep your blog private, or open to only a few invited people, depending on your purposes).

One excellent site for tips is David Lebovitz's "Living the Sweet Life in Paris." Though his focus is food blogging, his advice can apply to anyone. For example, he writes, "The main thing you want to do is to *find your niche* and *say something that people will enjoy reading or learning from you.* We all have different personalities and highlighting yours in your blog is the most important thing you can do to differentiate yourself from others." He goes on to discuss the importance of high-quality photos or other graphics in your blog to create interest; using lots of section breaks and white space to make it easier to skim (you have to surrender to the fact that much reading on the web starts as skimming, so you need to take that into account as you write); commenting on other blogs to attract attention to your site; and investing in a designer to be sure your blog is both attractive and usable.

Microblogging

As of this writing, Twitter is the most recognized microblogging site. Its users send out tweets that are 140 characters in length and can be anything as mundane as what you just had for lunch to sharing breaking world news. Bloggers often use Twitter hand in hand with their blogs in order to share links of interest and to keep followers apprised of new entries. With the restraint of so few characters, these microbloggers learn over time how to draw attention quickly.

The journal *Creative Nonfiction* has embraced the Twitter revolution, running a "tiny truths" contest that invites microbloggers to tell a true story in 130 characters or fewer (http://twitter.com/#!/cnfonline/favorites). The journal then retweets winning entries daily and publishes ten to twelve winners in each print issue. Some of their favorites include the following:

I take a deep breath and dial. She picks up on the second ring. Her voice doesn't sound like cancer, it sounds like Amy.

—Patty Wetli

She vows to eat (locally, seasonally, ethically, raw) a diet rich in fiber and adverbs. Vows and reaches for the Rice Krispies.

—Jo Deurbrouck

Teeter-totter talk: Girl asks, "How do you know two people are married?" Boy shrugs, says, "They're yelling at the same kids."

—Ceiridwen Terrill

Like traditional blogging, microblogging could act as a powerful daily practice, and the restriction of the short length might build your ability to compress key events into singular, vivid images. A collection of your own microblogs would be a fascinating form in itself, conveying an entire life in as few words as possible. The form is quick, spontaneous, catching the world on the fly; it is both intimate and incredibly public—the kind of contradiction that makes online writing so complex, pleasurable, and emblematic of the constant evolution in literary forms.

TRY IT

1. If you are not yet ready to jump into using HTML, try creating your own version of a "forerunner text." Look at Emily Dickinson's fascicles on the web (try Google Images); read Borges's "The Garden of Forking Paths." Write a work that violates the rules of the page, as Dickinson does, or offers multiple modes of reading and interpreting it, as with Borges. Let the writing sit for a few days, then consider it: What does your composition method add to your writing? Are you tempted to take it a step further and utilize a hypertext presentation?

2. Use an online medium you are familiar with, such as Facebook, Twitter, or MapQuest, to compose an essay.

3. Edward Falco, in response to a question about how authors start a piece in hypertext (with all its many components), said, "There are probably as many different ways of writing hypertext as there are hypertext writers." Some authors start with a print piece and gradually accrete other nodes of material; some write directly to a hypertext program like Storyspace. One method we've found useful is to have everyone assemble index cards and actually map out the architecture of a site—including visual elements like photos and art, if you plan to use them. Lay the potential screens out in front of you, see where links would occur, and practice different navigational options. Seeing your work spatially can ignite ways of using the form.

4. You can also begin by starting a simple piece directly in a hypertext program—look around for friends who can tutor you. Challenge yourself to use just three text links (text linked to other screens of text), and only use outside links for visual images. Remember, most museums and artists have websites you can link to—the back button will take viewers back to your site, or you can plan to end at an outside link. Starting out in hypertext by trying to include complicated animation or the like may give you the false impression that this form is too difficult to master. It isn't; it's a series of small steps. Start with a few little steps, and you will most likely be excited by the possibilities you see before you.

5. If you were to write a blog in the form of "The Year of Living _____ ," what would fill in that blank? Even if you don't write a blog for that title, it can still be interesting to see what comes to mind as a way to think about new material for your writing.

6. Spend some time reading blogs on a topic that's close to your heart. Take note of the voices that attract you, those that repel you, and those that leave you neutral. Write up a list of those attributes, and then see how you might learn from them for your own writing—on a blog or otherwise.

7. Start a blog with the idea of a finite number of entries: "Fifty Ways" or "Twenty-Five Views of" or "Thirty Considerations," etc. Commit to posting at least once a week, no matter what.

8. If you already have a blog, research how you might start attracting more traffic to it. Read one of the "tips" websites and commit to improving the quality and variety of the blog posts.

9. Practice "Twitterature." Every day for a week, write a short-short-short essay in 140 characters or fewer. You could also do this with a group to see what kind of work you come up with.

PART 3

HONING YOUR CRAFT

Let men and women make good sentences. Let them learn to spell the sound of the waterfall and the noise of the bathwater. Let us get down the colors of the baseball gloves, the difference in shade between the centerfielder's deep pocket and the discreet indentation of the catcher's mitt. . . . Let us enlist the Vocabulary, the Syntax, the high grammar of the mysterious world.

—STANLEY ELKIN

12

The Particular Challenges
of Creative Nonfiction

Of course a picture can lie, but only if you yourself are not honest or
if you don't have enough control over your subject. Then it is the
camera working, not you.

—ANDRÉ KERTÉSZ,
PHOTOGRAPHER

I'm writing an essay about my grandmother. I'm not sure why I'm writing
this; there are just certain scenes and images that haunt me and I have to
get them down on paper: my grandmother immobilized in a hospital bed,
the ties of her hospital gown undone around her collarbone; my mother
crying quietly in a restaurant as she tells me she can't bring herself to care
for her mother in her home. As I write, I have to make several questionable
choices: do I really remember massaging my grandmother's back that day in
the hospital? Now that I've written it, the scene's taken on the stamp of
truth, seems to have replaced any "real" memories I might have of that day.
And do I relate the scene of my mother's shame; is it really my story to tell?
Can I imagine a scene between my mother and my grandmother, the difficulty of touch between them?

In the end, several months later, I decide to leave in the massage scene—
it has an emotional truth to it, a resonance that indicates to me the memory
is valid, not only for the essay but for myself. But I delete the scene with my
mother in the restaurant; though the facts of this moment are more readily

145

verifiable, I've decided that it oversteps some boundary I've set up for myself. That part is not my story to tell—I don't have the authority or the permission—and it feels too risky. I also, therefore, need to cut the scene where I imagine my mother and grandmother together in our family home. This is a difficult cut—I love the writing in that section—but it needs to go because the scene no longer fits in with the trajectory of the essay.

Yet I know that none of this writing has been wasted. Through writing the scenes I eventually eliminated, I came to understand what was important for this particular essay: to focus my attention on the metaphors of touch, the difficulties of such simple gestures within the family. I also learned how I draw the theoretical lines for myself, how I choose to go about negotiating the ethical land mines of creative nonfiction.

—Brenda

A Few Caveats About Writing from Life

Creative nonfiction is a tricky business. On the one hand, you have the challenge—and the thrill—of turning real life into art. But on the other hand, you have to deal with all the issues that come attached with that "real life." When a fiction writer wants her character to remember the first time she ate ice cream, she can enter the problem imaginatively: place the character at Coney Island with a melting chocolate cone or at a birthday party with a neat scoop on a slice of cake. Can you do the same thing when you're writing from your own memory, even when you don't exactly remember the scene? A fiction writer is able to create the set amount of characters necessary for the story's action; can you do the same thing with the characters you encounter in your own life and research? When a fiction writer needs dialogue, she writes dialogue. As a nonfiction writer, can you make up dialogue you don't remember verbatim? When you're writing essays based on research, how much of your imagination can you use? Does "nonfiction" mean "no fiction"?

The self inhabits the prose of creative nonfiction, whether or not you write directly about your own experiences. It is this "I" that picks and chooses among the facts. This "I" re-creates those essential scenes and makes crucial decisions about what to include and what to exclude. The "I" decides on the opening line that will set up the voice of the piece, the essential themes and metaphors. The "I" gives the essay its *personality*, both literally and figuratively. The essential question, then, is how do you create a piece inhabited by the self without becoming self-centered? And how do you negotiate all the ethical and technical obstacles that come with writing from real life?

The "I" and the Eye: Framing Experience

A useful way of looking at how creative nonfiction employs the "I" is to align the genre with photography. Both photography and creative nonfiction operate under the "sign of the real" (a phrase coined by literary theorist Hayden White); both operate *as though* the medium itself were transparent. In other words, when you look at a photograph, you are lulled into the illusion that you see the world as it is—looking through a window, as it were—but in reality you are being shown a highly manipulated version of that world. The same is true with creative nonfiction. Because it operates under the sign of the real, it can be easy to mistake the essay as presenting life itself, without adulteration.

But both photography and creative nonfiction actually function just as subjectively as fiction and painting, because the personal "eye" is the mechanism for observation, and the inner "I" is the medium through which these observations are filtered. As Joan Didion puts it, "No matter how dutifully we record what we see around us, the common denominator of all we see is always, transparently, shamelessly, the implacable 'I.'" The minute you begin to impose form on experience—no matter how dutifully you try to remain faithful to history or the world—you're immediately faced with a technical dilemma: How do you effectively frame this experience? What gets left outside the confines of this frame? Are some frames more "truthful" than others? And the way you decide to frame the world directly reflects the "I" and the "eye" that perform this act of construction.

Wallace Stegner, in his book *Where the Bluebird Sings to the Lemonade Springs*, posits that our task as writers is "to write a story, though ignorant or baffled. You take something that is important to you, something you have brooded about. You try to see it as clearly as you can, and to fix it in a transferable equivalent. All you want in the finished print is the clean statement of the lens, *which is yourself*, [emphasis ours] on the subject that has been absorbing your attention." A good photograph will mirror the inner vision of the photographer, just as a good essay will reflect the unique sensibility of the writer, whether or not that writer focuses on material interior to the self.

The Persona of the First-Person Narrator

Just as the details of the world and experience may be framed or constructed by a mediating "I," so too is that "I" a fabrication for the purposes of the essay. We are not the same on the page as we are in real life, and we must be aware that the "I" is just as much a tool—or a point of view or a character—that we manipulate for particular effects. The "I" on the page is really a fictional construction, reflecting certain parts of us, leaving others out, or exaggerating certain aspects for the purposes of the essay at hand.

For instance, Bernard Cooper is not *always* obsessed with the sound of sighs, as he is in his essay "The Fine Art of Sighing," just as David James Duncan often has other things on his mind besides the baseball sent to his brother the day after the brother died, which he describes in his essay "The Mickey Mantle Koan." But, for the time span of the essay, they create themselves as characters with these obsessions that focus the piece and create its reason for existing at all.

In *The Situation and the Story*, memoirist Vivian Gornick writes about finding her voice in creative nonfiction. "I began to read the greats in essay writing—and it wasn't their confessing voices I was responding to, it was their truth-speaking personae," she writes. "I have created a persona who can find the story riding the tide that I, in my unmediated state, am otherwise going to drown in." The narrating "I," the persona you create, is the one who has the wherewithal to rescue experience from chaos and turn it into art.

Gornick further describes how this concept of the persona extends even to our characters—and how we, as narrators, essentially *become* characters—in her essay "Truth in Personal Narrative":

> Once, in Texas, at an association of engineers, I gave a reading from my memoir *Fierce Attachments*. No sooner had I finished speaking, than a woman in the audience raised her hand to ask a question: "If I come to New York, can I take a walk with your Mama?" When the laughter died down I

told her that, actually, she wouldn't want to take a walk with my mother, it was the woman in the book she wanted to walk with. They were not exactly the same.

Shortly afterward, I attended a dinner party in New York where, an hour into the evening, one of the guests (a stranger to me) blurted out in a voice filled with disappointment, "Why, you're nothing like the woman who wrote *Fierce Attachments*!" At the end of the evening she cocked her head at me, and said, "Well, you're *something* like her." I understood perfectly. She had come expecting to have dinner with the narrator of the book, not with me: again, not exactly the same.

The Pact with the Reader

As you create this persona, you also establish a relationship between yourself and the reader. In creative nonfiction—more so, perhaps, than in any other genre—readers assume a real person behind the artifice, an author who *speaks* directly to the reader. Just as in spoken conversations, it's a symbiotic relationship. The reader completes this act of communication through his attention to the author's story, and the author must establish right away a reason for the reader to be attentive at all. For this relationship to work, however, the author must establish a certain level of trust.

Simply presenting your work as an "essay" rather than a piece of fiction sets up certain assumptions. The reader will be engaged in a "true story," one rooted in the world as we know it. Because of this assumption, the reader needs to know he is in good hands, in the presence of, in Vivian Gornick's words, a "truth-speaking" guide who will lead him somewhere worthwhile. The reader needs to know he won't be deceived along the way, led to believe something that turns out to be patently untrue. Philippe Lejeune, in his seminal work *On Autobiography*, calls this the "pact with the reader." The essayist pledges, in some way, both to be as honest as possible with the reader *and* to make this conversation worthwhile. Without this pact, true communication becomes impossible.

As essayist Patricia Hampl puts it, "You tell me your story, I'll tell you mine." Without this understanding, we become more like the people you occasionally see in the park: men and women talking to themselves, rehashing past wrongs, their arms gesticulating wildly in the air. We don't really *listen* to such a narrator; in fact our impulse is to turn and walk in the opposite direction.

So, *how* does a writer establish this kind of pact with the reader? In the introduction to *The Art of the Personal Essay*, essayist Phillip Lopate writes that "part of our trust in good personal essayists issues, paradoxically, from their exposure of their own betrayals, uncertainties, and self-mistrust." When we reveal our own foibles, readers can relax and know they engage in conversation with someone as human as they are.

Good writers can also establish this pact through their skillful manipulation of the techniques that make for vivid writing (see Chapter 13). If we know we are in the hands of a literary artist—one who won't let us down with clichés or a weak infrastructure—then we're usually willing to go wherever he or she leads. We assume that the writer has shaped the material for its best literary effect, while at the same time remaining as true as possible to the "facts" of the world and history. Let's take a look at some famous essayists and see how they establish a pact with the reader early on in their work, combining craft with content:

> **Joan Didion ("Goodbye to All That"):** "That first night I opened my window on the bus into town and watched for the skyline, but all I could see were the wastes of Queens and the big signs that said MIDTOWN TUNNEL THIS LANE and then a flood of summer rain (even that seemed remarkable and exotic, for I had come out of the West where there was no summer rain), and for the next three days I sat wrapped in blankets in a hotel room air-conditioned to 35° and tried to get over a bad cold and a high fever. It did not occur to me to call a doctor, because I knew none, and although it did occur to me to call the desk and ask that the air conditioner be turned off, I never called, because I did not know how much to tip whoever might come—was anyone ever so young? I am here to tell you that someone was."

> **E. B. White ("Afternoon of an American Boy"):** "Seeing him, I would call 'Hello, Parnell!' and he would smile and say 'Hello, Elwyn!' and walk on. Once I remember dashing out of our yard on

roller skates and executing a rink turn in front of Parnell, to show off, and he said, 'Well, quite an artist, aren't you?' I remember the words. I was delighted at praise from an older man and sped away along the flagstone sidewalk, dodging the cracks I knew so well."

Margaret Atwood ("Nine Beginnings"): "1. *Why do you write?* I've begun this piece nine times. I've junked every beginning. I hate writing about my writing. I almost never do it. Why am I doing it now? Because I said I would. I got a letter. I wrote back *no*. Then I was at a party and the same person was there. It's harder to refuse in person. Saying yes had something to do with being nice, as women are taught to be, and something to do with being helpful, which we are also taught."

Bernard Cooper ("The Fine Art of Sighing"): "You feel a gradual welling up of pleasure, or boredom, or melancholy. Whatever the emotion, it's more abundant than you ever dreamed. You can no more contain it than your hands can cup a lake. And so you surrender and suck the air. Your esophagus opens, diaphragm expands. Poised at the crest of an exhalation, your body is about to be unburdened, second by second, cell by cell. A kettle hisses. A balloon deflates. Your shoulders fall like two ripe pears, muscles slack at last."

What do you find in common with these four very different essayists? Though they write about quite divergent subjects, and from widely varying points of view, they've all constructed an "I" voice that speaks directly to the reader, and they all give the reader some evidence that it will be worthwhile to remain in this conversation. In her long, breathless sentences, Joan Didion reveals her embarrassment and timidity at being in a city where she knows no one and is unsure of the social conventions. Not only does she reel us in because of the details (we get to be on that bus with her), but she also laughs at herself and invites the reader to laugh with her. "Was anyone ever so young? I am here to tell you that someone was." These two sentences establish that Didion has perspective on her experience. She has garnered some wisdom in the time between then and now, and so we won't be subjected to a rendition of raw emotion; rather the material will be shaped and presented by someone who is able to distance herself from the "I" who is a character in her story, and the "I" who narrates that story many years later.

E. B. White gains our trust because he is able to vividly describe a scene of childish delight and in such a way that we experience it along with him. Though we may never have had White's exact experience, he keys us into an experience that might be termed universal. Surely we've all experienced some moment of joy such as his, some moment when we were recognized by someone we admired. And if we haven't, White makes us wish we had, with his strong verbs ("dashing," "executing," "dodging"), and his powerful sentence structure that leaps and dodges and ends in a sigh of nostalgic satisfaction. White, like Didion, also shows us that he understands the difference between creating an "I" character in the story and a narrating "I" with the skills to render this story effectively. The line "I remember the words," while deceptively simple and commonplace, alerts the reader to the older writer's presence in the scene, looking on and rediscovering it along with the reader.

Margaret Atwood uses the form itself to establish that we're in good hands. She uses the interview question as a reason for writing in the first place, and then confesses that she'd rather do anything but write the essay we have in our hands. The tension between the question (which recurs nine times throughout the essay, an insistent voice that spurs the writer and reader on) and her tentative answers to that question provides dramatic suspense for an essay that could easily, in other hands, become clichéd or predictable. Also, by confessing her difficulty with writing, she allows us to relate to her experience. It's as though she's giving voice to the doubts we all carry in our heads, a daring move that we silently applaud. She creates a persona, forthright and strong, who is able to say the things we ourselves might find difficult.

Bernard Cooper reaches out a hand and tugs us into his essay by starting off with the second-person point of view. "You feel a gradual welling up of pleasure." He makes us a participant in his essay by re-creating a sigh on the page. Read the passage aloud and see if you can keep from letting out a long, hearty sigh. And the "you" makes an assertion that's difficult to deny. The experience he creates on the page does indeed become a universal sigh, exhaled in common with thousands of others.

All these writers, along with the multitude of creative nonfiction writers we admire, must immediately make a case for taking up a reader's time and attention. In doing so, they also take care of the "so what?" question that plagues writers of creative nonfiction and of memoir in particular. Why should anyone care about your personal story or your perspective on the world? What use will the essay have for anyone outside of yourself? By engaging you in their essays through vivid details and an authentic voice, through imaginative uses of form and structure, these essayists show that the personal can indeed become universal. We care about their stories because they have become *our* stories. They have verbalized for us what has previously remained silent or have at least rephrased these issues for us in such a way as to make them new. That's what we're after as readers of literature: a fresh articulation of the world so that we might understand it more thoroughly. These essayists do so through both personal revelation and careful crafting of their prose.

The Permutations of "Truth": Fact Versus Fiction

If you set out to establish a pact with the reader—to gain his or her trust—then you must make some critical decisions about how—or whether—you will employ fictional elements in your nonfiction writing. As we've noted earlier, the simple act of writing and the construction of the narrative voice are essentially creative acts that impose a form where none before existed. Beyond that, what kinds of fictions are allowable and what are not in creative nonfiction? Just how much emphasis do we put on "creative" and how much on "nonfiction"?

Some writers believe that nothing at all should ever be knowingly made up in creative nonfiction. If you can't remember what color dress you wore at your sixth-grade graduation, then you better leave that detail out or do some studied research to find the answer. If you had five best friends in high school who helped you through a jam, then you better not compress those five into one or two composite characters for the sake of efficient narrative. On the other hand, some writers believe that small details can be fabricated to create the scenes of memory, and they knowingly create composite characters because the narrative structures demand it. Some writers willingly admit imagination into factual narratives; others abhor it and see it as a trespass into fiction.

It's interesting to note that when a writer publishes a piece of fiction that contains highly autobiographical elements, no one flinches; in fact, such blurring of the boundaries is often presumed. But to admit fictional techniques into autobiographical work creates controversy and furious discussion. The nature of that essential pact with the reader—that sense of trust—demands this kind of scrutiny into the choices we make as nonfiction writers.

We believe that every writer must negotiate the boundary between fact and fiction for him- or herself. What constitutes fabrication for one writer will seem like natural technique to another. But what we can do here is show how some writers employ fictional techniques and the effects these choices have on your credibility as an essayist.

Memory and Imagination

If your work is rooted in memory, you will find yourself immediately confronted with the imagination. Memory, in a sense, *is* imagination: an "imagining" of the past, re-creating the sights, sounds, smells, tastes, and touches (see Chapter 1). In her essay "Memory and Imagination," Patricia Hampl writes, "I am forced to admit that memoir is not a matter of transcription, that memory itself is not a warehouse of finished stories, not a static gallery of framed pictures. I must admit that I invented. But why?"

We invent because our lives and the world contain more than simple facts; imagination and the way we imagine are as much a part of ourselves as any factual résumé. In creative nonfiction, the creative aspect involves not only writing techniques, but also a creative interpretation of the facts of our lives, plumping the skeletal facts with the flesh of imagination. Personal history sometimes demands this kind of elaboration for its full significance to emerge on the page. Hampl continues, "We find, in our details and broken and obscured images, the language of symbol. Here memory impulsively reaches out its arms and embraces imagination. That is the resort to invention. It isn't a lie, but an act of necessity, as the innate urge to locate personal truth always is."

Look back to the tonsil story at the beginning of Chapter 1. There's no real way to verify either the fact or fiction of the tonsils floating in a jar on the bedside table. What I, Brenda, can do with this image is admit the bizarre and unlikely nature of this mental picture that imagination has called forth in conjunction with memory. I can say, "Why do I remember this jar of tonsils at my hospital bedside?" In so doing, I readily admit the imagination into memory and can then proceed to construct an essay that both interprets the image for metaphorical significance and allows it to become a jumping-off point for a longer meditation on the topics this metaphor suggests. I do not discount or omit this image because its factual veracity is in question; rather I relish the opportunity to explore that rich boundary zone between memory and imagination. And I do so in full view of my audience, disclosing my intent, and so maintaining my pact with the reader.

Emotional Truth Versus Factual Truth

Mimi Schwartz in "Memoir? Fiction? Where's the Line?" writes, "Go for the emotional truth, that's what matters. Yes, gather the facts by all means. Look at old photos, return to old places, ask family members what they remember, look up time-line books for the correct songs and fashion styles, read old newspapers, encyclopedias, whatever—and then use the imagination to fill in the remembered experience." If we allow imagination into memory, then we are naturally aligning ourselves with a stance toward an emotional or literary truth; this doesn't mean that we discount factual truth altogether, but that it may be important, for *literary* purposes, to fill in what you can of the facts to get at a truth that resonates with a different kind of veracity on the page. Facts only take us so far.

Schwartz continues, "It may be 'murky terrain,' you may cross the line into fiction and have to step back reluctantly into what really happened—the struggle creates the tensions that make memoir either powerfully true or hopelessly phony. The challenge of this genre is that it hands you characters, plot and setting, and says, 'Go figure them out!'—using fact, memory, and imagination to re-create the complexity of real moments, big and small, with no invented rapes or houses burning down." Here, Schwartz herself draws the line. We may reconstruct certain details, imagine ourselves into the stories *behind* the facts, but certain facts, such as a rape or a house burning down, cannot be invented. Or as novelist and memoirist Bret Lott puts it in his essay "Against Technique," "In fiction you get to make up what happens; in creative nonfiction you don't get to mess with what happen*ed*."

Take a look at the case of a highly publicized memoir, *Fragments: Memories of a Wartime Childhood*. In this lyrical narrative told from a child's point of view, Binjamin Wilkomirski re-creates scenes from his experience as a child survivor of the Holocaust. He recounts his father's execution in graphic detail, scenes of rats scurrying over piles of corpses. The prose is beautifully rendered, and some scenes move the reader to tears. But shortly after publication of this memoir, critics began to question Wilkomirski's veracity. One journalist did some investigation and found evidence that showed the writer had never been in a concentration camp at all. Birth certificates and adoption records showed him born in Switzerland in 1941 and adopted into a family shortly thereafter. However, Wilkomirski stood by his memories, which were recovered, he said, in therapy. To him, these memories were as real—they carried just as much emotional truth—as the factual history.

Few people would argue that Wilkomirski hadn't crossed that ethical line for creative nonfiction. Though we've presented arguments that claim emotional truths can be just as veracious as facts, it is not acceptable to appropriate or wholly invent a history that has little or no relation to your own. You still need to use your own history as a scaffolding for the emotional truths you will uncover. While *Fragments* exemplifies this dictum in fairly obvious terms (to appropriate something as horrific and emotionally charged as the Holocaust leaves little room for debate), you need to see how it might operate in smaller ways within your own nonfiction writing. There are facts and then there are *facts*. Which ones are hard and fast?

For example, Annie Dillard has been brought to task simply for claiming to own a cat she never had. Her book *Pilgrim at Tinker Creek* begins with the line "I used to have a cat, an old fighting tom, who would jump through the open window by my bed in the middle of the night and land on my chest." Later in the paragraph she writes, "And some mornings I'd wake in daylight to find my body covered with paw prints in blood; I looked as though I'd been painted with roses." This image becomes important to her spiritual explorations throughout the book, and nowhere does she really acknowledge that the cat is a literary device or a fiction constructed for this purpose. For many readers, this constitutes a breach of contract; though Dillard uses the fictional cat to good effect, the fact that she has deceived the audience in some way undermines her credibility for the rest of the book. "How can we be sure of anything she says from here on out?" these readers would cry. Other readers are willing to exonerate Dillard for this fiction, claiming that it is not an important detail, and the cat is meant as a metaphorical device. After all, the book's subtitle is *A Mystical Excursion into the Natural World*. In the realm of mysticism, even nonexistent fighting toms might materialize to be our spirit guides.

One of the most publicized controversies in creative nonfiction came with the publication and promotion of James Frey's memoir, *A Million Little Pieces*. Chosen for the coveted Oprah's Book Club, this memoir told in riveting detail Frey's story of drug and alcohol abuse, criminal activity, and many other unsavory events. Oprah Winfrey, on her show, told viewers it was "like nothing you've ever read before. Everybody at Harpo is reading it. When we were staying up late at night reading it, we'd come in the next morning saying, 'What page are you on?'"

But something didn't sit right with several critics and watchdog groups. The Smoking Gun conducted an in-depth investigation, which revealed that most of what Frey had written was highly exaggerated, if not completely fictionalized. Frey defended his actions, saying that he had "embellished" the truth for "obvious dramatic reasons." Oprah had Frey back on the show to chastise him for this deception, and the publisher, Nan Talese, even went so far as to offer refunds to offended readers.

What do you think? Where do you draw the line for your own work?

It could be that the response to Frey's artifice was so strong because those who "stayed up late at night reading it" felt their own emotions had been trifled with. At the same time, when we read memoir, should we do so with a grain of salt? Five years after her admonishment, Oprah had Frey back on her show to apologize for her reaction; in this interview, Frey said he wasn't ashamed of his actions, because he believes all memoir writers "do what I did." Would you be comfortable inserting such fictions in your own nonfiction writing?

"The Whole Truth?"

Sometimes you'll be troubled not by "facts" that are made up, but by those that are omitted. In essay writing, it's nearly impossible to tell the "whole" truth. Of necessity, you'll find yourself needing to pare away certain details, events, and characters to create an essay that makes narrative sense. For example, if you're writing about something that happened in school when you were ten years old, you'll have to decide just how many members of your fifth-grade class will make it onto the stage. Who is important and who is not, for this particular essay?

This is an easy one: you'll naturally choose to flesh out the one or two characters closest to you at the time. More difficult will be knowing when and how to omit the characters that felt important in real life but just get in the way once you land them on the page. For example, Bernard Cooper included his brothers in his early book *Maps to Anywhere*, but when he wrote the essays collected in *Truth Serum*, he made a conscious decision to leave his brothers out. This left him open to criticism from reviewers who said he deceived his audience by implying he was an only child. Here is his reply to them, from his essay "Marketing Memory":

> I had three brothers, all of whom died of various ailments, a sibling history that strains even my credulity. . . . Very early in the writing of *Truth Serum* I knew that a book concerned with homosexual awakening would sooner or later deal with AIDS and the population of friends I've lost to the disease. . . . To be blunt, I decided to limit the body count in this book in order to prevent it from collapsing under the threat of death. . . . There is only so much loss I can stand to place at the center of the daily rumination that writing requires. . . . Only when the infinite has edges am I capable of making art.

"Only when the infinite has edges am I capable of making art." Perhaps that should be a credo we creative nonfiction writers etch on the walls above our desks. For that is what we're up to all the time: creating those edges, constructing artful containers that will hold some facts and not others.

These "edges" might also be formed by choosing to create "composite characters," or to compress events in time. A composite character is a fictional construction; the author blends the traits of several characters into one or two, thereby streamlining both the cast of characters and the narratives needed to take care of them. Compression of time means that you might conflate anecdotes from several trips home into one composite visit. As a writer and a member of a writing community, you'll want to think about these devices—and talk about them—to see how they conform to your own writing ethics.

Cueing the Reader

As you continue to develop your own guidelines for the permutations of truth in creative nonfiction, you'll find that you'll create your own tools for negotiating some of these tricky areas. Some simple ones to keep in mind, however, are *taglines* that let the reader in on what exactly you're up to. Phrases such as "I imagine," "I would like to believe," "I don't remember exactly, but," "I would like to remember," or even a simple "Perhaps," alert the reader to your artistic agenda. Once you set the terms of the discussion—once you situate the reader in that boundary zone between fact and fiction—then you most likely will be free to go wherever you wish.

For example, what would have happened if Annie Dillard said "I never owned a fighting tom, but I would like to imagine . . ." Or she might have disclosed where she received the image: "I once had a friend whose fighting tomcat left paw prints of blood on her chest. I wish I had such a creature. . . ." For Dillard, this kind of tagline may have lessened the literary effect of the passage. But it would certainly diffuse any accusations against her credibility as well.

Cueing the reader can be accomplished even more subtly. If you have trouble writing a scene for a family event because it happened ten years ago, try beginning it with a line like, "This is how my father sounded," or, "This is what Sundays were like at my house." Then watch the pieces fall into place. These statements are unobtrusive, but they make it clear that you're not claiming to provide a verbatim transcript of an event.

Writers can also directly tell the reader what they're up to. Full disclosure lets readers know what we're in for. In a daring move, Lauren Slater titles a book *Lying: A Metaphorical Memoir*. Though this book is full of details that prove to be untrue, notably her descriptions of having epileptic seizures, Slater stands by her work with an obvious defense. The title tells us, quite bluntly, that she's fabricating metaphorical experiences. Though you may or may not buy this as a reader, you can't claim that she didn't warn you.

Pitfalls to Avoid: Revenge Prose and the Therapist's Couch

Ironically, while creative nonfiction can be a tool of self-discovery, you must also have some distance from the self to write effectively. You must know when you are ready to write about certain subjects and when you are not. If you are crying while crafting a piece of nonfiction, the tears will smudge the ink, ultimately making your work unreadable. If your hand shakes with anger while writing, the words will veer wildly across the page with no sense of control or design.

This is not to say that creative nonfiction is devoid of emotion; on the contrary, the most powerful nonfiction is propelled by a sense of urgency, the need to speak about events that touch us deeply, both in our personal history and those that occur in the world around us. The key to successfully writing about these events is *perspective*. Earlier in the chapter, we aligned creative nonfiction with photography. Perspective is the way a photographer chooses to frame and compose her photograph, and it is just as vital when you approach the tough subjects for personal essays. Perspective defines the difference between a journal entry meant only for private venting and the essay designed for public consumption.

As readers, we rarely want to read an essay that smacks either of the therapist's couch or revenge prose. In both cases, the writer has not yet gained enough perspective for wisdom or literature to emerge from experience. In therapist's couch prose, the writer is still weighed down by confusing emotions, or feelings of self-pity, and wants only to share those emotions with the reader. The depth of these emotions does not allow for a literary design to emerge. In revenge prose, the writer's intent seems to be to get back at someone else who has wronged him. The offender does not emerge as a fully developed character but only as a flat, one-dimensional incarnation of his awful deeds. In both cases, it is the writer who comes out looking bad, because he has not stepped back enough from the person or events to gain perspective.

As a writer, it is important for you to start recognizing when you can write about certain material and when you cannot. Perhaps it will take another twenty years before you are fully ready to deal with traumatic events in your childhood. It might take years before you're really able to deal with the breakup of your marriage. Or perhaps you will be able to write about a *small* aspect of the experience, focusing your attention on a particular detail that leads to a larger metaphorical significance outside of the event itself. For instance, remember David James Duncan and his koan of the signed baseball? He deals with the death of his brother years after the fact by focusing his attention on that signed baseball sent to his brother by Mickey Mantle. This baseball leads him to a philosophical rumination on the nature of life itself. This *peripheral vision*—this ability to sidle up to the big issues by way of a side route—is the mark of an accomplished writer, one who has gained enough perspective to use personal experience in the service of a larger literary purpose.

The best writers also show a marked generosity toward the characters in their nonfiction, even those who appear unsympathetic or unredeemable. For example, Terry Tempest Williams, in "The Clan of One-Breasted Women," writes an essay that is clearly fueled by anger, but it does not come across as personally vengeful or mean-spirited. Most of the women in her family died of cancer, an illness that could have been caused by the government's testing of nuclear weapons in her home state. By channeling her energy into research, she shows herself as someone with important information to impart, aside from her own personal history. She creates a metaphor—the clan of one-breasted women—that elevates her own story into a tribal one. By directing her attention to the literary design of her material, she is able to transcend the emotional minefield of that material. "Anger," she has said, "must be channeled so that it becomes nourishing rather than toxic." Her work is passionate, yes, but not shrill in a way that might lose her readers.

The Warning Signs

In your own work, always be on the lookout for sections that seem too weighed down by the emotions from which they spring. Here are some warning signs. Read the piece aloud and see if the prose has momentum. Where does it lag and become plodding? Those are the sections that probably haven't been refined enough to avoid melodrama. And seek out any sections that too directly explore your feelings about an event rather than the event itself. Where do you say words such as "I hated," "I felt so depressed," "I couldn't stand"? The "I" here will become intrusive, repeating itself into infinity: a monologue of old grievances.

If you find yourself telling the reader how to feel—and in a tone that's more like aggrieved chatter at a bar than convincing narrative—then you're probably headed right into revenge prose. You don't want to end up sounding like this, "And then you know what else that no-good jerk did? You won't believe this, even after *I* was the one to put him through medical school, and *I* was the one to bear his children, he says *he* needs some space, can you believe that? Space? What the hell does he need *space* for?" Channel your creative energy, instead, into constructing the scenes, images, and metaphors that will allow the reader to have her own reactions, *apart from the ones you had at the time*. On the page, your life is not just your life anymore; you must put your allegiance now into creating an artifact that will have meaning outside the self.

TRY IT

1. Have an individual or group session in which you plumb your own sense of nonfiction ethics. What would you do and what wouldn't you do? Would you re-create a scene or invent dialogue for someone without a clear cue to the reader? Would you invent a fact? It's useful to proceed in your writing with a defined sense of your own boundaries.

2. Practice writing cueing lines. This can be fun to do in a group, while passing one another's essays around or just writing inventive cueing lines to pass ("If I dreamed this scene, this is how I would dream it."). Sharing ideas will get you in the habit of using cueing lines creatively.

3. Try writing out a memory in scene from the perspective of at least two people who were present (members of your family, perhaps). Get their memory down as accurately as you can by questioning them, and write it as carefully and lovingly as you write your own. Think of this as an exercise in the quirks of individual perspective. If you like the results of this exercise, try juxtaposing pieces of each narrative, alternating the voices, to create a braided essay.

4. Try compressing time by creating one scene out of several similar events. For instance, take moments from several Christmas dinners and create one specific scene that encapsulates all of them. What do you gain and/or lose by doing this to your material?

13

The Basics of Good Writing
in Any Form

I was delighted to find that nonfiction prose can also carry meaning in its structures and, like poetry, can tolerate all sorts of figurative language, as well as alliteration and even rhyme. The range of rhythms in prose is larger and grander than it is in poetry, and it can handle discursive ideas and plain information as well as character and story. It can do everything. I felt as though I had switched from a single reed instrument to a full orchestra.

—ANNIE DILLARD

People need maps to your dreams.

—ALLEN GURGANUS

I am working with a group of novice nonfiction writers, and we're about two-thirds of the way through our time together. My students have plumbed their lives in ways they never thought possible: as environmental records, as living history, as a movement through various forms—scientific, spiritual, cultural, aesthetic—of inquiry. They sort themselves through the door of my classroom with varying degrees of eagerness, and pull out their notebooks, pens cocked and waiting. They're used to coming in and interrogating themselves in different ways: Who are they really? How have they lived? Today, however, I know I'm going to make them groan. Instead of prompts like writing about the explosion of Mount St. Helens or the World Trade Organization riots in Seattle, I have them pull out a piece of their own prose and count the number of words in each sentence for three paragraphs. I also have them jot down comments on the kinds of sentences they use: simple declarative (basic subject-verb), complex, fragmented, and so forth. They do the assignment, because it would be even more boring to sit and do nothing, I suppose. Suddenly a little exclamation breaks out from a corner of the room.

"Ohmigod!" says one young woman. "All of my sentences are eleven words long!"

This young woman has been concerned about what feels to her like a flatness or lifelessness to her prose. Here, in one rather mechanical but not painful exercise, she's put her finger on the reason, or one of the reasons. On further analysis she discovers that she has a penchant for writing one simple declarative sentence after another: "I drive to the forest in April. My car is almost ready for a new clutch. The forests are quiet at that time of year." The metronomic beat of same sentence structure, same sentence length, has robbed her otherwise sparkling essays of their life.

For the sake of comparison, listen to the difference created in those three sample sentences by a little more rhetorical inventiveness: "In April, a quiet time of year, I drive to the forest. My car almost ready for a new clutch."

—SUZANNE

Scene Versus Exposition

Generally speaking, scene is the building block of creative nonfiction. There are exceptions to this statement—more academic or technically oriented writing, the essay of ideas perhaps—but overall, the widespread notion that nonfiction is the writer's thoughts presented in an expository or summarizing way has done little but produce quantities of unreadable nonfiction. Scene is based on action unreeling before us, as it would in a film, and it will draw on the same techniques as fiction—dialogue, description, point of view, specificity, concrete detail. Scene also encompasses the lyricism and imagery of great poetry. We have, as the Dillard quote at the head of this chapter indicates, access to the full orchestra. We need to learn to play every instrument with brio.

Let's begin by defining our terms. *Expository* writing, as the term implies, exposes the author's thoughts or experiences for the reader; it summarizes, generally with little or no sensory detail. Expository writing compresses time: *For five years I lived in Alaska.* It presents a compact summation of an experience with no effort to re-create the experience for the person reading.

On the other hand, *scene*, as in fiction, uses detail and sensory information to re-create experience, generally with location, action, a sense of movement through time, and possible dialogue. Scene is cinematic. Here is a possible reworking of the above sentence, using scene: *For the five years I lived in Alaska I awoke each morning to the freezing seat of the outhouse, the sting of hot strong coffee drunk without precious sugar or milk, the ringing "G'day!" of my Australian neighbor.*

The latter version of this sentence clearly presents the reader with a more experiential version of that time in Alaska, with details that provide a snapshot of the place: the slowness of time passing is stressed by the harsh routine of the coffee and outhouse; we get a sense of scarcity of supply; the neighbor even has a bit of swift characterization. Of course, for an essay in which Alaska is totally unimportant the expository summation might be the better move. But if you find yourself writing nonfiction with very little scene, you are likely to produce flat writing readers have to struggle to enter.

Remember "The Knife," by author/surgeon Richard Selzer? This essay moves fluidly between scene and exposition; Selzer forces us to *live* the awesome power and responsibility of the surgeon before allowing himself the luxury of meditating about it.

> There is a hush in the room. Speech stops. The hands of the others, assistants and nurses, are still. Only the voice of the patient's respiration remains. It is the rhythm of a quiet sea, the sound of waiting. Then you speak, slowly, the terse entries of a Himalayan climber reporting back. "The stomach is okay. Greater curvature clean. No sign of ulcer. Pylorus, duodenum fine. Now comes the gall-bladder. No stones. Right kidney, left, all right. Liver . . . uh-oh."

Selzer goes on to tell us he finds three large tumors in the liver. "Three big hard ones in the left lobe, one on the right. Metastatic deposits. Bad, bad." Like fine fiction, this passage contains a clear setting—the hospital room, characterized appropriately enough by sound rather than appearance: the silence of life and death. There is action mimicking real time, containing the element of surprise. We learn along with the surgeon about the patient's metastasized cancer. There's dialogue, as the surgeon narrates to himself, to his surgical assistants, seemingly to the fates, his discovery of the patient's mortality. And, like fine poetry, this piece of writing also organizes itself through imagery: the "quiet sea" of the passive patient's breathing versus the labored voice—like a "Himalayan climber's"—of the surgeon emphasizes the former's loss of control.

Selzer's passage would be easy to change to an expository sentence: *Often in surgery I found unexpected cancer.* But the author's final purpose—an extended meditation on the relationship of human and tool, soul and body—would fall flat. The reader, lacking any feel for the grandeur and potential tragedy of exploring the body, would dismiss expository statements such as, "The surgeon struggles not to feel. It is suffocating to press the feeling out," as merely odd or grandiose.

There are several other moves worth noting in this passage. One is that, like the sample Alaska sentence given above, Selzer's surgical description is *representative scene*. In other words, he doesn't pretend this operation occurs at one specific time and place, but it represents a typical surgical procedure, one among many. Another technique to note is his use of the second person for a speaker that is presumably himself. Second person—the *you* rather than the *I*—is a point-of-view choice, discussed in more detail further on in this chapter.

In contrast, here's an example of a specific, not representative, scene, from Jo Ann Beard's essay "The Fourth State of Matter." The scenes comprising the essay all occur at very specific moments in time. Here is Beard at work, with her physicist colleagues having a professional discussion around the chalkboard:

"If it's plasma, make it in red," I suggest helpfully. We're all smoking illegally, in the journal office with the door closed and the window open. We're having a plasma party.

"We aren't discussing *plas*ma," Bob says condescendingly. He's smoking a horrendously smelly pipe. The longer he stays in here the more it feels like I'm breathing small daggers in through my nose. He and I don't get along; each of us thinks the other needs to be taken down a peg. Once we had a hissing match in the hallway which ended with him suggesting that I could be fired, which drove me to tell him he was *already* fired, and both of us stomped into our offices and slammed our doors.

"I had to fire Bob," I tell Chris later.

"I heard," he says noncommittally. Bob is his best friend.

This is a very pinpointed event, not representative but presumably unlike any other moment in Beard's life. Notice how much suggestive detail Beard packs into a short space. These characters break rules, argue, and exist in complex relationship to one another. Her relationship with Bob is established in this scene—a relationship that seems suffused with a genuine but relatively harmless tension, given their ability to issue dire threats to each other without consequence. The dialogue sounds real and secures the characters, capturing the nuanced pretense of Bob's stressing the "plas" part of the "plasma." Chris, the man in the middle, seems to have heard all this bickering before.

We all tend to use too little scene in creative nonfiction. We especially forget the possibilities of representative scene. Even when we're reporting a typical rather than a specific event, use of scenic elements, as in Selzer's surgery, conveys a sense of character and situation far more effectively than does summary.

Specificity and Detail

Scene forces us to use specificity and detail, elements that get lost in the quick wash of exposition. Even in discussing the largest ideas, our brains engage with the small workings of the senses first. And the specificity of a piece of nonfiction is generally where the sensory details lie: the aroma of honeysuckle, the weak film of moonlight. While it is possible to go overboard with detail, generally in drafting it's best to keep going back and sharpening as much as possible. You leaned not just against a tree but against a weeping silver birch; the voice at the other end of the phone sounded like the Tin Man's in *The Wizard of Oz*. Your readers or writing group can tell you when you've gone too far. When you write scene, your job is to mimic the event, create an experiential representation of it for the reader.

Look at the examples given before, and think about how much the details add to those scenes: the hushed silence of the hospital room and three hard tumors on the left lobe of the liver in Selzer's essay. In Beard's, we see the bickering but ultimate acceptance of this close group of coworkers. We sense the author's ambivalent position in the group—shut out of their "talking physics," as she tells us earlier—but also her authority within the group. We sense, in the hyperbolic description of Bob's pipe smoke ("like daggers"), a bit of foreshadowing of a coming tragic event.

In *The Elements of Style*, William Strunk, Jr., explains that the one point of accord among good writers is the need for detail that is "specific, definite, and concrete." (We also address this point in Chapter 1.) Concrete detail appeals to the senses; other writers call such details "proofs." If Selzer told us readers that sometimes in surgery he found cancer, we might abstractly believe him, but it's hard to associate that fact with real life and death. In this passage, we're convinced by the specifics: three hard tumors on the liver, the surgeon's voice mumbling, "Bad, bad."

Abstract language—the opposite of relying on concrete detail—refers to the larger concepts we use that exist on a purely mental level, with no appeal to the senses: *liberty*, *justice*, *contentment*, and so on. These terms may contain the implication of sensory detail (you may flash on "warmth" when you hear "contentment," but that's a personal reaction that wouldn't make sense to, say, a penguin), but they are in themselves broad categories only. Of course, within the details you use emerges a wealth of abstract information. Beard could have summarized her relationships with her coworkers; Selzer could have presented a few expository sentences about soul and body, surgeon as God. We want experiences, not lectures; we want to enter into events and uncover their meanings for ourselves.

Paying attention to concrete detail and the input of our own senses also helps save us from the literary pitfall of cliché, an expression or concept that's been overused. Frequently, clichés are dead metaphors, so overused we don't pay attention anymore to the comparisons they contain. (Do you actually think of a yellow metal when you hear "good as gold"? Do you even realize this phrase comes from a time when the gold our country held validated our money?) If Beard had described Bob's pipe tobacco as smelling like "dirty socks," or "killing" her nose, she would have been indulging in cliché. Instead, she used the information of her senses to create a fresh image.

Chances are, you know more than you need to know to write effective scene, but your natural expressiveness has been stifled, often by misguided advice from academic writing classes. Next time you work on a piece of creative nonfiction, hear yourself talking through the story to friends in a crowded coffee shop or club. There's plenty to divert their attention: music, people-watching, smoke, and noise. Which details do you use to hold their attention? Do you imitate the look of someone's face, the sound of a voice? Do you screech to demonstrate the sound of car tires on asphalt? Your reading audience will be equally distractible. Think about how to render these attention-grabbing devices in your prose. You may want to consult Chapter 1, "The Body of Memory," to remind yourself how to use sensory detail.

Developing Character

Character development, like learning to write effective dialogue, is part of writing scene. It's another particularly easy-to-miss demand of good creative nonfiction. After all, *we* know what our parents, children, or lovers look like. Unconsciously, we tend to assume that everyone else does as well.

Suzanne has, by marriage, a very funny grandmother. She wasn't intentionally funny, but nonetheless the mere mention of her name tends to bring down the room when the family's together. The family bears in mind, as courteous people, that we need to break through our uncontrollable giggling and clue other listeners in to the source of our amusement: "Well, she came from a tiny town in south Georgia and talked about nothing all day long but her ar-ther-itis and her gallbladder that was *leakin'* plus she lied compulsively and pursed her mouth in this funny way when she did. . . ." After a few minutes of this our auditors understand why we find her so endlessly amusing. This kind of filling in, also natural in conversation, is the essence of character development.

Nothing demonstrates the power of fine characterization like studying writers who, in a few strokes, can help us apprehend someone sensually (through sight, sound, or feel) as well as give us a sense of their essence. The following are examples of quick, effective character development from essays we love:

- **Albert Goldbarth in "After Yitzl"**: "My best friend there shoed horses. He had ribs like barrel staves, his sweat was miniature glass pears."
- **Lawrence Sutin in "Man and Boy"**: "In the case of my father and myself, I had the fullness of his face and his desire to write, which had

been abandoned when he came to America with a family to raise. . . . He was a middle-aged man who was sobbing and sweaty and his body was heavy and so soft I imagined his ribs giving way like a snowman's on the first warm winter day."

- **Judith Kitchen in "Things of This Life":** "Mayme would step onto the platform wearing a dark purple coat, her black braids wound tightly around her head. Her skin was too soft and wrinkly. When you kissed her cheek, it wobbled, and you wished you didn't have to do that."

Details that give a sense of the essence of an individual—in all his or her typicality (commonness with their type; grandmothers typically have soft and wrinkly skin) and individual, specific glory (sweat like miniature pears)—are hard to define, but blazingly effective when you come upon them. Think, when you write about someone close to you, how you would characterize that person in a stroke or two for someone else.

Dialogue

It can be difficult to allow ourselves to use direct dialogue in creative nonfiction. After all, memory's faulty; we can't recall conversations word for word, so why try? The answer is that we need to try, because insofar as nonfiction attempts to be an honest record of the observant mind, dialogue matters. We recall voices, not summaries; we observe scenes in our head, not expository paragraphs.

Dialogue generally moves action forward. Selzer quotes himself finding the metastasized cancer, and Beard gives a sense of the dynamics of her office. Dialogue must characterize and capture the voice of the speaker, however, not simply give information. The latter is called in fiction writing "information dumping," and it occurs when you have people say things like, "Well, Carmen, I remember you told me you were taking the cross-town bus that day only because your white 1999 Volvo had developed a gasket problem." Information dumping is less of a problem in nonfiction because this genre is reality based (and people really *do not* talk that way). But, if you cue your readers that you are re-creating a conversation, it may be tempting to lard the dialogue with information you can't figure out how to get in any other way. Don't do it.

Everyone has a natural cadence and a dialect to his or her speech. We nearly always speak in simple sentences, not complex-compound ones. We might say, "When the rain comes, the grass grows," which has one short dependent clause beginning with the word *when*; we aren't likely to say, "Whenever it happens the rain comes, provided the proper fertilizer's been applied, the grass grows, unless it's been masticated by cows grazing thereon"— a simple sentence or *main clause* ("the grass grows") festooned with wordy subordinate clauses. We frequently speak in sentence fragments or ungrammatical snippets—e.g., the how-are-you question "Getting along?" instead of the grammatically correct "Are you getting along?" One exception to these rules of natural speech might be a person who *is* pompous and wordy. Perhaps you're writing dialogue to capture the voice of a stuffy English professor you know. In that case, go to town. Just bear in mind that what bores you will bore others fairly quickly. In the case of people who are boorish, dull, or otherwise hard to listen to, give readers a sample of the voice and they will fill in the rest. A little goes a long way.

One final caveat: beware of elaborate taglines, which identify the speaker, such as "he said," "she argued," and so forth. In dialogue between two people taglines are often dispensable after the first two. Even when you must use them, stick as much as possible to "said" and "asked," two fairly invisible words in the context of dialogue. It's an easy mistake to make—and a difficult one to overlook as a reader—to have all of your characters "retort," "storm," or "muse." And make sure the words themselves contain tone as much as possible. (Tone can also be conveyed in a character's gesture, as in Beard's colleagues casually breaking the rules by smoking in their office.) Don't follow each speech tag with an adverb such as "angrily," "sadly," and so on. If you feel the need to use those words, ask yourself why the dialogue itself doesn't seem to contain those feelings.

Point of View

Every story is told by a storyteller (even in a piece with multiple speakers, one speaker dominates at a time), and every storyteller must be situated somehow within the frame of the work. This situating is called *point of view* (POV), and we express it through choice of pronouns. To put it simply, the tale can be told by an "I" (first-person POV), a "you" (second person), or a "he" or "she" (third person). Though it may seem at first blush as though all nonfiction must be told in first person, skillful writers do use the techniques of second- and third-person POV to wonderful effect in nonfiction. And the more the genre stretches its limbs, takes risks, and remakes its rules, the more such untraditional devices appear, and the more aware we become as writers of what they can do.

Of the three point-of-view choices, second person is the rarest, in nonfiction as well as in fiction and poetry. It's not hard to figure out why: second-person POV calls attention to itself and tends to invite reader resistance. Imagine recasting "For five years I lived in Alaska" as "For five years you lived in Alaska." That's exactly what a POV shift to second person would do; it places the reader directly in the shoes of the author, without narrative mediation. Clumsily used, second person screams out for the reader to say, "No, I didn't" with an inner shrug of indignation and stop reading. Skillfully used, however, that blurring of line between reader and author can be very powerful.

Here's a sentence from "The Fourth State of Matter" again, a classic first-person approach: "It's November 1, 1991, the last day of the first part of my life." Compare that with a short passage from Richard Selzer, who uses second person liberally throughout his essay. Watch the careful way he slips from first- to second-person POV, as if inviting the reader to experience the fearfulness of a surgeon's power:

> I must confess that the priestliness of my profession has ever been impressed on me. In the beginning there are vows. . . . And if the surgeon is like a poet, then the scars you have made on countless bodies are like verses into the fashioning of which you have poured your soul.

In contrast, Judith Kitchen's essay "Things of This Life" uses third person throughout the piece to create a sense of freshness and excitement in a childhood memoir:

> Consider the child idly browsing in the curio shop. She's been on vacation in the Adirondacks, and her family has (over the past week) canoed the width of the lake and up a small, meandering river. . . . So why, as she sifts through boxes of fake arrowheads made into key chains, passes down the

long rows of rubber tomahawks, dyed rabbits' feet, salt shakers with the words "Indian Lake" painted in gold, beaded moccasins made of what could only in the imagination be called leather, is she happier than any time during the past week?

Kitchen, further along in the essay, tells us, "Now consider the woman who was that child." It seems at first an odd choice, to write about the self as if it were someone completely apart, a stranger. But as Kitchen unfolds her sense of her life as "alien," a space she's inhabiting that raises questions she still can't answer ("How can she go on, wanting like this, for the rest of her life?"), the strategy becomes a coherent part of the architecture of the essay.

Imagine the paragraphs it would take to explain such an alienation from the self—a sense of distance from one's own desires—and the relative powerlessness such an explanation would have. Annie Dillard writes in our introductory quote that she "delighted" to learn that nonfiction, like poetry, can carry meaning in its structures. Kitchen here has wisely chosen a structure to convey her feeling—a feeling open only to the clumsiest articulation.

Image and Metaphor

Janet Burroway, in her text *Writing Fiction*, describes metaphor as the foundation stone "from which literature derives." Image—any literary element that creates a sense impression in the mind—and metaphor—the use of comparison—form the heart of any literary work. Notice how, trying to impress this importance upon you, we strain to make strong metaphor: metaphors are the foundation stones of a building; they're the pumping hearts of literary writing. The ability to make metaphor is the most basic constituent of human thought and language. Yet, too often we leave direct consideration of these devices to the poets.

While essays can be organized many ways—through topic, chronology, or passage of time—organization through image and metaphor has become much more common. Clustering thoughts through images and loose associations (and metaphors are, at the most basic level, associations) seems fundamental to the way the human mind works. You may mentally jump from a look at a leaky faucet to a memory of watching the 1970s TV show "Charlie's

Angels" because of the name of the actress Farrah Fawcett. You may then glide effortlessly from that thought to a sense memory of the powdered hot chocolate with marshmallows your mother made for you on weeknights while you watched television. As we grow more aware of and sophisticated about the way human consciousness operates, it makes sense that our literature will come closer to these basic thought rhythms. In the Beard excerpt we used earlier in this chapter, within a few sentences we see images of daggers and hissing and the use of the word *fire*. The imagery in this essay tells its own story—of a deadly event about to overtake the lives of these people.

You can often find clues to your own imagistic or metaphoric organizations when you recall the sensory association a thought or experience calls to mind. If the summer your best friend was killed in a diving accident always comes back to you with a whiff of honeysuckle, stay with that image and explore it in writing for a while. Does it lead to concepts of sweetness, youth, temptation, the quick blooming? If you let yourself write about the image alone for a while— not rushing to get to the subject your mind may insist is "the real story"—a more complex, more true, series of themes in your story will probably emerge.

The Rhythm of Your Sentences

It's a well-known fact that sentences must contain some variation. You must have become acquainted with this fact already. It's clear if you read a certain kind of prose. A work must use different kinds of sentence structures. Different kinds of sentence structures help alleviate that numbing feeling. It's a feeling you don't want your readers to have.

The previous paragraph contains six sentences, each composed of about ten words, and each is a simple sentence, beginning with a subject and its verb. Unlike this sentence you're currently reading, none begins with a clause. None is short. None, unlike the twenty-five-word sentence introducing this second paragraph, engages us for very long. Read both of these paragraphs together. Do you sense a difference? Do you, as we do, begin to go blank by the middle of the first paragraph, and finally feel some relief at the second one?

Notice that the second paragraph in this section of the book, while clarifying many of the ideas that the first paragraph contains, varies sentence structure and length. It also varies voice. One sentence uses the *vocative* or *command* voice ("Read both paragraphs together"), two are cast in the *interrogative* voice—they ask questions. Clauses like "Unlike this sentence" and "as we do" appear at the beginnings, middles, and ends of sentences to break up that repetitive simple structure.

The Poetry of Prose

Virginia Woolf, who many writers would list as "favorite poet," began work not with an idea but with a "rhythm," writing to a friend, "Style is a very simple matter; it is all rhythm. Once you have that, you can't use the wrong words." Though it's become popular, and helpful at times, to divide up non-fiction into lyric essays and non-lyric essays, doing so can obscure the fact that all language is controlled by rhythm—especially a highly stressed, Germanic language like our own. If you learn to see how language operates through rhythm and sound, or *prosody*, within prose, as well as how sentence structure affects meaning, you will be delighted at the new power of your prose.

Let's examine a paragraph of Woolf's prose, one that appears at the start of her novel *Mrs. Dalloway*:

> What a lark! What a plunge! For so it had always seemed to her, when, with a little squeak of the hinges, which she could hear now, she had burst open the French windows and plunged at Bourton into the open air. How fresh, how calm, stiller than this of course, the air was in the early morning; like the flap of a wave; the kiss of a wave; chill and sharp and yet (for a girl of eighteen as she then was) solemn, feeling as she did, standing there at the open window, that something awful was about to happen; looking at the flowers, at the trees with the smoke winding off them and the rooks rising, falling; standing and looking until Peter Walsh said, "Musing among the vegetables?"—was that it?—"I prefer men to cauliflowers"—was that it?

Woolf begins with two short, emphatic sentences that illustrate the joyous, "plunging" movements of her heroine, Clarissa Dalloway, going out on a trip to purchase flowers. She follows that with two long sentences, the first ending with the prepositional phrase "into the open air," the sentence structure itself mirroring—and stressing—the protagonist's entry into the larger world beyond her doors. The second of the long sentences contains a parenthetical phrase (Clarissa thinks of her age in the memory as a parenthetical afterthought, a reflection of how we recall just how young we were at some of life's key moments!). Those emphatic semicolons that first set off the arrival of waves in her mind cue us that the "kiss of a wave" may not be an entirely pleasant thing, and prepare us for the "foreboding" feeling Clarissa remembers. So does the strong stress—the many accented syllables—contained in the first part of this sentence. The final use of dashes to set off the question "was that it?" enables that phrase to "float" syntactically, not clearly connected to anything else in the sentence—is she wondering what Peter Walsh said, what she was thinking then, or something else? The dashes perfectly capture the artless wandering of her mind at this moment. While many writers understand Virginia Woolf as an originator of the "stream of consciousness" narrative style, few examine how she achieves the effect stylistically.

Author Virginia Tufte uses the term *syntactic symbolism* to describe syntax that creates emotional effects. Here is an excerpt from writer Dorothy Parker, a description of a breakup:

> But I knew. I knew. I knew because he had been far away from me long before he went. He's gone away and he won't come back. He's gone away and he won't come back, he's gone away and he'll never come back.

Here the repetition of "knew" captures the author's sense that she cannot drive this devastating knowledge out of her mind. Even the tense shifting—past "knew" to present "He's gone"—reflects her inability to cease feeling the painful emotion.

Sentence length and structure, pattern of stressed syllables, and placement of dependent clauses and phrases all deeply influence meaning. In her book *Holy the Firm*, Annie Dillard writes about a tragic plane crash that disfigures a child. Dillard begins with a sentence with a clause placed in an unexpected order. "Into this world falls a plane," she writes, rather than "A plane falls into this world," choosing to place the clause ("into this world") at the introduction to the sentence rather than after the subject it describes, the plane. The last position in a sentence always gets the most attention, so her sentence structure puts our attention squarely on the plane, with the swoop of the opening clause beginning with "into" causing the plane to "fall" into our reading ear.

Prose, not just poetry, avails itself of rhyme too—its beauty and, at times, its feelings of comfort and closure. In the novel *Jane Eyre*, Charlotte Brontë describes her heroine waking up as the closeted madwoman in the house rampages through the rooms on her floor: "I sat up in bed by way of arousing this said brain; it was a chilly night; I covered my shoulders with a shawl, and then I proceeded to *think again* with all my might." Notice the rhyme between "brain" and "again" and "night" and "might." Brontë has written a couplet in prose! Somehow, reading this beautifully rhyming sentence lets us know Jane will think her way out of this danger.

TRY IT

1. Go through a piece of your writing and find a passage of summary that could or maybe even should be in scene. Don't fret right now about whether scene is absolutely necessary here: the point is to develop the skill of automatically asking yourself whether that option will help you.

Sometimes we stymie ourselves by imagining we must remember *everything* or we can't describe *anything*. So work with what you do remember. You may forget the look of a room but remember the sound or smell of it (think of Selzer's defining silence in that hospital room). Or create a bridge, such as writing a few sentences about how this is what a dialogue sounds like in your memory as you try to re-create it, giving yourself permission to fill in what you don't remember word for word. Remember that almost any device for reconstruction is fine, as long as you let readers in on what you're doing.

2. To get a feel for writing scene, re-create an event that took place in the last week—one with characters you can delineate and dialogue you can remember. It doesn't have to be important— it probably will help if it isn't. The point is simply to write two to three pages in which a location is established through description, people are characterized and talk, and something happens.

3. Finally, when you feel confident of your basic skills, remember a scene out of your own life that does contain the utmost importance. For everybody this will be different. It could be something as obviously important as the birth of a child or an argument leading to the end of a marriage; or its importance could be subtle but real to you—a conversation leading to a new closeness or a new distance between you and someone critical in your life. The point is, you must have a strong sense memory of this scene, one you can play back in your head over and over again; and it must matter to you.

Write the scene with as much fidelity as possible. Have the people in it enter and leave, describe what you saw, heard, and felt. If you still remember exactly how your mother asked, "Where were you last night?" describe the question in all the sensory detail you can muster, along with the wrench in your gut that came with it. Don't question right now why what matters matters. Trust your intuition, and tap into all of the passion you have invested in this scene.

Now question yourself. Why was a certain gesture or inflection so important? Why did you spend most of this conversation staring at a loudly ticking clock on the wall? Why did you notice the caramel color of your drink? The chances are that, like Selzer and Beard, your emotional story is locked into the details you remember of your life. When you begin to question the scene in this way, scrutinizing every detail, you'll probably discover an essay waiting to be written about this crucial moment.

4. Write a portrait or character sketch. Think of someone close to you and try to convey their essence, through clothing, sound, dialogue, gestures, and so forth, in two or three paragraphs. Don't aim to write scene; this portrait doesn't need to contain action, merely characterization.

When you're reasonably finished, trade your piece with a writing partner. Read each other's sketches and then elaborate on the person described, giving an overall, abstract sense of that individual's personality. How close did you come? Discuss with your partner ways this sketch could be refined: important details that may have been omitted, or others that could be misleading. Is this character sketch on its way to becoming an essay? Articulate to yourself why this character matters, why she is different, or why he is intriguingly typical.

5. Write a page or two of dialogue. Practice for this by using your notebook to record snippets of speech verbatim: exchanges with classmates, friends, spouses, parents. Pay attention to the syntax of speech. How much is grammatically correct or incorrect? How much slang or dialect appears in different speakers' voices? When you feel ready, write a page or two of typical dialogue—you can record it and write it down, or try to re-create it—with someone fairly close to you. Do the same partner swap with this dialogue you did with characterization, and see how much of the person you're describing comes through in his or her voice.

6. The only way to fully understand point of view is to experiment with it. Pull out an earlier essay of yours, or write a simple paragraph about some subject you've thought about as a likely one. Then recast the point of view, from first to second or third. Force yourself to keep going through at least one paragraph; don't look at the clunkiness of a sentence such as "For five years you lived in Alaska" and give up. Push through, and open yourself up to moments when the point of view works, when you feel interesting possibilities arise. (You can also refer to Chapter 10, "Playing with Form: The Lyric Essay and Mixed Media.")

Traditionally, point-of-view *shifting*—moving from the narrative position of one character to another within a piece—has been a problem area for fiction writers. Unintentional shifting is a common error for young writers; masterful shifts can make a story, as in Flannery O'Connor's famous shift to the Misfit's point of view at the end of "A Good Man Is Hard to Find." As nonfiction expands its reach, we see point of view shifting in this genre as well. Richard Selzer does it, as we've shown earlier in this chapter. See if such a switch can enrich a piece of your own writing.

7. Do a quick diagnostic of two to three paragraphs of your own prose (less might not be representative enough). How long do your sentences tend to be? How do you structure them? Do you vary voices or speech acts, such as questioning, stating, and commanding, or do you simply use the declarative or simple statement voice? Challenge yourself to approach a piece of prose in a way you haven't in the past—more short sentences or sentence fragments, perhaps, or more shifts in voice. See how this change alters your work and opens up the possibilities of the essay.

8. This is an exercise that may turn into an essay, and one that will demonstrate how fundamental well-crafted titles are to good writing. Titles should not summarize or merely reflect what is to come—they should add interest, torque meaning, open new dimensions to your work.

Write a narrative, avoiding self-censorship as much as possible, about one of the following events, or something equivalent that interests you:

- Doing a favor for someone whom you anticipate will be ungrateful
- Falling asleep when you didn't mean to
- Buying groceries
- Doing laundry
- Cooking a meal for a person you have mixed feelings about
- Filling a prescription you're not sure you can afford, for something you're slightly ashamed of

Then, select a title:

- Why My Mother and I Will Never Get Along
- How to Understand the Gulf War
- Why We Invaded Libya
- Why I Chose Not to Have Children
- How to Be a Postmodern Author
- Composition as Explanation
- What I Know About the Tea Party Movement
- Civilization and Its Discontents
- Beyond Good and Evil
- Why I Am Glad (or Sorry) I Live Now
- Why I Am Not a Rock Star (or Movie Star, Astronaut, Politician)

Don't interrogate too much why you choose the title you do; pick what you are drawn to. Then write a final paragraph that ties your narrative to your title. Be subtle if possible, or as explicit as you need to be.

If you do this exercise with a group, have the group generate title ideas before the writing begins.

14

The Writing Process and Revision

The writing has changed, in your hands, and in a twinkling, from an expression of your notions to an epistemological tool. The new place interests you because it is not clear. You attend. In your humility, you lay down the words carefully, watching all the angles. Now the earlier writing looks soft and careless. Process is nothing; erase your tracks. The path is not the work. I hope your tracks have grown over; I hope birds ate the crumbs; I hope you will toss it all and not look back.

—ANNIE DILLARD

In graduate school, I once submitted a workshop story that nobody liked—not one person. I remember one woman in particular: she dangled my work in front of her and said, her lips curling in distaste, "I don't understand why this story even exists!" Of course, at the time, I huffed and I puffed, and I spoke derisively of this woman at the bar that night. My friends cooed words of support, patted me on the back, and scanned the bar for more lively companionship. But even as I walked home that night, I could tell that her comment, though poorly worded, had something in it I needed to hear. It has stayed with me throughout the years, and now, when I'm at the final stage of revision, it's her question I hear in my head: *Why does this essay exist?* I go back to work with a grim determination. No longer do I coddle the newborn prose, but hold it up roughly, probing for weakness, drawing blood. I try to identify and slash out all that is mere indulgence and platitude.

At this stage in the writing process, the draft becomes nothing more than a fruitful scavenging ground. Right now, as I write, I'm in the middle of Wyoming, and down the road a huge junkyard lies at the intersection of two minor highways. Against the rolling fields of wheat grass, this junkyard rises as ten acres of glinting metal, bent chrome, colors of every hue. One of my fellow colonists, a sculptor, began buying scraps to incorporate in her work: gorgeous landscapes with ribbons of rusted metal juxtaposed across blue skies. Now I've come to see the junkyard as a place of infinite possibility. What useful parts still hum in the innards of these machines? How will they be unearthed? What kind of work would it take to make them shine?

—BRENDA

The Drafting Process

Writing is easy; all you do is sit staring at a blank sheet of paper until the drops of blood form on your forehead.

—GENE FOWLER

When you first sit down to work, you may have no idea what the writing will bring. Maybe it even scares you a little, the thought of venturing into that unknown territory. Perhaps you circle your desk a while, wary of the task at hand. You pick up your cup of coffee in two hands and gaze out the window; you remember an e-mail you meant to answer. You get up and check the mailbox, picking a few dead leaves off the coleus plant in the window. You sit down. You get up and change your shirt, appraise yourself in the mirror a long time, and come back to your desk. Maybe you pick up a book of poetry and read a few lines, put it down. You pick up your pen and write a word, then another. You go back and erase. You begin again.

Or maybe you are the type of writer who can sit down and start writing without hesitation, training yourself to write at least one full paragraph before stopping. You know you'll go back and trim and revise, so you just keep the words coming. You give yourself one hour, and you don't move from your chair in all that time. That hour, if the writing goes well, turns into two or three. You work steadily and pile up the pages.

Either way, the important thing to know, for yourself, is your own style. In the first case, to the untrained eye you may appear engaged in nothing but mere procrastination; certainly you are not writing. But if you know yourself well, you understand that this puttering is essential to your writing process. Some thought has been brewing in your brain now for several days, perhaps weeks, or months. This idea needs your body to occupy itself while the essay forms itself into something fleshy and sturdy enough to survive outside the mind and on the bleak terrain of the page. Or, in the second case, you act more like an athlete in training, knowing that routine and discipline are essential for your creative process. You write quickly because that's the only way for you to outrun your inner critic. Neither way is "correct." The only correct way to write is the way that works for you.

The writing process is just that: a *process*. You must have the patience to watch the piece evolve, and you need an awareness of your own stages. You must know when you can go pell-mell with the heat of creation, and when you must settle down, take a wider view, and make some choices that will determine the essay's final shape.

First drafts can be seen as "discovery drafts"; much of the writing you did from the prompts in Part 1 will fall into this category. You are writing to discover what you know or to recover memories and images that may have been lost to you. You are going for the details, the unexpected images, or the story line that reveals itself only as you go along. The best writing you do will have this sense of exploration about it; you allow yourself to go into the unknown, to excavate what lies beneath the surface. It's important to allow yourself permission to write *anything* in a first draft; otherwise you might censor yourself into silence. The first draft is the place where you just might light upon the right *voice* for telling this particular story; once you're onto that voice, you can write for hours.

No matter how good (or bad) this material seems at first glance, most often it will need some shaping and revision before it is ready for public eyes. Writer Natalie Goldberg calls revision "envisioning again," and this gets at the heart of true revision: you see your work in a new light and rework it for a specific effect. Revision, perhaps, is an acquired taste, but you may find that revision actually becomes the most "creative" part of creative nonfiction. At this stage you've already produced the raw material; now you have the opportunity to dig into it with your sleeves rolled up, all your tools sharpened and at the ready. It is in revision that the real work begins. The short-story writer Raymond Carver often wrote twenty to thirty drafts before he was satisfied. "It's something I love to do," he said, "putting words in and taking words out." Or listen to Vladimir Nabokov: "I have re-written—often several times—every word I have ever published. My pencils outlast their erasers."

Global Revision Versus Line Editing

Revision can often be mistaken for line editing. There is a time, naturally, for going back to your prose to fine-tune the grammar, change a few words, and fix typos. But first you need to look at the essay as a whole and decide what will make this essay matter. What is the *real* subject of the piece? Where does the voice ring out most strongly? What image takes on more significance than you realized? What now seems superfluous, mere deadweight that hinders the essay's momentum?

It's beneficial to take some time between drafts at this stage of the process. After that first, heady flush of creation settles down, you'll better be able to pinpoint the areas that sing and those that fall flat. You'll be able to notice an unexpected theme that emerges organically through the imagery you chose. You'll hear how the ending may actually be the beginning of your piece. Or the beginning may make for a better end. At this point you need to see the work as a fluid thing, with infinite possibilities still to come. What you may have intended to write may not be the most interesting part of the essay now. Be open to what has developed in the writing process itself, and don't be afraid to cut out those areas that no longer work.

Ask yourself this question: what is the essence of the topic *for this particular essay*? Many times it's easy to think that we have to put in everything we know or feel about a topic in one essay. For instance, if you're writing about a big issue, such as sexual abuse in childhood, you may be tempted to write a gigantic essay that incorporates every incident, every feeling you ever had, and the entire cast of characters involved. Or if you're writing about a life-changing travel experience, you might feel you need to put in every stop along the way. You have to figure out what is necessary for this essay *and this essay alone*. You will write other essays about the topic, don't worry. As writer Natalie Goldberg put it, "Your main obsessions have power; they are what you will come back to in your writing over and over again. And you'll create new stories around them."

You may keep only a small portion of the original work, perhaps even just one line. But by doing this kind of pruning, you enable new, more beautiful and sturdy growth to emerge. Take comfort in knowing the old work may find its way into new essays yet to come. Keep a file on your desk or in your computer called "fragments." If it's hard for you to let go of a section completely, put it in this file and know that you will call it back sometime in the future, in a new incarnation. Time and again, we have found new homes for those bits and pieces of prose that just didn't work in their original homes.

"Profluence": Moving It Forward

As we described in Chapter 9, "The Tradition of the Personal Essay," essays often have two lines of movement: the horizontal (plot, story, linear development) and the vertical (insight, reflection, delving below the surface). When you are at the stage to revise your work, you can envision your essay in these terms. Is it more horizontal or vertical? Does the balance between the two feel adequate, or is it unbalanced in some way? Is there a beginning, middle, and end?

Even in experimental or lyric work—works that aren't dependent on plot—we need to figure out what is creating forward movement in the piece. John Gardner, an eminent fiction writer, has translated the archaic term *profluence* (which literally means "onward") onto literary craft, using the term to describe the way a story lets us know that it is getting somewhere. In creative nonfiction, we can think about profluence too: are we "getting somewhere"? What kind of container or structure will help this movement along?

Sometimes, the story itself will lend itself to profluence: for example, a travel narrative often has a natural starting and ending point. Other times, we need to find a small thread that will act as this propellant, perhaps even something quite mundane. For instance, in his essay "Burl's" (from his book *Truth Serum)*, Bernard Cooper "bookends" his essay with a simple task: at the beginning of the essay, Cooper's father sends the boy outside the diner to get a newspaper from the vending machine. While doing this task, the child narrator notices two transvestites teetering down the sidewalk. This observation leads him into a rumination on how things are not always as they seem:

Any woman might be a man; the fact of it clanged through the chambers of my brain. In broad day, in the midst of traffic, with my parents drinking coffee a few feet away, I felt as if everything I understood, everything I had taken for granted up to that moment . . . had been squeezed out of me.

He breaks from this scene to the heart of the essay, where Cooper ruminates for several pages on the concrete memories that gave him his first inklings of his own blurred sexual boundaries. We then return to the paper at the end of the essay: "I handed my father the *Herald*. He opened the paper and disappeared behind it. My mother stirred her coffee and sighed." Though we have almost forgotten about the small task at this point, it returns to provide a satisfying, small "plot" for the piece. He has suspended a small moment in time, and in the few moments while he performed this task, the narrator has gained new insights into his experience.

In your own revision, think about the structure of your essay and whether there might be some small "plot" like this one, a container that will hold your deeper musings in place. Read several essays with this idea in mind: How do these writers begin and end their essays? What creates profluence? How do we move across space and time?

The Role of the Audience

When you're writing a first draft, it's often necessary to ignore any concept of audience just so you can get the material out. An attentive audience, hanging on your every word, can be inhibiting at that stage of the writing process. But when you're revising, some concept of audience will help you gain the necessary distance to do the hard work that needs to get done. This audience can be a single person. What would your writing teacher from high school—the one who drove you into writing in the first place—think of this essay? Where would she say you're being lazy or timid? What would your most trusted friend say about that last paragraph? Sometimes by merely placing yourself in another person's perspective, the problems of the piece become readily apparent and you can fix them with ease.

Or the audience can be much larger. Many times, having some kind of reading venue or publication in mind can focus your attention in a way that nothing else can. Many towns have open-mike readings in cafés or bookstores where beginning and experienced writers are invited to read their work to an audience. If you are brave enough to commit yourself to reading one night, you will find yourself in a fever of revision, reading the piece aloud many times and getting every word just right. Or, you might decide that you're ready to start sending your work out for publication. Find one journal and read as many copies as you can, then revise your piece with this publication in mind. You'll surprise yourself with the focus you can generate once the piece leaves the personal arena and goes public. (See Chapter 16 for more details on the publication process.)

Three Quick Fixes for Stronger Prose

After you've done the hard labor on your essay, you'll want to do the finish work, the small things that make the prose really shine. (We don't mean to suggest these two processes are mutually exclusive; naturally you will find yourself adjusting the prose as you go along.) We have three quick fixes that make any piece stronger: "search and destroy," "the adjective/adverb purge," and "the punch."

Search and Destroy

The most overused verbs in the English language are variations of *to be*—these include *is, are, were, was,* and so forth. While these verbs are necessary (note how we just used one of them in this and the previous sentence), often you can sharpen your prose by going over the piece carefully and eliminating as many of them as you can. To do this you will need to look closely at the words surrounding the *to be* verbs; often you can find a stronger verb to take its place or a more juicy noun. Even when you eliminate an *is* here or a *was* there, the resultant prose will seem much cleaner and lighter. It's the kind of work the reader won't notice directly (except for word nuts like us), but it will immediately professionalize your prose.

Take a draft of an essay that is nearly finished. Go through it and, with a red pen, circle all the *to be* verbs. Go back and see if you can rework any of those sentences to replace them with verbs that feel more "muscled," have more impact to them. Sometimes you'll find you don't need the sentence at all, and you'll have eliminated some deadweight. If you're working in a group, exchange essays with one another and do the same thing. Suggest new lines that eliminate the *to be* verbs.

The Adjective/Adverb Purge

Often, adjectives can be your enemy rather than your friend. Adjectives or adverbs can act as crutches, holding up weak nouns or verbs, and they actually water down your prose rather than intensify it. As with the search-and-destroy exercise, the point here is not to eliminate adjectives and adverbs altogether, but to scrutinize every one and see if it's necessary for the point you want to get across.

Take an essay you think is nearly finished and circle every adjective and adverb. Go back and see if you can rework the sentences to eliminate these words and replace them with stronger verbs and/or nouns. Or you can take stronger measures. For at least one writing session, ban adjectives and adverbs from your vocabulary. See how this exercise forces you to find more vivid nouns and verbs for your prose.

The Punch

Professional writers develop a fine ear for language. Writers are really musicians, aural artists attuned to every rhythm and nuance of their prose. And when you study the writers you admire, you'll invariably find that they tend to end most of their sentences, all of their paragraphs, and certainly the closing line of the essay, with potent words that pack a punch. They do not allow their sentences to trail off but close them firmly and strongly, with words that leave the reader satisfied. When you work toward strong closing words in your sentences, the prose also takes on a new sense of momentum and trajectory, the sentences rearranging themselves in fresh ways to wield that satisfying "crack."

Read your essay aloud, paying attention to the sounds of the words at the ends of sentences and paragraphs. Do they ring clearly and cleanly, firmly ending your thought? Or do they trail off in abstraction? Circle any words that seem weak to you; then go back and rework these sentences for better closing effects. Pay particular attention to the word you use to end the entire essay. How do you leave your reader? What will he remember?

An Example of the Writing Process

We asked the writer Bernard Cooper for his thoughts on the writing process. Here is what he had to say:

> A friend of mine once said that she needed two things in order to write: paper, and Liquid Paper. This was before she used a computer, of course, but I think her statement illustrates the importance of revision, the necessity to change and perfect what one has written down. I edit relentlessly—have already revised this very statement. My prose itself tends to come in short bursts, while the bulk of my time is involved in trying different words and sentence structures and punctuation so those word-bursts say exactly what I want them to. Revision seems to me the writer's most crucial task; you are given the chance to make your work as powerful as possible. "Words are all we have," said novelist Evan Connell, "and they'd better be the right ones." Anyone who has written for long knows the pleasure in finding the word that makes a description suddenly more vivid, or finding the structure that makes a sentence more taut, surprising, rhythmic, or funny.

When you write well, revision becomes not a chore, but the essence of the writing act itself. What came before cleared the way for what is to come; no writing is ever wasted, no time spent at the desk useless. Writing creates its own rhythm and momentum, and you must be willing to go with it, to become absorbed in the task, to let go of the writing you once thought precious. It's exhausting work, requiring stamina and rigor, but the rewards keep you going.

At one time or another, many writers experience what they call "gifts"—essays or poems or stories that seem to come effortlessly, full-blown onto the page with little revision or effort. But as the poet Richard Hugo put it, "Lucky accidents seldom happen to writers who don't work. . . . The hard work you do on one poem is put in on all poems. The hard work on the first poem is responsible for the sudden ease of the second. If you just sit around waiting for the easy ones, nothing will come. Get to work."

The Writing Life

Time, motivation, money: all these things can be important in sustaining a writing life, one in which you can create unexpected raw work, as well as spend the time necessary for detailed revision.

Time: For focused, intensive writing time, consider applying for a residency at a writers' or artists' colony. Most of these provide time and space for writing at no or nominal charge (including meals). Besides the benefit of sustained writing time, you also will meet other writers and artists who will inspire and support your work. Lists of retreat centers can be found at www.awpwriter .org and www.pw.org. You can also, of course, create your own retreat for a day, a weekend, a week, or longer by renting a place by yourself or ideally with others. Vacation rentals by owner (VRBO) is an excellent resource for finding reasonably priced rentals: http://www.vrbo.com.

Many writers these days are also creating "virtual retreats": a group agrees to spend anywhere from a day to a weekend with a predetermined writing schedule and goals; each member checks in regularly via e-mail or on a blog with what has been accomplished. National Novel Writing Month (November) and National Poetry Writing Month (April) have also become popular ways to motivate oneself to write intensely. Participants in these challenges pledge to write a novel in a month or a poem a day, respectively. Imagine what your version of such an Olympic writing challenge in nonfiction might be: a short-short essay a day? Two rough drafts a week? Have your group share results, with an agreement of no critique (critique tends to stifle the muse in rapid writing stints), and you may be delightfully surprised with your stamina and at least some of your results.

Money: Grants do exist to help support your writing. There are clearinghouse sites to find grants for writers, such as http://www.fundsforwriters.com/grants .htm. Often there are fairly large grants available for specific types of writers (younger writers, certain ethnic groups, religion, geographic region, etc.). Bigger grants, such as the NEA ($25,000), the Guggenheim, The Whiting Foundation ($30,000), the Lannan Foundation, and the Rona Jaffe Award ($25,000) exist, but they require you to establish your work in literary journals first. Many of these you can't even apply for, but anonymous panelists nominate your work. So you need to have your work out there in the public eye.

Motivation: You might consider creating a writing group to provide motivation and deadlines (see Chapter 15, "Sharing Your Work"). Or you might consider investing in additional schooling. MA, MFA, and Ph.D. programs provide you with the time, motivation, community, and sometimes money to write. On the *Tell It Slant* website, we provide the document "MA, MFA, and Ph.D.: What's the Difference?," which explains the benefits of various graduate creative writing programs, such as studio MFA's, low-residency MFA's, Ph.D.'s with a creative dissertation, and MA's in publishing.

TRY IT

1. Take a writing session to observe everything you do around writing. What is your routine? How does it serve or sabotage you? What keeps you from writing? What helps you? What happens when you change your routine?

2. Do you have an inner critic that immediately censors or criticizes your writing? Take a piece of paper and draw a line down the center. On the right side of the paper, begin writing, perhaps from one of the writing exercises in Part 1. On the left side, write down any critical thoughts that come to mind as you write. (Don't worry if the session becomes only critical thoughts; it happens all the time!) Do this for about five or ten minutes, then go back and read what the critic has to say to you.

   On a new sheet of paper, begin a dialogue with your inner critic. How does the critic both enable and sabotage your writing? For example, you may realize that the critic is merely trying to protect you from the harsh criticism the world might heap on you; rather than a hostile presence, the critic may actually be quite benevolent.

3. Take out a piece you wrote at least a month ago. Read it aloud, either to yourself or to a kind audience. Make note of the paragraphs that feel full and rich and those that are not as strong. Are there any areas that surprise you? What is the essay *really* about? What can be cut out and saved for another time? What needs to be included that was left out at first?

Here are some specific questions to ask yourself as you go about the global revision process:

- Is there one image that can be used as a cohesive thread throughout the piece? How can you amplify this image and transform it from beginning to end?
- Have you chosen the most effective point of view for telling the story? What happens when you experiment with third person? Second person?
- Look closely at the beginning paragraph of your essay. Do you begin in a way that draws the reader in? Often, the first few paragraphs of a rough draft act as "clearing the throat." Is the true beginning really a few pages in?
- Look closely at the end of the essay. Do you end in a way that leaves the reader with a compelling image? Often it's tempting to "sum up" the essay in a way that can be wholly unsatisfying to the reader. Can you end on an image rather than an idea?
- How do the beginning and ending paragraphs mirror or echo one another? The first and last paragraphs act as a frame for the piece as a whole. They are, in a way, the most important places in the essay, because they determine everything that happens in between. If you make an effort to connect them in some way—repeating a key image from the beginning, bringing back on stage the major players for a final bow—you will find a stunning finish to the piece.

4. Make a plan for yourself about your future writing life. What would you do if you could devote time and money to writing? What is your wildest dream?

Next, break this down into steps you can take to fulfill at least part of that dream. Consider starting small, maybe even just writing a "contract" with a friend for a certain amount of writing per week. You'll be amazed at how much motivation such a small step can create.

15

Sharing Your Work: The Writing Group and Workshop

The fiction that artistic labor happens in isolation, and that artistic accomplishment is exclusively the provenance of individual talents, is politically charged and, in my case at least, repudiated by the facts. While the primary labor on *Angels* has been mine, more than two dozen people have contributed words, ideas and structures to these plays.

—Tony Kushner

I have just received a joyous e-mail from my friend Dan, telling me he has placed his latest manuscript with a university press he admires. It is an outpouring of both personal and group pride. My husband and I have been part of Dan's writing life for more than a decade, since the two of us met him in graduate school. That was fourteen years ago.

Originally, a group of six graduate students comprised our workshop. I can't remember whose casual suggestion it was that we begin meeting in a special room in a Charlottesville tavern that's always been something of a grad student hangout. The small room holds old Moët & Chandon Champagne posters crammed on every wall, curvy Art Deco women holding bottles. Each piece we put up for discussion we distribute the week before and talk about for twenty minutes to half an hour. The feedback is smart, bracing, encouraging. We find both value in everything and room for the writing to flower into something even finer. And, of course, there's always time for chat and catching up before and after the workshop part of our get-togethers. In addition to our workshop meetings, we soon celebrate each other's successes, throw each other parties, help each other search out publication venues.

Now, almost a decade and a half later, we have mail and e-mail. We still share our work, albeit less regularly and much more slowly. We still feel a kudo for one of us is a kudo for the group, as we have nurtured, edited, and prodded each other for much of our writing careers. Between us we've gone from beginners at the art of literary writing to having published twelve books. And all of us know, as Dan's e-mail shows, we couldn't have done it alone.

—SUZANNE

The Need for Feedback

Tony Kushner, in the quote introducing this chapter, states the case strongly but not, we think, too strongly. Writers need feedback. The myth of writers as loners who follow their vision and remain true to their inner muse, bucking rather than embracing outside help, is very much a myth. It was created largely by the writers of the British Romantic period, whose artistic mythologies we still cling to, though those writers themselves used one another unceasingly as idea sources and sounding boards. Virtually all writers do. "I write," said Terry Tempest Williams, "in a solitude born out of community."

The modern writing workshop or writing group is not an innovation but a form of learning that can be traced back as long as literature and the arts have flourished. You can use this chapter to find ways to create your own workshop group—one with members you trust, who can grow with you and your work—or to get the most productive working relationship you can out of a classroom workshop or an established writing group. Even if this desire seems improbable now, trust us: if you keep writing, you will want caring and responsive readers.

Setting Guidelines for Discussion: A Practice Approach

In the following section on learning to give useful responses, we will provide very specific suggestions for shaping workshop discussion. You may use or adapt these as your group sees fit. For now, it is a good idea to have a preliminary talk with your peers about what does or does not work for you as a group in receiving feedback. You can and should discuss the entire process of workshopping, come up with a procedure, and devise your own workshop etiquette—a collective sense of what is OK and not OK in talking about your writing. Logistical questions to discuss include how far in advance you will share your work, whether you will read pieces aloud at any point, and whether you want to include written comments or limit yourself to oral critique. If you are doing this as a workshop leader or teacher, consider having the group create a specific "contract" that you will all try to follow.

It is essential to find a method of discussion with which the group feels safe and comfortable; don't flounder around trying to shape your valuable writing without first defining what helps you. To guide this process, find an essay, perhaps from a literary magazine, for practice. Read the piece and offer comments as you would in a workshop setting, and together monitor the discussion for responses that seem diminishing, unconstructive, or unhelpful.

You may want to ask the group to rule out feedback based on "I do like," "I don't like" formulas. These are by their very nature subjective comments and hard to use in the revision process. One way to train ourselves out of the "I like, I don't like" reflex is to begin the discussion by using the phrase "I notice" instead. For example, "I notice the image of the maple tree recurs three times in the essay," or "I notice the strong connection between the dog and the woman," or "I notice the momentum of your sentences." By noticing, instead of judging right away, the reader allows the writer to hear what stands out in the piece, and to hear it in a way that does not automatically flatter or degrade the writer. It takes away some of the emotional energy—both positive and negative—that can get in the way of a writer really absorbing what the reader sees in his or her piece. Once several readers have "noticed" what is happening in your piece, you will get an in-depth sense of what stands out and what has not yet emerged. Your respondents can then go on to explicate the meaning or theme they see developing in the things they noticed, and how these images or scenes or sentences can lead to fruitful revisions.

All of you together can watch out for unhelpful critical language— "stinks," "lame," "one cliché after another." Of course we don't advocate only praise; those words probably do hold suggestions for revisions that need to be made. What's important is that you work together as a group to find more constructive approaches. "This doesn't come up to the level of the rest of the essay," "I'm not seeing this scene yet," or "The language here could be more original" might be suitable comments to replace the offending ones.

Even when you hear responses that feel appropriate, use this practice session to sharpen them. If someone says he or she can't quite get a feel for a character, question why that is and try to formulate the most specific response possible. "I can't quite see David because he's never described and never speaks until you find him crying in the kitchen." Try reformulating your feedback comments two and three times to make them as specific as possible. Practice together until you feel good about one another's feedback style and the comments flowing from your discussion feel supportive, encouraging, and full of ideas to take back to your writing desk.

The Agenting Approach

One workshop strategy we have had great success with is the agenting approach. It is a role-play method. All the members of the writing group agree to function as one another's literary agents for the duration of the group.

Literary agents take on their author-clients because they believe in them. Agents feel certain they can sell their clients' essays and books. They derive their income from sales of their authors' work, so their faith in their authors is concrete and tangible. At the same time, agents become valuable critics and editors. They must bring their clients' work to the publishing market in its finest possible form.

As literary agents, then, you believe absolutely in one another and in the value of the group members' writing, and the fact that it can be brought to a final, polished form worthy of publication. At the same time you have an interest in making the essay or book extract the best it can be. And so you will provide substantial encouragement and substantial feedback.

As an agent your comments are always couched in terms like, "I think this will really work once the dialogue feels more authentic/Jack has a fuller character/we know where Luke ended up." Like an agent, you will always begin your responses by citing what *does* work, and, where appropriate, providing ideas for transferring that success to less polished parts of the essay.

When beginning this approach, it can help to write out comments in the form of letters—the type of communication you'd likely get from a literary agent. These letters will begin with an affirmation of your faith in your client;

a summary of what works well in the piece; and a careful, detailed listing of what needs to be addressed before the piece is finally ready. These letters can be used to fuel discussion and passed to the author at the end of a workshop session. A wonderful side benefit of the agenting approach can be, when you reach a phase in your group relationship where lots of revision has taken place, you can decide to devote an hour or two to browsing at the periodical section of a bookstore or a library or looking online to find suitable publication venues for one another's work. (See Chapter 16.)

Here are a few more guidelines to consider.

- Don't be subjective or start talking about your own experience unless there's a specific reason to, such as an expert knowledge you can add to the work at hand. ("I've worked at an emergency room and I don't think it would be painted bright pink," not "I've worked at an emergency room; isn't it weird?")
- When you give praise, see if you can add even more to your comment by suggesting another place where the same writing tactics can help the essay. Do provide revision suggestions freely, along with support and encouragement. The other side of the workshop coin from the pick-it-all-apart session is the lovefest, which ultimately disrespects the writer's ability to bring his work to a higher level, and does him no good.

Remember always that as you give to others in your group, you will get back. You have a deep commitment to their growth as writers and to the productive workings of the group as a whole, so always act accordingly. Also, we often learn the most about our own writing while listening carefully to critiques about someone else's work. What is true for that person struggling with a satisfying ending is probably true for you as well. Don't assume that the only time you learn anything is when your own piece is up for discussion.

Some Useful Workshop Guidelines

Here are a few tips for making the group work.

- **Agree to distribute copies of writing to be workshopped no less than forty-eight hours in advance of your meeting.** Provide clean, typed copies, not handwritten ones that will be hard to read professionally. Even with all the goodwill in the world, things come up, and with less than two days to prepare comments, members will come in scanning the essays as they go, a frustrating experience for reader and author. Consider using an online venue for distributing your work. Google or Yahoo Groups, Dropbox, Blackboard, or an e-mail list are all easy ways to ensure everyone gets copies in time, and some readers will also appreciate being able to make typed comments directly on the manuscript.

• **Set an amount of time you will spend on each essay, with a five- or ten-minute degree of flexibility.** Twenty minutes to half an hour usually works.

• **Have one of you agree to facilitate the discussion.** Facilitating means making sure the conversation stays within or lasts until the assigned period. Facilitators can also throw out topics or questions as necessary (each piece under discussion can have a different facilitator). We remember one poorly run graduate workshop in which the instructor simply allowed the group to go on as little or as long as it liked, leading to discussions that ranged anywhere from five minutes to an hour. That's a frustrating, insulting experience for an author, so agree in advance to monitor your time and keep comments on track. If you are the facilitator of the group, you can decide whether to guide each discussion or to assign others to lead for one another.

One method we've found useful for some mature groups is to have the teacher or leader hold off on making comments on the manuscript itself or during the workshop, but instead to take on the role of "scribe," writing down as much as possible during the discussion, being the impartial observer on behalf of the writer. Then, after the workshop, the leader can write up a summary of what she heard, as well as revision suggestions based on the group's comments and her own opinion. For example, she can couch responses with phrases such as, "I heard many voices saying _____ , while others disagreed and felt the most important part of the essay was _____ . You have a few choices here in how to revise." In this way, the writer—who is often too nervous or overwhelmed to clearly hear what is being said—can relax, knowing another is listening carefully. This technique also models how to begin sifting through comments and dealing with contrary opinions, understanding that there is always more than one way to approach revision. The writer must learn how to both trust his own intuition and take guidance from others.

This method also gives the teacher or leader a chance to think about his or her own response in light of the group's feedback, and by doing so validates the democratic nature of group discussion. The leader is often a privileged responder, which can make the group members lax in their own feedback; by sitting back and taking on the role of invested listener, facilitators empower the group process itself and may also hear responses that shift their own perception of the piece.

Small-Group Versus Large-Group Workshops

The workshop approach we have described works well in a group of eight to fourteen people; often, at the high school or college level—or in a larger community group—your class sizes are likely to be much larger. You can still choose to do a whole-class workshop, but one way to help modulate the responses is to have every other person in the circle respond directly to the writer (it is helpful to structure the discussion loosely on the "Workshop Checklist" later in this chapter), varying the order for different questions.

Another way to approach discussion is to break the group down into smaller workshop circles. The advantage to this method is that all participants will be heard and will feel more free to speak; the writers all gain a certain amount of trust and understanding with one another over time. The disadvantage, of course, is that the leader cannot oversee each discussion group. Leaders can offset this by handing out workshop guidelines ahead of time and by assigning each person in the group to be the "advocate" for one other person in the group. This advocate is responsible for ensuring that the discussion stays on track, that the group answers the writer's questions, and that a positive, helpful atmosphere takes precedence. Leaders might consider varying small-group with large-group workshops to provide a variety of responses.

A Workshop Checklist

In addition to the general suggestions outlined earlier, here is one intuitive way to read an essay to be discussed. We suggest you use the following questions when you read, picking and choosing as seems appropriate, rather than marching through them one by one in the group. Facilitators can also keep this checklist handy as a way of sparking conversation when it begins to lag.

1. Jot down the scenes, descriptions, and images that stick with you: the "Velcro words and phrases," as writer and teacher Sheila Bender puts it. Put the essay down and make note of the first thing you remember about it. Generally these passages are the ones that not only are the best written, but the most key to what the essay is doing at a deep level.

2. Identify the emotional tones of the essay and its prose. You may sense the pleasure of a friend's visit, of a hike, the anxiety of sentences that all begin with "I think" or "I believe." Do you get the sense of overformality in a phrase like "I am perturbed"? Do you wonder why the author calls her mother by the definite article, "the mother"? Does it feel somewhat chilly? In all cases, are these feelings ones the author intended to convey, or do they seem unintentional and perhaps working against the movement of the essay?

3. Identify your curiosity. Make note of where specifically you want to know more. "I want to know more about that distant definite-article mother," "about that feeling of perturbation in the pit of the stomach," "about the author's uncertainty," "about the rest of the family," and so forth. Which locations/characters would benefit from more description? Which characters' voices do you want to hear? Where do you want to know more about the author's responses and feelings? These curiosities help locate places for expansion.

If you need help going deeper with your comments, here are some **content questions** to consider:

- What is the organizing force of the essay, and does it sustain the piece? If this essay has a clear narrative (a story to tell), is the story clear? If it is a lyric essay organized around images, do the images keep it going?
- Are characters effectively presented and fully developed?
- Is dialogue believable, important to the overall essay, and used where it needs to be? Does it help shape character?
- Are there places where exposition should be replaced by scene for greater reader involvement or scene replaced by exposition for greater compression?

- Is the point of view working well? Would it help to try another point of view, e.g., substitute first person for second?
- If this is a meditation or essay of ideas, is there an ideology behind it? Is it presented clearly? Is it presented in a way that respects the reader, rather than becoming preachy or heavy-handed?
- Are the images used fresh and interesting? Do they work together in a way that supports the essay?
- Is the language fresh throughout, avoiding sentimentality and cliché?

Here are some **form questions** to keep in mind:

- Does the form of the essay add to/enhance its content?
- Is the organization effective? Look closely at elements such as collaging, the use of white space "jumps" between material, and whether the piece's organization is purely chronological, following the order in which events happened, or something else.
- Does the piece begin and end in a way that feels satisfying? Note that "satisfying" does not necessarily mean providing closure, or full answers to any questions it might raise. Does the essay open in a way that makes you want to keep reading, and end in a way that provides some sort of aesthetic stopping point?

These samples will help you with **diction questions**:

- Does the language seem appropriate to the subject? Is it at times overly fussy or formal or overly slangy and flip?
- Does the essay contain any archaic or outmoded language—a trap we all fall into in literary writing—that doesn't belong?
- Are the sentence structures and rhythms appealing and effective?

You might also look back to Chapter 14, "The Writing Process and Revision," and think about feedback in terms of "global" versus "local" responses. Train yourself to begin with "big picture" responses: What is the piece *really* about for you? What theme or idea seems interesting, ripe for future development? What connections are being made in an original way? What one image really stood out for you? Why? Then shift your group's feedback to more "local" concerns, looking at what can be cut, what can be modified, what can be added, and what can be moved around.

Creating Your Own Writing Group

The veteran publisher Stanley Colbert wrote, "Your journey to the best-seller list begins with a single reader." All of the people you come in contact with who share your interest in writing and literature are resources for forming a writing group.

Who are your friends or acquaintances who love to write? If you've never talked with them about forming a response group, try it. Most writers spend their lonely writing time dreaming of an audience of enthusiastic readers—chances are, you will be proposing something they'll regard as a dream come true. If you're shy about your writing and find it hard to think about sharing it with your cat, let alone a group, try this. Look at the questions in the intuitive list, given previously in this chapter. Now think of a piece of your writing and imagine answers to those questions. Chances are the thought of hearing a list of your Velcro scenes and images, the places you've made a reader curious, will actually seem pretty pleasant.

The fact is, when we worry about sharing our work, we imagine ourselves handing an essay to someone and saying, "What do you think?" and standing, knees trembling, for the final judgment. Well, first of all, no one has the all-knowing literary judgment to do that (a contemporary of poet John Milton, author of *Paradise Lost*, wrote of him, "His fame is gone out like a candle in a snuff and his memory will always stink"). Second of all, delivery of verdicts is not what writing groups are for, and you should never let yours drift into that destructive habit. Remember, you can and should exert control about the feedback process, and talk about it as a group until you get it right.

Kate Trueblood, an author and teacher of writing, formed a group with three other writers she knew who seemed compatible. Though the group was friendly and supportive, the workshop did spend a few meetings having to fine-tune their discussion style. "At first it was a little jumbled and unfocused, and feelings were hurt," Kate remembers. The group communally generated a list of rules that's kept them going successfully for many years now. "We talk about what's successful first, then acknowledge amongst ourselves when we're moving to critique. We work from global issues to smaller issues. And each time we pass out a manuscript we designate what kind of feedback we want, and what stage the work is in."

If you don't know anyone interested enough or compatible enough to form a workshop group with you, you still have another excellent resource—your local bookstore. It's a well-kept secret that many bookstores have active writing groups that meet regularly and often welcome new members.

If you find your bookstore(s) does not have a workshop group, start one. Ask to speak to the store manager of a bookstore you like or, in a larger store, the community relations coordinator. These folks will generally help you, by posting signs and advertising in store newsletters and calendars, to find other folks in your community interested in sharing their writing. From the interviews we've done with bookstore personnel, the response will almost certainly be strong: there are a lot of writers seeking readers out there. From the bookstore's point of view, it's a way to lure literature lovers into their store on a regular basis. From your point of view, it's heaven: a group of peer reviewers, and a comfy place to meet.

Most of all, be excited about one another's work, and your own. Use your writing group as a place to generate writing as well as to critique it. Set aside time to create writing prompts together, or agree to try separately to tackle a difficult subject, providing each other support as you go along. Have writing time together with music that inspires you playing in the background. Meet at museums. Bring a piece of writing each week you've fallen in love with and share it, then talk about what it can teach you.

For many writers, an online writing group works very well, too, as it can bring in people who don't live in your area, as well as be adapted to everyone's schedule. This could be a generative writing group, where you give each other writing prompts (perhaps from this very book!) and deadlines, or it could be focused on providing feedback on work written on your own. Again, Google or Yahoo groups can be utilized quite effectively for this kind of virtual meeting place, as can a simple e-mail list or Listserv. Since you won't have the advantage of face-to-face conversation, it will be even more important to negotiate how you will respond to each other's work so that the nuances of personal communication online can remain positive and helpful. If it is a generative writing group, you might want to stay focused simply on "Velcro" phrases and images, speaking back to the reader the areas that seem rich with meaning and beauty. You might want to rotate the duties of facilitator so that there can be some order and cohesion in how you function together.

Remember that a group of writing friends once sat in the house during a thunderstorm and challenged each other to write a ghost or horror story, and then met again to share their efforts, one of which was Mary Shelley's classic *Frankenstein*. It was a book that would never have been created any other way.

16

Publishing Your
Creative Nonfiction

Essays end up in books, but they start their lives in magazines. (It's hard to imagine a book of recent but previously unpublished essays.) . . . The influential essayist is someone with an acute sense of what has not been (properly) talked about, what should be talked about (but differently). But what makes essays last is less their argument than the display of a complex mind and a distinctive prose voice.

—Susan Sontag, from her
Introduction to *The Best
American Essays, 1992*

It's 1993, and I've just received my copy of the *Georgia Review*, where my essay "A Thousand Buddhas" sits among the pages. It's my first acceptance by a national literary journal, and I can hardly believe it. It took a long time to write that essay, and even longer to figure out where to send it, to wait through the evaluation process, and then to work with the legendary editor, Stan Lindberg, over the phone. It's both thrilling and terrifying to finally see it in print.

It's 2011. I've submitted a piece to a journal using the online submission manager Submishmash. The program creates an account for me so that I can see where my submission is at every stage of the process. Within a week,

I have my answer from the editor, and a couple of weeks after that, the essay actually appears in the online edition. The process seems a little dizzying in its swiftness. And I'm still both thrilled and terrified to see the piece in print.

The publishing world has changed a lot in the last twenty years, but some things never change: the need to write the best creative nonfiction I can, and then to do the necessary work of finding it a good home—whether that home be in a traditional print journal or in a quality online publication. The writing process, for me, does not feel complete until I've sent the work out into the world to stand on its own.

—Brenda

Getting published involves more than just writing your best work; it means knowing where that work will get a good reception and how to revise so that the essay makes it past the eyes of the first readers. It means understanding the type of publication that might be receptive to your work: A literary journal? An online publication? A venue that can offer multimedia capabilities? Or perhaps what you have written belongs in a slick magazine like *Harper's*, a women-oriented magazine like *O* or *Elle*—both of which publish quality nonfiction—or a specialty magazine like the environmental slick magazine *Orion*. All of these venues are possibilities, but it is vital to learn how to gauge and approach your potential audience.

Once you start aiming toward publication, your writing will take on a new level of professionalism. You may find focus where before there was just a blur, or you'll finally figure out the dead prose that's slowing down your first paragraph. Think like an editor, with hundreds of essays crossing your desk or your computer every month: what will make your essay stand out from the crowd?

Publication Venues

Literary Journals

These journals are literary publications, generally but not always housed at colleges and universities, run by people who are in the business of publishing mostly because they love literature. They offer prestige, a small (around the low thousands, typically) but devoted readership, and exist on the low end of the payment scale. Acceptance rates are low, too, frequently 1 to 2 percent, and even fewer for very prestigious journals like the *Kenyon Review*. Literary journals often have particular editorial directions, such as *Image*, a journal of spirituality and the arts, or *Seneca Review*, which leans strongly toward the lyric essay. Some literary journals do print artwork and other media. It's important to read carefully as you select potential homes for your work.

The good news? You can develop warm, even mentoring relationships with editors of literary journals, who are passionate about great writing. Literary agents also read literary journals to get ideas about potential new clients whose writing they find exciting.

Online Journals

Online literary journals (sometimes called e-zines) are currently as important a venue for literary writers as print journals. Print journals tend to have readerships in the low thousands; online journals may average ten thousand or more "hits," or views, per issue. The difference is largely due to accessibility and reading habits on the web—most web users surf and sample many different websites. Finally, the cost of creating an online publication is minimal—you have to learn the programming, which isn't hard, and find a server that can accommodate your files. Most universities have servers students can request space on—two former students of ours, Jeremy Voigt and Jordan Hartt, started an online publication, *Arbutus*, that is still going strong. The low cost of start-up, however, means online journals frequently pay little to nothing.

The relative ease of creating an online publication means that there are many of them, and their quality varies somewhat more than that of print journals. Many of the online journals named at the end of this chapter, however, have published work that has been awarded Pushcart Prizes and inclusion in *Best American Essays* and *Best of the Web* anthologies.

There's a distinction between online publications that publish traditional print literature—posting it as it would appear on the page—and those that publish a mix of traditional print literature and hypertext. There are also online journals that publish only hypertext and hypermedia (more truly mixed-media works that may not include print). In the first category would be a quality online journal like *Brevity*, which publishes short—750 words or less—creative nonfiction. *Brevity* is housed on the website of the literary journal *Creative Nonfiction*, a site worth a look in and of itself: generally *Creative Nonfiction* has three or four essays posted, plus lots of news and discussion of the genre. In the second category would be journals like *TriQuarterly Online* and *Shadowbox*—whose formats encourage interactive reading—and in the third category would be *The New River*, a gold standard site publishing some of the best hypertext and hypermedia around.

Browse online journals using a site such as LitLine and the list hosted by Every Writer's Resource (see the list of websites at the end of this chapter). Enjoy the spirit and experimentation of this medium: streaming audio, streaming videos, art, even virtual communities are common. Let both your mind and your eye become engaged, and new possibilities will open for your own nonfiction.

The Slicks

Touch the cover of any of these magazines—a category that includes *Harper's*, *The Atlantic*, *The New Yorker*, and smaller specialty magazines like *Orion*—and you'll see how they got the name the "slicks." Glossy paper and visually alluring covers are part of the package these magazines offer, and they tend to have wide readerships. Much of the time, slick magazines contract for the articles they want, and they pay a "kill fee" if they ultimately choose not to run the article. Authors approach these magazines with "pitch letters" explaining the article or essay they wish to write in a few paragraphs. Editing tends to be heavy at these magazines, but pay is the best in the business: many slick magazines can offer payment of several thousand dollars per piece. Many slick magazines will also look at unsolicited writing, either overall or for particular departments of the magazine. To get this information, you need to read the magazines well enough to get a sense of their editorial voice, and visit their websites. The more prestigious slick magazines can be difficult, but certainly not impossible, to approach without a literary agent.

A final note: there are slick magazines like *The Sun* that function editorially as literary journals do, accepting a range of open submissions. Discovering these opportunities is one of the joys of wide reading.

Preparing for Publication

Read, read, read! Read publications that run quality creative nonfiction. Browse in the library, bookstores, and newsstands as well as on your computer. Send away for sample issues of magazines. Target your work to the markets most likely to publish your particular brand of nonfiction writing. This will save you time and money. Editors hate getting work that comes from writers who obviously have never even cracked the covers of one of their issues.

Visit the websites of your target publications and read the submission guidelines posted. These guidelines will let you know whether the publication prefers electronic or print submissions, and they give further details on how to submit, such as the publication's reading period—most do not read unsolicited material year-round—payment, and length limits. Also try the following link from the Association of Writers and Writing Programs' website for a list of quality literary journals: www.awpwriter.org/magazine/link7.htm. Look through resource books, such as the *CLMP Literary Press and Magazine Directory* or *Writer's Market*, to find out contact information.

More and more publications are using online submission services. Many use a service called Submishmash, which allows you to upload your work onto a host site for editors to consider. Online submission through services like Submishmash enables you to check in on your submission, drop the requirement for a prestamped self-addressed envelope, and even click a box to withdraw your work if it should be accepted elsewhere. Just because you are using online submission services, do not skip the cover letter! It should be as polished and complete as with a print submission.

Aim high, but not unrealistically so. It's important to start establishing a publishing history, so don't hesitate to send off to smaller, lesser-known journals. Getting your name out there in the publishing world will lead to greater and greater opportunities. Finally, look for contest and anthology submission opportunities. Good resources for these are *The Writer's Chronicle* (published bimonthly by the Associated Writing Programs) and *Poets and Writers* (published bimonthly, available in bookstores).

Elements of Your Submission

1. Your essay, polished to perfection, with extra care taken on the first and last paragraphs. There should be no typos, grammatical errors, punctuation

errors, messy print, or anything else that will undermine the professionalism of your work. Put your name, address, phone number, and e-mail address on the upper left-hand corner of the first page. Number the subsequent pages on the upper right-hand corner, using your last name as part of the header. Example: "Miller—2." For print submissions, do not staple; use clean paperclips.

2. Your cover letter. Use standard business format. Keep it short and simple. Avoid the impulse to be jokey or overly familiar. If you can offer sincere praise of the publication that shows you are a reader as well as a would-be author, do. Do *not* tell the editor what your essay is about! The essay should stand on its own.

3. A business-size self-addressed stamped envelope (SASE) for the magazine's response, for print submissions. If you want your manuscript returned, use a large enough envelope and sufficient postage.

For print submissions, put all these in a nine-by-twelve-inch manila envelope. Keep a record of your submissions, noting the date, the place sent, the title of the essay, and the result of the submission. Make sure you include in your log any online submissions you do as well; they can be easy to forget with it all happening at the click of a button.

Literary Agents

The function of literary agents tends to be something of a mystery for many writers, even for those well along in their careers. The fact is, many writers write and publish successfully without a literary agent. You should aim to work with a literary agent only if you feel you have a book project well under way, or have amassed excellent publication credentials, *and* you do not see yourself placing your work at a smaller, independent publisher or a university press. Agents exist to get your work placed at the larger publishing houses, many located in New York City, that pay substantial advances and publish books that they anticipate receiving substantial royalties. These are the publishing houses that exist, whatever individual editors may feel about literature, to earn money and maintain a healthy bottom line. Agents, too, earn their living by taking about 15 percent of their authors' earnings. In return for that, they talk up your work to editors they know and have a strong working relationship with, submit your work for you, and make sure your interests are represented when an offer comes along. Bear in mind that no reputable agent ever charges a "reading fee" or any fee other than what can be deducted from your advances and royalties, along with compensation (once the book is placed) for copying and messenger costs for the actual submission process.

Publishing a Book

If you think your writing might lead you to a book-length project, it's useful to know that many nonfiction books now—particularly the ones placed at the larger publishing houses—are sold on proposal. Writing a good book proposal has become an art in itself—proposals can range anywhere from twenty to forty pages long or longer and may take months to complete. Philip Gerard spent four months researching and writing the book proposal for *Secret Soldiers: The Story of World War II's Heroic Army of Deception*, a time commitment that's not unusual. Proposals take the reader through the narrative arc of the book itself and usually cite other books that have covered similar territory, establishing a sense of what the market for such a book would be like, as well as its possible competition. There are several examples of successful book proposals on the website for this book, along with an explanation of the components of the proposal.

As with publications of individual essays, book publications cover a variety of venues. There are the large, mostly New York–based houses that would include W.W. Norton, Knopf Doubleday, Penguin, Random House, Harper-Collins, and other imprints. These are the publishers that pay top dollar in advances and have access to the best publicity machines in the business, the kind that can get valuable TV and radio spots and take out prestigious and visible advertisements.

These large houses are, of course, the hardest publishers to get interested in your project, and the hardest to keep interested in you as an author: they publish books for the purpose of making money, and the fact is, in this competitive arena, the majority of books do not earn out their advance money. Large houses are also notorious for losing interest in a book and dropping publicity campaigns. With the exception of W.W. Norton, these publishers are owned by large conglomerates, so you may find that many prestigious book imprints—Viking, Penguin, Putnam, Tarcher—are all housed in the same company. When you try your manuscript with one editor in the conglomerate, the rejection is typically final; much of the time you cannot go back and try other editors in the firm. Agents are particularly qualified to know what editor in the maze of imprints owned by one publishing conglomerate would be best for your project.

Small Presses

You are not stuck if you cannot get a press like Knopf interested in your book. Small, independent presses and university presses publish books that win major awards and reach important audiences. These presses may not offer the same advance money as the larger houses, but they are less likely to overedit your work and more likely to commit to you as an author over the long term. Their marketing can be hit-and-miss; you should always check out how well any smaller publisher is able to distribute its books—actually get them into bookstores—as well as get them reviewed and advertised. It is not unusual for smaller houses to become passionately devoted to a nonfiction title and actually do superior marketing to a larger press.

There are many presses in this field, but to cite a few, the University of Georgia and University of Nebraska are publishing beautiful books in the field of creative nonfiction, and among independent presses, Graywolf Press and Sarabande Books are exemplary. Check out the information at the end of this chapter to find more university and small presses, and buy and read the books they produce.

Self-Publishing

Finally, a word on self-publishing. At one time publishing your own work through a so-called "vanity press" or subsidy publishing house of some type (meaning, you, the author, put some resources into the publishing process) was considered a sign of failure. But this is no longer the case: given the very tumultuous state of publishing in recent years, even bestselling authors like Steve Almond are making very public decisions to self-publish some or all of their literary work. In the current state of publishing, writers are often given the directive to do most of their own publicity anyway; with self-publishing, you can also enjoy all of the monetary fruits of your labor. Given that you, or a professional you hire, need to create your own publicity campaign, self-publishing works best with books that have a clear focus. You should also be prepared to put a reasonable sum of money into marketing your book, in addition to the publishing costs.

Successful self-published books are often picked up by publishing houses. Print-on-demand books, which can be published through a variety of venues, including Random House's self-publishing branch Xlibris and Amazon.com's BookSurge, are created only when a buyer wants to buy a book, thus eliminating the enormous fees for book distribution and book returns (the policy, going back to the Great Depression, whereby bookstores can return unsold books for full price to publishers). Services also exist, such as one offered by the prestigious review journal *Kirkus*, to review self-published books—the author pays *Kirkus* several hundred dollars for this service and reviews may be negative, but the point is, there are ways of getting your self-published book in front of an appropriate audience.

There are many online forums offering advice and how-tos for self-publishing. Start with www.selfpublishingreview.com.

A Final Note

It is wonderful—and a privilege—to think ahead to a lifetime of being a writer. Self-expression constitutes one of the great joys of life. And one of life's most common—and keenest—regrets remains, "I should have written it down." People lament not having written down their stories for a book-buying audience, for children and grandchildren, for others who have shared similar experiences, and ultimately for themselves. You, our reader, have this to look forward to: the fact that your own indelible imprint on the world can be captured in the nearly indelible medium of language, be it ink or pixel. You need to ask yourself the question of what you want your written legacy to accomplish, and set your publishing goals accordingly. All the while, keep in mind that most important of all, you are building the tools of self-expression you need to satisfy the one you most need to satisfy in life—you.

Following, we offer the resources you'll need to start out into the sometimes nail-biting, sometimes magical world of publishing.

First, here is a sample cover letter for a print submission:

March 6, 2012

Marcia Aldrich, Editor
Fourth Genre

Dear Ms. Aldrich:

I've enclosed the personal essay "The Road Home" for your consideration.
    My work has appeared or is forthcoming in _____ (and/or)
I am currently studying nonfiction writing with _____ .
    There is no need to return the manuscript, but I've enclosed an SASE for
your reply. Thank you for your time and consideration.

Sincerely,
Signature

Print your name, street address, phone number, e-mail address, and website address, if you have one, at the bottom of the page.
Here are some good markets for creative nonfiction:

Print
Another Chicago Magazine
Ascent
Bellingham Review
Boulevard
Calyx
Crab Creek Review
Creative Nonfiction
Cutbank
Fourth Genre: Explorations in Nonfiction
The Georgia Review
The Gettysburg Review
Gulf Coast
Harpur Palate
Hayden's Ferry Review

The Iowa Review
The Journal
The Kenyon Review
Michigan Quarterly Review
Mid-American Review
The Missouri Review
New Letters
The Normal School
The North American Review
Orion
The Packington Review
The Paris Review
Ploughshares
Prairie Schooner
River City
River Teeth: A Journal of Nonfiction Narrative
The Seattle Review
The Seneca Review
The Sewanee Review
Shenandoah
The Sun

Online
Agni Online (http://www.bu.edu/agni)
Brevity (www.creativenonfiction.org/brevity)
Evergreen Review (www.evergreenreview.com)
Narrative (www.narrativemagazine.com)
Shadowbox: A Showcase of Contemporary Creative Nonfiction
(http://www.shadowboxmagazine.org)
Superstition Review (http://superstitionreview.asu.edu/n7)
Sweet: A Literary Confection of Poetry and Creative Nonfiction
(www.sweetlit.com)
Thumbnail (www.thumbnailmagazine.com)
Timothy McSweeney's Internet Tendency (www.mcsweeneys.net)
TriQuarterly (www.triquarterly.org)

Web-Based Resources
- American Association of University Presses (http://www.aaupnet.org /aaup-members/membership-list) offers a listing of university presses.
- Association of Writers and Writing Programs (www.awpwriter.org) has links to numerous journals, magazines, and presses, as well as other useful information.
- Electronic Literature (www.eliterature.org) offers a portal site for a great deal of nonfiction published on the web.
- Every Writer's Resource offers an excellent list of literary publications and a wealth of other information (www.everywritersresource.com).
- LitLine (www.litline.org) contains many literary publishing listings.
- New Pages (www.newpages.com/book-publishers) offers a listing of independent presses.
- Poets and Writers (www.pw.org)
- Self-Publishing Review (www.selfpublishingreview.com)
- WritersNet (www.writers.net) offers a variety of useful resources and advice on everything from agents to freelance writing for writers looking to publish their work.

Print Resources
- *How to Write a Book Proposal*, by Michael Larsen
- *Literary Market Place*
- *Write the Perfect Book Proposal: Ten That Sold and Why*, by Deborah Levine Herman and Jeff Herman, presents ten actual book proposals that resulted in book deals, with analysis.
- *Writer's Digest*

Epilogue:
Last Words

Lately I've been reading the selected poems of William Stafford, which includes some of the poetry he wrote the year before he died. Stafford was in the habit of getting up every day at 4 A.M. He wrote, by hand, during the dark, quiet hours in his study. He wrote about the simple things, the small things, in a voice that carries with it that sense of early morning meditation.

I don't know if Stafford was cognizant of his approaching death (he was eighty years old, after all, and perhaps at some point we can no longer deny that particular specter at our door), but the poems written during those final days have the quality of "last words": stripped of artifice, speaking from a self that wants only to understand and be understood. These are poems that want us to pay attention—not to abstract ideas and philosophies, not to idle worries or regrets, but to the world as it unfolds before us, every minute, every day. And as I read these poems I'm thinking that all of our writing, perhaps, could be written with this kind of disposition: with the tenor of "last words," the essays we would leave behind if no further writing were possible.

—BRENDA

There is a certain kind of reading I know in advance I will find endlessly fascinating: historical diaries, letters, and the like—works like the seventeenth-century diaries of Samuel Pepys or the Civil War diaries of Mary Boykin Chesnut, which provided the inspiration for Ken Burns's epic film *The Civil War*. While both of these authors have historical moments in their diaries, what captures our imagination in their work is the sense of inhabiting the everyday in a time and place now gone: Pepys admiring the beauty of the king's mistress and fretting over a flooded basement, Mary Chesnut's feminist yearnings and tension with her husband. The quality of the writing draws us in with authors like Pepys and Chesnut, but their particular skill lies in understanding how to chronicle their lives with enough respect and focus to bring them headily close in our imagination.

It's hard to believe. Our lives—secret, banal, and full of Kleenexes and bus schedules as they are—form stepping-stones to the future and vital links to the past. What we have lived through and done will define the world as it exists hundreds of years from now. We are the only witnesses to this our time, which is as wondrous and banal as any moment in history, and which carries its full complement of world-changing events: wars fought, great art made, rights hard won. Value your own life and the experiences you've had: they are priceless. At the same time, learn to love the world you live in. Hike urban streets, mountain trails, or better yet, both. Go to places you've never thought of going before; talk to everyone you meet with the assumption that his life is just as interesting as yours. Fall in love, be passionate, and the stories of your time will be yours to tell.

—SUZANNE

Regaining Passion

Sometimes when you're in a writing class or studying writing intensively, it's easy to temporarily lose the passion that brought you to writing in the first place. It's easy to feel as though you've taken all the magic out of it, and you sit at your desk, bored or resistant, unable to find one thing worth writing about. Especially when you write creative nonfiction, it's easy to feel as though you've "used up" all your material, plumbed all your memories, reflected on everything there is to reflect about. Your mirror has lost its luster, your pen run dry of ink.

When this happens (and it happens to all of us), you must do whatever it takes to refill the well. This might mean just taking some time out to roam the city or spending a week on the couch with your favorite books and comfort food. It might mean making a date with your writing group or deciding to write poetry or fiction for a while instead. The important thing to remember is *it will come back*. Your passion for writing will always return, doubled in force, after its period of dormancy. The writing life is one of patience and faith.

As you've read through this book, you've received all kinds of writing prompts to trigger new work; you've read about techniques; you've learned a bit about the philosophical and ethical challenges of creative nonfiction. You've perhaps learned new ways to approach your own memories, research interests, and ideas. You've thought about preparing your work for the public eye. Now, with all this knowledge still settling inside your head, we will tell you one last thing:

Forget it all.

Don't forget it forever. But just forget it for now. Take a moment to be quiet in the space where you do your best work, at the time when the muses are most present. Try to remember what it's like to be a beginner; regain what the Zen masters call "beginner's mind," open to all possibility. When you're ready, we offer you this one last "Try It":

TRY IT

1. What are your "last words"? What would you write if you knew your time was up?

What Should I Read Now, and Where Can I Find It?

Read, read, read. Read everything—trash, classics, good, and bad, and see how they do it. Just like a carpenter who works as an apprentice and studies the master. Read! You'll absorb it. Then write. If it is good, you'll find out. If it's not, throw it out the window.

—WILLIAM FAULKNER

There's no getting around it. Reading and writing go hand in hand. You cannot be a good writer without also being a good reader. You *must* read widely, with the eye of a writer, engrossed not only in the plot or the characters or the descriptions, but attuned to the craft that makes these things come alive on the page. You read to hear other writers' voices, but you also read to tune up your *own* voice, to remember what gets you excited about writing in the first place. Through reading, you continually learn the craft all over again.

Throughout *Tell It Slant*, we refer to many fine essays to illustrate key points in writing creative nonfiction. Space and money prohibit the inclusion of those essays in this book, but we've compiled a list for you to keep in mind the next time you're prowling the bookstore or shopping online. You can find this list of individual essays and anthologies—along with detailed suggestions on how to use them—on the *Tell It Slant* website. Many of these readings are available online as well as in print. This is by no means a comprehensive accounting of great creative nonfiction! Such a list would be long and wide, but we hope to give you at least a place to begin. Meanwhile, we offer an essay by each of us (in the "Sample Essays" section) to illustrate our thoughts on process and say welcome to the community of writers.

Sample Essays

The Hazing of Swans
Suzanne Paola

Every year they come back, along with the wind and other hunkered-down survivors of November. Trumpeter swans don't come because of the wind, or on it, but, I suppose, in spite of it. They come in November to the place I live, the northernmost, westernmost tip of Washington State—Bellingham; Skagit and Snohomish counties below us; and the abutting Sumas Plain in British Columbia.

When I first saw trumpeter swans, a Seattle friend called and told us to meet her on a Skagit County road. My husband and I went for the outing, watching with binoculars as the swans bobbled along. We had lived in the area eight years but somehow never heard of them, though they're the proverbial rare bird, desirable to see, and 75 percent of the trumpeter swan population winters here. The swans, hard to find, prove hard to miss when found: they're the country's largest water bird, topping out at 35 pounds. They roost in marshes and lakes but come inland to feed; we saw them in a field off a country road. The birds shoveled their black beaks in the muck, slinking their necks to swallow, or just sat. Swans can be great slackers. Unless they've spent time in a tannic marsh, which tints them a little red, their white is extremely pure, their necks curved as question marks, oval heads sunk on that long arc intestineward. All-grace at rest but graceless up. When swans walk it's like seeing a piece of your grandmother's ceramic collection rise and waddle.

Our sons, mine and my friend's, hung on the chain link fence, too high. Don't kill yourselves, I said unthinkingly, then, please *look*.

The boys found both self-preservation and swan-watching equally unworthy. Finally we all went off to eat oysters.

223

It's a testament to the natural hardiness of the trumpeter swans that they fly here now, with the weather's switch from summer's high placid to windstorm. A storm blew two weeks ago; we watched the crazed churn of leaves, branches and the occasional shingle through the windows, obeying the Weather Service warning to stay in. Most people injured by the wind have flying limbs crash into them or their cars. The wind blustered, forty miles an hour sustained, gusts up to one hundred. A roof sheared off. Last year my neighbor's weeping silver birch, an ancient tree, split down the middle and began to crash in my direction as I went numb, admiring the rich streak of heartwood the tree exposed, veering toward me. The birch turned and sank on the fence between our houses.

When my husband and I moved here in the fall, we said *eldritch*. Eldritch tonight, as the wind rattled the trees, the house: those cages we didn't recognize without the wind's touch. Eldritch means weird, supernatural, uncanny—that state so beloved of Freud—and it comes to mind every time we perch on the couch watching our roof blow away, especially as we live just off an avenue with almost the same name, Eldridge, over which the wind climbs to get to us. Crows always try to fly in this weather, and end up stalled, wings out, above the trees.

The wind put the fear of God into my son when he was younger—I lay with him in his room under the eaves, sleepless together, in the blow.

What is that, he said, of the branches pounding on the house.

Nothing, I told him, the wind, a reassurance only literally true.

The eldritch or uncanny, *unheimlich* in German, obsessed Freud, though he confessed he didn't appreciate the sense of it. ("The writer of the present contribution must himself plead guilty of obtuseness in the matter," Freud wrote in his great work "The Uncanny.") Perhaps he simply lived in the wrong place. I say that a bit less than facetiously, as Freud discussed the uncanny in terms of home—the German heimlich, most simply, means of the home, domestic, but in an odd secondary meaning it means secretive, closed off, fearfully homey. The unheimlich, wrote Freud, is that class of the fearful leading back to what is known of old and long familiar. The heimlich and unheimlich intertwine, "two words that develop such ambivalence they finally coincide with their opposite," as Freud wrote. He may have needed a weirder home than repressed Vienna, with its file of mother-obsessed, dreamy neurotics.

When the storm's all over—which may be a day or two—we go forth and gather up. Neighbors pull limbs from the street; cars get diverted. We glean the squares of our roof, wondering if eight, ten, fourteen fewer shingles will be a bad thing. Our neighbor rebuilds the fence. Over the last ten years the windstorms have become more frequent and more violent, in the rhythm of erratic global weather. Our friend Connie got concussed by her car door, just trying to get out. A door of our outbuilding pulled off and flung itself across the yard, not at the hinges, but down the middle. It's a chicken-wire life we live. At least in November.

In all this, the swans come back, to their version of a Florida getaway. Carpeting the sides of the road, when you find them, along with the snow geese. It's easy when you're driving and using peripheral vision to wonder if you've hit on a strange storm. Not long ago—a blip in historical terms—we would have been shooting them to use their bodies: skin for powder puffs, quills for pens, feathers for fine ladies' millinery. Or flesh for a bit of sustenance meat. Considered extinct and now back again, the swans have a magic for us, who live in fellowship with all who rise and fall from the species dead: the salmon we doggedly breed in little jars, then slip into the water; the whales who pass by twice a year; sea lions; pods of orcas; golden eagles; all endangered, beings who seem to live with one fin or claw in the next world. We have our Lazaruses, like the bald eagle, highly endangered when my husband and I moved here sixteen years ago, now merely a threatened species, and a bird we see all the time.

I think this age may be intrinsically uncanny, maybe here in the maritime Northwest more than elsewhere. Most of the reading world knows we live in an era of unprecedented (without an outside event like an asteroid) extinction: a median estimate from Conservation Watch is that a quarter of the globe's species will be gone by 2050, in forty years. Everyone lives within this erosion, but I see the larger, iconic faces of it: whales, eagles, falcons, spotted owl. A horned puffin fills my eyes one day, and I know that hair follicle shiver folklore calls *someone stepping on a grave*. Not for the puffin, a slick, comic guy with tuxedo feathers and huge orange bill: like a Venetian carnival character in dress clothes and a mask. It's just knowing that this image, slipped into my eyes when I'm thinking about, say, dinner, is one I will probably never see again. My son will probably never see it, or my son's children. By then, there may be no horned puffins. How would it feel to see the last few passenger pigeons zip down in front of you?

Cars arrive, where I live, from everywhere in spring and summer: they want to look at what is left.

In recent years a dead fin whale and a dead gray whale washed up, on their sides in their pier-heavy barnacles. The dead gray flopped, half in and half out of the water, a mile from my house, at the foot of a plant that made toilet tissue and, on the side, lots of mercury to pour into the bay. (My students used to argue about the exact image they would use for the odor of that plant—sulphur, bad ham.) The gray stayed for a week before disposal, working its way slowly onto the beach as the tide rocked it up.

That whale I visited every day, enjoying the new flipper, the new patch of barnacles or kelp unveiled on a tidal tease from its lace. It felt almost chummy. First the face, undifferentiated from the rest of it, except for a propped eye and long downturn of mouth. The grays have repopulated some and are no longer critical; a judge even granted a local tribe the right to hunt them again. The population has reached 20,000, give or take a few, still, it seems to me, a shaky number. (Three hundred grays swim the coast of Korea, stubbornly clinging to existence; none remain in the Atlantic, that whale-road of the Anglo-Saxons.) As I try on twenty thousand, I come up with an American small town, a mid-sized university. The number one, I felt as I considered that body, put a dent in the overall, making 19,999, a different sort of number altogether. It's not like taking one out of six billion, as in us, humanity.

On a recent trip to the Olympic peninsula my husband and son built sand forts to see them get licked away and I walked along a huge spit, narrow enough to toss a beach ball from one side to the other. I saw the puffin there. A group of Pacific brants swam: a small, pretty goose with a white chinstrap also under watch due to its dwindling population, its habit of migrating yearly from the Canadian tundra to the same eroding spot in Baja California.

I relaxed on the ferry to the peninsula with *In Touch* and *People*. I love these magazines but have a guilty sense I ought to read something smarter, so I hoard them for moving vehicles: ferries, planes. I read how Jennifer Lopez and Marc Anthony just had twin babies. (The astonishingly rich couple, smooth-faced and tinted, had sold the right to take the first photographs of their babies—wrinkled, larval, hard to imagine emerging from the parental gleam—to *People* for six million dollars.) The article highlighted the babies' sumptuous lives: newborn outfits of cashmere and real fur tucked around their seam-eyed, puffed faces, enameled strollers worth thousands and thousands of dollars, diamond pacifiers. If time fluctuated just a little, these babies, scrunched and out of it, might wear trumpeter swan-skin onesies, be rubbed with ambergris oil. Perhaps the singer/actress's couture hospital gowns would have been covered with white feathers.

In 1999, the trumpeters fell into a sustained and inexplicable, an unheimlich, dying. Hundreds of dead swans have appeared, four hundred one year, three hundred the next. Landowners find bodies frozen in iced ponds, apparently unable to keep swimming. On land the swans collapse in on themselves in a soft spiral, beak to the side, dying slowly and balletically, like Anna Pavlova performing *The Dying Swan*.

A species already on the imperiled list, swans were autopsied by teams of state biologists and found full of lead: shot from shotguns, once used to hunt fowl, with the odd fishing sinker thrown in. Swans, like all birds, swallow pellets and break them down in their gizzards to grind food; in the process, the lead leaks into the swans' bloodstream, causing paralysis, starvation and asphyxia. It probably takes just one to two pieces of shot to kill them, but autopsied swans have had as many as eight hundred.

I wonder what Anna Pavlova would think if I put her here, in her lush hats and outfits, maybe with Jack, her pet swan, beside her. She loved the birds and made the *Dying Swan* her signature dance; not a great work, as critics point out, because a dancer on pointe can resemble a swan on land, with its clumsy webbed walk, but because the dance captures the plangency of a swan's death, the death of a bit of beauty. At her own death Pavlova had her swan costume brought to her bedside. She would appreciate our wind-whipped swan watch; a Hot Line to report dead and dying swans to the Department of Fish and Wildlife, weekly, even daily newspaper stories on numbers lost, dying swan etiquette. Along with our newspaper stories on weather records: the warmest, the coldest, thirty-eight glaciers on our mountain severely receding or gone to alpine pools, lessening the spring melt the salmon need to spawn. Our swan dying has slowed the swans' recovery, and in an imperiled species—and with no clear reason—It has worried everyone and led to the formation of an intercountry Swan Research Team to find and try to eliminate the lead.

Trumpeter swans appear in large flocks, a field of white pillows. A hundred years ago this sight would have been a sign of angels or apocalypse. Trumpeter swans were considered extinct then (until 1913 a specimen preserved in a museum was the only evidence trumpeter swans had been in my county). A few in remote mountains had escaped the massive hunting and birds began to come back.

How strange, like our finding the extinct fish, the coelacanth, presumed gone for hundreds of millions of years, alive off the coast of Africa in 1938. It spooked people, this six and a half foot, splotched, lobe-finned, presumed-dead fish, and inspired a B movie where a squirt of coelacanth blood caused the living to revert to primitive stages of evolution—dogs went wild, humans went australopithecine and loped around the screen in glued-on fur. Obtuse Freud would have been a poor writer of B movies.

I put Freud, with his heavy frames and whiskers pruned like an obsessive's hedgerow, in the scene when those first swans returned to the wets of our dim mining and brothel town. Massive, white in the way of sundrained vision, and as far as anyone knew, dead and gone. At the time in Bellingham people would have been pulling plentiful salmon out of the water, logging, umber cedars bobbing like the fish. Many mines collapsed, and the town would have been fresh with stories of ghosts, the houses built on filled mines as white wing-spans the size of a man and a half returned.

Eldritch, unheimlich. Sigmund Freud, call yourself.

The swans' comeback was neither widespread nor stable. Just as the swans came close to making the newly created national endangered list in the 1960s, a few thousand were discovered in Alaska (quite a statement on the stats of those who did make the endangered list). The majority of the birds still live there—about 25,000 now exist, under various protections. Again, the figure strikes me as shaky. Trumpeter swans used to live across a great deal of North America and now they're hemmed in, where the winds rage: one avian disease (Atlantic brants are currently dying by the hundreds of what's probably a hepatitis), a few natural disasters, and then what? I live in earthquake and tsunami country. (As I strolled along the Dungeness Spit with the brants, signs stressed that in the event of a tsunami I should get to higher land. Helpful, with six feet of gravel beach and driftwood on each side.) Geologists find new faults here every day.

Perhaps at the time of the swans' return, with fewer extinctions and those less noted, the sight of trumpeter swans made no difference beyond the return of a resource. I can imagine we would seem strange, fetishistic to that age, crowding in whale watching trawlers to chase orcas and whatever, blackening our eyes with binoculars. Do you have the pileated woodpecker? said the old man walking by in the peninsula's temperate rainforest. And are they so rare you never see them?

I have felt that old man's almost querulous need, drawing up lists of things I want to see in the wild: cougars, moose, whales, bears, elk, so meticulous and driven I could be hunting them. I drag the family I love along, demanding, much to their irkedness, that they turn their eyes this way, that way. I have seen the pileated woodpecker (candidate for endangered), out the window of a camping cabin on one of my state's many islands, and felt that ripple through my chest, the flutter of the uncanny, as the bird poked simply in a Douglas fir. I saw it, and the sight was both exhilarating and queasy, loaded with the same anxiety not seeing it would have held. We see so much here— the spotted owl, the flipping chinook— no one in the future is likely to see again. The gray whale's spume out in the water: it is there, breathing, one individual behaving as if this week's krill is its biggest problem.

I tote my child around to these things: Jin, son, please look.

Hundreds of us on shore, trying to drive the image up our retina, as if that could be a permanent record of anything.

We drive to Skagit County with binoculars, the mob crowding the tomb of Lazarus when Jesus raised him. Unheimlich can mean things that ought to have remained hidden that have come to light, Freud said, the return of the repressed—or, as he combed the uncanny tales of E.T.A. Hoffman, a blurring between the lines of life and its opposite. Please lord, yes, begged sister Martha at the tomb, while someone in the crowd said, Don't do it, it's been too long, he'll stink.

Unheimlich, Freud noted in his essay, shares more with heimlich than a root. Both words can mean the same thing. Unheimlich doesn't just exist in opposition to the home but can mean it, a return, Freud thought, to a more primitive stage of our personal or species existence. Some australopithecine moment caught in the heavy-lipped jaw of the coelacanth. *Eldritch* is of obscure origin, though it may come from the Old English *el* for strange and *riche* for land. Freud's conclusions presumably would have changed with a different language and a different landscape. Or not. The land of the strange means the land of the long familiar.

Once Lazarus rose he faced the wrath of the local priests, who immediately wanted to kill him, keeping things in their proper place I guess. Legend has it he fled.

I spent a day recently looking for trumpeter swans with my family—whine of wind out of car, whine of kid in—though I only found a meadow with snow geese about to return to the water for their sunset roost; up down, up down they rose and fell; like seeing someone shake out a pure white sheet. Twice in the past week, though, I've come across trumpeter swans along the highway, where my binoculars prove futile and I barely have time to see. Still, I got my husband to slow down (both times we were in BC, where drivers are far too nice to honk) and took in the sight of them, fairy tale beautiful until they got up and lumbered along, more Shrek in gait than Snow White. Oddly enough a handful of bald eagles stood amid the skein of swans—balds normally wouldn't share ground with trumpeter swans—and the eagles had their yellow eyes fixed on their rivals, with the uncanny look of kids keeping the cuter kids from their stuff.

I look at my son, thinking of him as a bizarro version of the Lopez/Anthony twins. He's bigger, of course, and singular, and more to the point, follows my practice of wearing only consignment store clothing. I make an exception for fair trade, but fair trade clothes tend to be very expensive, so we're consignment store for the most part, both of us with holes here and there, things that don't quite match or fit. I began doing this to avoid feeding mega-corporations my money, or buying clothes for me or my child made by children earning slave wages. I feel partly smug about this practice and partly absurd. Jin at 10 can look pretty much how he wants without social stigma, but with holes and mismatched clothes I'm far out of the realm of any professional dress code, the flamboyant or the buttoned-up. My choices don't hurt Ralph Lauren or Nike or Jennifer Lopez, who owns a chic clothing line herself. My gesture is a small gesture, perhaps aimed only at feeling good when I read my magazines. Or, in this landscape of revenants, a fool's hairshirt.

The swan die-off remains, in its eighth year now, about 306 trumpeters lost per year. The birds consume mostly what's called "historical lead"; the use of lead shot has been banned in Washington since 1989, and most lead dates back considerably farther: the lead in the ground can go back to the Lewis & Clark expedition, when settlers hunted and traders swapped shotguns to the First Nations. Some newer, recreational shot exists, from clay shooting (legal) or illegal hunting, though it's not the bulk of what the swans eat. Under the tulip fields that we love, the raspberries and occasional acreage of corn, lie kernels and seeds, bulbs and bullets.

"It shouldn't happen," Doug Zimmer, a biologist with the U.S. Fish and Wildlife Service and member of the Swan Research Team, told me. "Lead sinks fast and it shouldn't be accessible. And why would swans just start eating it over the last eight years? It's a mystery. There's nothing we can see, no change in roosting habits. We've found a few hot spots [where unusually large numbers of swans die], but mostly, we haven't got a clue."

The trumpeter swans have taken back up, with a vengeance, their burden of eating our lead. They are, Martha Jordan of the Swan Team reminds me with unintentional irony, the canaries in the coal mine; large carcasses that reflect all the birds, and secondary scavengers like coyotes, dying of lead because dead swans form a food source. (When I mentioned the bald eagles on the ground to Doug Zimmer, he pointed out that they may have been waiting for swans to die.) When my son talks about guns, as ten-year-olds do, I react with shameless emotion; I say, Don't you ever get near a gun, even if it isn't loaded, don't *touch* one. Don't let anyone around you get near one.

I worry about his body and I have metaphysical worries. A gun is designed to do one thing, and perhaps to fire it is to make a pact, of sorts.

I will die. This is not news and I am used to the fact. What is fascinating to consider, through the window of my life, is the fate of my six billion comrades in this hairless-primate-as-top-predator experiment. We do not have enough food, water or fuel to keep us going in our present form; this we know. Climate's changing rapidly, ice caps melting. Apocalypse is a human weakness—most generations find some reason to believe they may be the last—but it's hard to avoid the fact that our problems go beyond the metaphysical: there isn't enough. Around the world right now people riot for food, from Haiti to Senegal. The World Food Program blames scarcity and soaring prices on a convergence of the bloated price of petroleum, natural disasters linked to climate change, and competition for grain used to make biofuels because fossil fuels are running out.

(I'm not the only one thinking apocalyptically: a History Channel series called *Life After People* enacted the collapse of civilization—our buildings, our infrastructure—after humans get wiped out; it was very popular. On the website for the show, inexplicably, there's a long and detailed survival guide in case you find yourself in the position of last human on earth. Take shelter in abandoned buildings; drink water from gutters; seek out canned food. Why?)

I grow a great deal of our food, and contract for much of the rest of it through a local organic farm. I deal with the feast-or-famine rhythm of harvest by canning and freezing, having an improvised cold cellar for root vegetables. I make cooking my household job, mostly, and find my family's eating (we always eat dinner together) mystically tender: the alchemy of plants I have grown or preserved becoming my son's sprouting body. Or my husband's, whose 50-point cholesterol drop I secretly hold to be my chemistry at the table. I remember my mother's 1960s meal-planning rules: you balanced the plate with a meat, a starch, and a vegetable. Now the balancing has changed: the omega-3s in the tuna and salmon Bruce needs for his cholesterol versus public health warnings never to consume more than one or two small servings of these fish a week (or none, if you're pregnant, very young or immuno-compromised), as mercury nests in their tissues. Our helpings of local salmon go *mano a mano* with my homegrown chard, tomatoes, and whatall, and I imagine the organic stuff, grown from my soil, my own compost and chicken manure I raked up at my son's school, chasing away the heavy metals.

We may well find a technological way around our dilemma, or flee the planet, or compress our numbers enough to continue. Or go the way of the long parade of top predators before us. Once the human population on earth went down to 10,000 (this bottleneck event happened about 80,000 years ago), a near-extinction level, and bounced back. And we still find the coelacanths of the world, members of what biologists call *Lazarus taxon*, who disappear from the fossil record and return. Then again we have the opposite, those extinction events, like the Permian one that took out 95% of the earth's species—including most of those well-adapted proto-mammals, the therapsids. A few straggling members of this class survived, and thanks to a lucky asteroid, went on to step over the carcasses of lots of dinosaurs and evolve into people, who would find those carcasses in the ground again, in the midst of a gas-emitting fuel.

The swan working group has begun a practice of hazing swans away from sites, like Judson Lake in my county, particularly high in lead deaths. This strategy began two years ago: wildlife workers raced around the lake with noisemakers, stomped, shone lasers, swung painted cardboard tubes with crude coyote heads and vroomed in airboats to haze the swans away. Judson Lake swan mortality went down, but perversely mortality went up by 22 deaths elsewhere; a new hot spot established itself in Snohomish County. The swan deaths seem to have established their own uncanny set point.

I said, articulately, Wow, when Doug Zimmer told me this.

"I get wow a lot," he said, adding with a touch of rue, "This is the most puzzling mystery of my career. I don't know of anything like it. We don't know why these three northern counties are so bad. There are places in the country with more lead in the ground and similar birds, and the birds don't eat the lead. And here, not all swans who use the same places die; not all swans who die use the same places. Swans [who mate for life] are very family faithful. They stay in family groups, and in the same group one will die and no others, though they feed next to one another."

The windstorms drive us to windows (the Middle English *eyes of the wind*). Ours are of hundred-year-old glass so it has flowed—glass is not a true solid—and there are waves and ripples toward the bottoms of the panes. My son leans his dark head into the bay window in the living room. He's picked up my habit—learned from my grandmother—of calling this *reading the newspaper*. She said this of her cats when they sat in the windowsills: *He's reading the newspaper*. I'm reading the newspaper, says Jin to me.

Oh yeah? What does the newspaper say?

It seems to say the bamboo is pulling from the ground, not, from my son's point of view, a bad thing—an instant sword, a javelin. It's been a long fall for windstorms and I'm ready for an end to it: the eldritch squawl, the sense of a wind turned on us with almost-human purpose. It becomes difficult to make decisions, even to cook, and not be captured by the upturning of gravity, the unmetaphorizable sound, the full stops and starts.

I imagine the swans would like an end to things, not just the wind driving the rivers over their banks but the planes and the coyote-like tubes waving and the red lights. "It may be the problem is too pervasive in this area to solve. The birds may have to be their own extraction system," said Zimmer. "The swans may simply have to eat the lead up. It's not what we want, but the swans may have to solve the problem for future generations of swans."

A Braided Heart: Shaping the Lyric Essay
Brenda Miller

On the first day of my class "Writing the Lyric Essay" I bring in a loaf of *challah*, the braided bread traditionally eaten for the Jewish Sabbath dinner. I take it out of my bag and set it in on a white cloth at the center of the table. Before I say anything at all about it, I watch my students' reactions: some eye it warily, their eyes narrowed in suspicion. They know there must be *some* reaction I'm looking for, and so they sit back and refuse to give any at all; they cross their arms over their chests or begin to rustle through their backpacks for pencils or pens. Some of them, the ones who recognize the *challah*, are worried that this is going to be one of those "spiritual" writing classes; they look at the bread and glance away, then lean over to whisper something to their neighbors. Some gaze at the bread only with suppressed delight, hunger evident in their eyes. *Snack time*, they think, and with it the promise of an "easy" class, one that coddles and nurtures.

Any of them could be right. I pass out the syllabus and watch the stapled packets make a circuit around the room, the *challah* still sitting placidly in the center of the table, innocuous yet full of mysterious power. I don't talk about the bread, but I begin some forays into the "lyric essay" in general. What is it? That is the main question we all have; I might even write it on the board. *What is the lyric essay?* Not only *What is it?* But *how do I make it?* What's the definition? What's the answer?

And I might tell them: *I don't know.* I might tell them, though they won't want to hear it, that we've entered a realm of unknowing, a place where definitions are constantly in flux, a place where answers are not as important as the questions to which they give rise.

The Challah

I loved *challah* when I was a child. It had to be bought from a special kosher bakery, the "Delicious Bakery" in the Hughes Shopping Center, and we had to get there at just the right time on Friday afternoons: before the loaves were sold out, and after they had just come from the oven, still warm, the egg wash and the sesame seed gleaming like gold. They seemed, in fact, the golden loaves of some fairy tale, minted from a factory deep inside a hidden cave, emerging on a conveyer belt and counted out for all the Jews of Northridge. There were a good many conservative congregations in the San Fernando Valley, the "California Jews" whom the east coast Jews frowned upon, or dismissed. There's a joke: California Jews are not really Jews, they're Jew-*ish*.

And I suppose my family fit that description. We went to synagogue when necessary, and my brothers and I went to Hebrew school, and I thought the men looked both distinguished and ridiculous with their *yarmulkes* on: it was the contrast between the elegant black silk, and the womanish bobby pins used to hold them in place. My brothers took them off as soon as they could, but sometimes my father absentmindedly left his *yarmulke* on throughout the rest of that sanctified day, preoccupied with a piece of wood in his vice grip on the bench in the garage, or sitting with his feet up on the Lazyboy recliner, watching a Lakers game, waiting for dinner to be served.

Though we were secular Jews, we were still Jewish enough to appreciate the quality of the Sabbath Bread, that beautiful, glowing *challah*. I recently asked a rabbi on the Internet why the *challah* is braided, what is symbolic about it, and his e-mail reply said (in a voice so much like the rabbis of my youth! Slightly contemptuous, a little annoyed . . .) that the Sabbath bread must only look *different* than everyday bread, that it need not be braided; it could be circular or oblong or in the shape of a rhomboid, for that matter. The braid had become custom for eastern European Jews; some bakers used three strands, some four; this rabbi, he said with a hint of pride, used six!

As a child, I knew only that the braided bread simply tasted *better* than ordinary bread, the way texture will often affect flavor, and the way presentation and form can sometimes offer sustenance in itself. I loved watching my mother cut through that jeweled crust, the heft of the buttered slice in my hands, the convoluted, lacquered outer surface giving way to the dense bread beneath. The inside was moist and delicious, tasted like an entire meal in itself. I often closed my eyes when I bit into it. Here was a bread that spoke of what it meant to have a sacred day: to bring the divine into one's small and common body.

Braiding the Challah

"Divide dough into four equal portions; roll each between hands to form a strand about 20 inches long. Place the 4 strips lengthwise on a greased baking sheet, pinch tops together and braid as follows pick up strand on right, bring it over next one, under the third, and over the fourth. Repeat always starting with the strand on the right, until braid is complete. Pinch ends together. Cover and let rise in a warm place until almost doubled. Using a soft brush or your fingers, spread egg yolk mixture evenly over braids; sprinkle with seed. Bake in a 350° oven for 30–35 minutes or until loaf is golden brown and sounds hollow when tapped."

The Lyric Essay

"Lyric. Essay. How do you think the two fit together?" My students mull over the question, avoiding my eyes, their gaze landing on the glowing *challah* at the center of the table. "What would be the recipe for a lyric essay?" I ask, "What are the ingredients?"

"Imagery?" one student tentatively offers. I nod my head eagerly and lean forward in my chair. "Poetic language?" another asks. I get up and start writing on the board, as my students begin to call out words and phrases; *fragments, personal experience, metaphor, sentences, gaps, structure, white space, thesis, sensuality, voice, meditation, repetition, rhythm.* When we're done I have a blackboard full of possibilities, really a panoply of all the ways of writing itself. It's a little daunting. I sit down and ask them again: so what makes the lyric essay a lyric? What makes it an essay? Why not just write a poem, instead, if you want to be lyrical? Why not just write an essay, if you want to be prosaic?

Silence falls, so I tell my students that the lyric essay is quite an ancient form; it's nothing new. Writers like Seneca, Bacon, Sei Shonagon in the 10th century, Montaigne, hundreds of others: all could be said to write essays whose forms were inherently lyric. That is, they did not necessarily follow a linear, narrative line. Many excellent writers and thinkers have tried to pin down the lyric essay, defining it as a collage, a montage, a mosaic. It's been called disjunctive, paratactic, segmented, sectioned. All of these are correct. All of these recognize in the lyric essay a tendency toward fragmentation that invites the reader into those gaps, that emphasizes what is unknown rather than the already articulated known. By infusing prose with tools normally relegated to the poetic sensibility, the lyric essayist creates anew, each time, a form that is interactive, alive, full of new spaces in which meaning can germinate. *The Seneca Review*, in its 30th anniversary issue devoted to lyric essays, characterized them as having "this built-in mechanism for provoking meditation. They require us to complete their meaning."

So, I underline *fragmentation* on the board. I underline the word *gaps*. I write the words *explode the narrative line!!* over the whole thing. My students nod; they write this down.

Then I go over and, with chalky hands, pick up the bread.

The Braided Essay

Writing has always—and always will, I'm sure—scared the hell out of me. I'll do just about anything to get out of it, and have been known to spend whole afternoons circling my desk like a dog, wary, unwilling to commit to writing a single word. What is so frightening about it? I still don't know. Perhaps it's the horrible knowledge that no matter how well you write, the resultant product will never correlate exactly to the truth, will never arrive with quite the melodious voice you hear in the acoustic cavity of your mind.

When I first started writing personal essays, I didn't know that's what I was doing. I had written poetry for many years, but at some point felt restricted by the poetic line. So I started wandering past the line break and ended up writing autobiographical prose that had a lilting, hesitant quality to it, as if it still didn't trust itself in this unfenced yard.

But what I found was that this yard had just as many fences, just as many restrictions. I was struggling to write an essay that seemed very important to me, an essay about being a massage therapist for several years at a small hot springs resort in northern California. This work had defined me and created a center of self based on serving others. By the time I was writing the essay, in 1989, this center had dissolved: I no longer practiced massage, and had yet to find another guiding principle to replace it. The urge to write was the urge to explain the sense of loss I felt, to bring coherence to an identity that now seemed fragmented, in flux, chaotic.

While I wrote, I kept looking at a photograph of myself from that time: I'm naked, in the hot tub of Orr Springs. The photographer (my boyfriend) chose to frame this scene through a windowpane misty with steam; we get a fragment of Jasmine bush, the blur of the water, my hands lifted to shield my face. The diffuse light centers on my abdomen (the site, it turns out, where much of my autobiographical material resides). I looked at this picture often, much the way I might gaze in a mirror: looking for a way into this body, a way for this image of the body to give up its secrets and make itself manifest in language. But as I tried to order this material of memory and image into a logical, linear narrative, the essay became flat, intractable, stubbornly refusing to yield any measure of truth.

By chance, I happened to be studying the personal essay form for an Independent Study class at the University of Montana. One of my class-mates brought in an essay by the poet Albert Goldbarth. It was called "After Yitzl," and I had never before read anything like it. Written in numbered sections that at first seem to have little do with one another, the essay worked through a steady accretion of imagery and key repetitions; it spoke in a voice that grew loud, then whispered, that cut itself off, then rambled. I found myself tripping over the gaps, then laughing delightedly as I found myself sprawled on the ground. Something cracked open inside me. I saw how cavalierly Goldbarth had exploded his prose in order to put it together again in a new pattern that was inordinately pleasurable.

So I turned to my own essay and tried the same thing. I deserted a narra-tive line in favor of images that intuitively rose up in the work. I allowed for silence, the caesuras between words, and the essay began to take on voices that hardly belonged to me. This fragmentation allowed for those moments of "not knowing" which, to me, became the most honest moments in the essay. I abandoned my authority, and with that surrender came great free-dom: I no longer had to know the answers. I didn't have to come to a static conclusion. Instead, the essay began to make an intuitive kind of sense.

When I arrived at the final draft, I had fragmented three different nar-ratives—my work as a massage therapist, the story of a life-threatening miscarriage, and the birth of my godson. All of this material was highly emotional to me; the fragmentation, however, allowed me—almost forced me—not to approach this material head-on but to search for a more circuitous way into the essay. I had to expand my peripheral vision, to focus on images that at first seemed oblique to the stories. Sometimes our peripheral vision catches the most important details, those you might not have expected to carry significance. You give yourself over to chance sightings, arresting the image on the verge of skittering away. In the resultant essay, "A Thousand Buddhas," it was the image of my hands, those hands fluttering up in the photograph, that became a contextualizing force, yoking together the juxtaposed meditations on birth and death that surrounded it.

Taking Risks

"For many bakers, kneading the soft dough is a lovely sensation, a sort of relaxing therapy. For others, the glorious moment comes with the first buttered bite of the fresh warm loaf. For everyone, the yeasty aroma wafting from the oven as the bread bakes crowns the day with a sense of delicious achievement. . . .

Yeast bread baking has the reputation of being chancy and difficult. . . . It's true that you do need to be careful at first. You have to protect the baby dough to get it started. But after that the bread almost makes itself."

Making Challah

There was a time in my life when I made all my own bread. I loved every part of it: reading the recipes, gathering the ingredients, kneading the dough, allowing it to rise. And all the praise I reaped from the task didn't hurt either. I remember, when I was in college, laying out perfectly browned loaves of whole-wheat French bread on the kitchen counter in a house I shared with four men in Blue Lake; such love in their eyes, such devotion! I remember baking bread every day for children in a summer camp: big, oversized loaves of white bread that we cut and spread with churned butter. And the *challah*, of course: sometimes I got ambitious and tried the kind of loaves you saw in synagogue: a four-strand base, with a smaller, three-strand braid on top, so that the whole thing became a monstrous labyrinth. Mine always emerged a little lopsided, but that only added to its charm.

All good bread makers develop a finely honed sense of intuition that comes into play at every step of the process: knowing exactly the temperature of the water in which to proof your yeast, testing it not with a thermometer but against the most sensitive skin at the underside of your wrist, with the same thoughtful stance as a mother testing a baby's formula. You add the warm milk, the butter, the salt, a bit of sugar. After a while you stop measuring the flour as you stir, knowing the correct texture through the way it resists your arm. You take the sticky dough in your hands and knead, folding the dough toward you, then pushing away with the heel of your hand, turning and repeating, working and working with your entire body—your legs, your abdomen, your strong heart. Your work the dough until it takes on the texture of satin. You poke it with your index finger and it sighs against your touch.

You cover it and let it rise. You keep it in your mind as it combusts in the warm dark. You return to it, this living thing you've created with your hands. You shape it to please the eye and the mouth. You pull it apart and roll the dough into yeasty ropes and begin to braid it back into a different form. You hope it will come out all right, that the strands aren't too thick or too thin, that they aren't too long or too short, that they won't fall apart in the middle, or break. Sometimes you have to unravel what you've done, start again. You keep braiding with your heart in your throat, hoping for the best. You have the egg wash at the ready, to add the finishing touches, the small bowl of poppy seeds. In your mind you have a vision of the perfect *challah*, gleaming on its special platter.

You do what you can. At some point the bread *"almost makes itself."*

French Braids

When I first met Hannah and Sarah, the way into their hearts was to plait their hair in French braids. They had faith in all women over a certain age to be able to braid hair, and so when they came to me with combs and ribbons in hand, I didn't have the heart to disillusion them. It was like a test of my merit as an adult female companion, and their eyes were so eager, so trusting: how could I refuse?

But braiding hair is not as easy as braiding bread. Especially French braids which require a certain dexterity of the fingers, an intuitive feel for the slippery hair of young girls. The hair slides from the fingers, breaks off, becomes unruly. I had to start over, again and again, and when I was finished they looked terrible, not really like braids at all but like some old sailor's rope, knotted and twisted and frayed.

But the girls were satisfied enough. They ran to the mirror and tilted their heads; luckily they couldn't see all the way around to the back. They patted their hair as if it were a nice, strange new animal and thanked me for my trouble. I knew why they wanted it so badly: braided hair has an allure so much more exciting than "normal" hair, it has texture and substance and mystery. Where does one strand originate and the next one begin? The eye travels, dizzy with delight, over the highlights and the hair seems to shimmer more fully, takes on a coy illumination that beckons the hand to touch, to feel, to love.

The Braided Essay

After that first essay, "A Thousand Buddhas," I began to adopt the structure of fragmented, numbered sections for much of my prose. And I began to see more clearly that this form wasn't just about fragmentation and juxtaposition; it wasn't really mosaic I was after. There was more of a sense of weaving about it, of interruption and continuation, like the braiding of bread, or of hair. I had to keep my eye on the single strands that came in and out of focus, filaments that glinted differently depending on where they had been. At the same time, I had to keep my eye focused on the single image that held them all together. As William Stafford wrote a few weeks before he died, "There's a thread you follow. It goes among/things that change. But it doesn't change."

As I began to adopt the braided essay more and more in my work, a strange, wonderful and mysterious thing began to happen. While I was still writing "personal" essays, essays that mainly relied for their material on the experiences of my life, I found that they started to expand more outward, taking on myriad facts and stories of the outer world as well as the inner. New strands began to develop, but which still intersected with memories most important to me. I liked this. It was as if I were creating the more complex, double-braided bread of the synagogue.

For instance, while at my first writing colony on an island in the Puget Sound, I happened to pick up an encyclopedia of Jewish religion from the library in the farmhouse. "Happened to" is the key phrase here; the essays of my own that I like the best arise out of happenstance, out of the material finding its way into my hands rather than vice versa. We must train ourselves into this state of "meditative expectancy," as Carolyn Forché calls the writer's stance; the world, after all, flies by us at millions of miles an hour, spewing out any number of offerings—it is the writer at her desk, the artist out perambulating, who will recognize a gift when she sees one. As I turned the pages of this marvelous book, I was struck by how little I, a Jewish woman who had gone to Hebrew school for most of her formative years, knew about my religion. In fact, I realized, I didn't have the foggiest idea how to pray.

I started writing down the quotes that interested me the most, facts about the Kaballah, and the ritual baths, and *dybukks,* and the Tree of Life. At the time, I was also writing about a recent trip I had taken to Portugal, and the news I had gotten there of my mother's emergency hysterectomy. I was also writing about my own yoga practice, and the volunteer work I did at a children's hospital in Seattle. As I kept all these windows open in my computer, the voice of the encyclopedia emerged as the binding thread, a way for me to create a spiritual self-portrait in the form of a complex braid.

This is what I love about all braided things: bread, hair, essays, rivers, our own circulatory systems pumping blood to our brains and our hearts. I love the fact of their separate parts intersecting, creating the illusion of wholeness, but with the oh-so-pleasurable texture of separation. It is not the same as a purely disjunctive form, the bits and pieces scattered like cookies on the baking sheet. Rather, the strands are separate, but together, creating a pattern that is lovely to the touch, makes the bread taste even better when we finally lift a slice of it to our tongues.

Poets, of course, have known this all along. They blow the world apart and put it back together again. Cornell wanders the city and is "lunged into a world of complete happiness in which every triviality becomes imbued with significance." Charles Simic comments, "The commonplace is miraculous if rightly seen, if recognized."

A Braided Heart

Bread has always been a miracle. As has poetry. And language itself, this tremendous urge to communicate. To live our lives in our shattered ways and still be happy: this is miraculous. The Sabbath bread helps us see that an extraordinary pattern binds our days together. The braided loaf, set on a table, makes of that table an altar. Our hearts may give the illusion of one muscular organ, but think how the florid chambers converge, and of the many veins and arteries that wind their way by design to reach this fleshy core. They come together; they intersect; they beat an urgent rhythm beneath our skin.

Music

I once wrote for a month at an artist's colony in upstate New York, and one of my fellow residents was a composer of operas. I am tone deaf, have no pitch whatsoever, and music for me has always been the most esoteric of languages. He played for us, on the piano, one of his arias. When he was done, we applauded, and I asked him: "How do you know when a piece is finished?" I know now it was a naive question, even a little foolish.

But he answered me without pause. "When what I hear up here," he said, clasping a palm to his forehead, "corresponds to what's written down here." He pointed to the score. I followed the line of his fingers, saw a page full of inky hieroglyphics that wound in and out of the lined bars.

A writer must spend a great deal of time ushering her piece into the world. There is the creation of bulk, then the cutting down to the essential, resonant, notes. This process takes a terrible amount of patience, more than an inkling of faith. I wanted to spy on that composer through his window and see if he does what *I* do when I'm writing: sitting with a blank stare, my pen poised over the empty page, my mouth hanging slightly ajar, waiting.

When I read the lyric essayists that I consider great—Albert Goldbarth, Anne Carson, Annie Dillard, Charles Simic, to name just a few—they all have the quality of a piece of music arrived whole from some distant place and played anew. I can go back and read these essays again and again because they seem neither static nor fixed. It's always a live performance: the white space expands and contracts, and I feel like a guest in a charmed province, the same one occupied by prayer.

The Challah

We pass the bread around the seminar table. I ask my students each to tear off a chunk, and hold it in their hands a moment, waiting until everyone has a piece. I want them to notice the heft of it, the yolky texture, the subtle yet amazing fact that within the loaf itself, once you cut it open, you see nary a sign of the braiding. You have a chunk of bread: whole, fine-grained, delicious.

The bread, of course, is good. All *challah* is good. And there are many ways to eat it. Some take it apart with their fingers, separating the strands, unwinding them and putting them one by one in their mouths. Some take big bites into the center of the bread, saving the golden crust for last. Some nibble at it, then leave it on their desks. After we're done brushing off the crumbs, taking quick sips of water, we look at each other again. Some of the students seem a little more relaxed now, a little more willing; they look at me expectantly, their eyes bright, wondering what will happen next. Some of the students seem even more annoyed, already putting their pens away; I doubt I'll see them on the roster at the next class meeting.

What I'm hoping, for the students that remain, is that the idea of *braiding* has entered us, become a viable, perhaps natural, way of shaping our material, and even our lives, for the brief ten weeks we'll be together. What I'm hoping is that by the eating of this bread together we begin to respond to a hunger unsatisfied by everyday food, unvoiced in everyday language. We'll begin to formulate a few separate strands; we'll mull them over, roll them in our hands, and bring them together in a pattern that acts as mouthpiece to the sacred.

Index